THE EQ Difference

A Powerful Plan for Putting Emotional Intelligence to Work

Adele B. Lynn

AMERICAN MANAGEMENT ASSOCIATION
New York | Atlanta | Brussels
Chicago | Mexico City | San Francisco
Shanghai | Tokyo | Toronto | Washington D.C.

Special discounts on bulk quantities of AMACOM books are available to corporations, professional associations, and other organizations. For details, contact Special Sales Department, AMACOM, a division of American Management Association, 1601 Broadway, New York, NY 10019. Tel.: 212-903-8316. Fax: 212-903-8083. Web site: www. amacombooks.org

This publication is designed to provide accurate and authoritative information in regard to the subject matter covered. It is sold with the understanding that the publisher is not engaged in rendering legal, accounting, or other professional service. If legal advice or other expert assistance is required, the services of a competent professional person should be sought.

Library of Congress Cataloging-in-Publication Data

Lynn, Adele B.
    The EQ difference : a powerful program for putting emotional intelligence to work / by Adele B. Lynn.
        p. cm.
    ISBN 0-8144-0844-3
    1. Emotional intelligence.   2. Work—Psychological aspects.   I. Title.
    BF576.L96 2004
    152.4—dc22   2004018816

Printing number

10 9 8 7 6 5 4 3 2 1

CONTENTS

PART 1 *Emotions: The Fuel of Life*

PART 2 *Training Your Self-Coach*

PART 3 *Five Areas of Emotional Intelligence at Work*

YOUR INNER BIRD DOG

Knowledge of what is possible
is the beginning of happiness.
—*George Santayana*

M ost people's ideals are noble. To achieve these ideals, however, sometimes requires wisdom far beyond what we are able to deliver on a daily basis. We are likely to get caught in the fray of life. Little things, like rush hour traffic, the line at the deli counter, or a coworker's comments become our focus and take us away from our ideal. We sometimes get stuck in the unimportant, and unleash our energy in the wrong direction. We intended to go north, but find ourselves heading south. Emotional intelligence, as defined and outlined in this book, can serve as a compass so that we can be assured that we are on the road to living our intentions and our ideals every day.

This book is for all of us who aspire to live up to our own greatness. It is for all of us who have caught a glimpse of our wisdom, warmth, depth, and charm. It's for all of us whose intentions or ideals are sometimes greater than our actions. It's for all of us at home and at work who care enough to study ourselves and use that knowledge *to manage ourselves and our relationships with others so that we truly live our intentions.* That, in essence, is the definition of emotional intelligence (EQ).

Emotional intelligence can make a huge difference in both our personal lives and our work satisfaction and performance. Emotional intelligence is the distinguishing factor that determines if we make lemonade when life hands us lemons or spend our life stuck in bitterness. It is the distinguishing factor that enables us to have wholesome, warm relationships rather than cold and distant contacts. EQ is the distinguishing factor between finding and living our life's passions or just putting in time. EQ is the distinguishing factor that draws others to us or repels them. EQ is the distinguishing factor that enables us to work in concert and collaboration with others or to withdraw in dispute.

All of us have done or said something that later we regretted. In these circumstances, we walk away muttering, "I didn't mean . . ." or "I wasn't thinking . . ." During these times, our actions did not support our good intentions. At other times, our intentions might be fuzzy, so we act inconsistently. Still at other times, our intentions may be totally lost in a sea of emotion. Whatever the divide between intentions and reality, one thing is certain. For each day of life, the human experience will present opportunities so we may try again to bridge the divide and to live our intentions.

Emotional intelligence increases our capacity to discover and express our greatness. Why? Because emotional intelligence demands a complete disclosure of our strengths. As a result, we can begin to fully understand our ideal selves and compare this ideal to how we behave each day. Our ideal self is the self that emerges when we are unencumbered by the burden of irrational thoughts and emotional upsets that can sometimes distract us from our intentions. It's that glimpse of self that does and says the right thing at the right time in the right manner. It's that self that is centered and assured. It's that self that doesn't feel a need for other people's approval or a need to compete at the expense of others. It doesn't fear making mistakes. It doesn't lash out in anger or spend time fretting or fearing things that it cannot control. It's that self that takes confident, assured steps in both our personal and work lives that produce satisfaction and success. It's that self that inspires others. It's that self that we're proud of. I'm not talking about ego pride. I'm talking about satisfaction deep down when we know we've lived our best today.

This book is not to change who you are, but to allow more of your ideal self to come through in daily living. The fact is everyone has gaps between their true intentions and reality. If, however, you are serious about bridging this gap and living your greatness, this book will not only inspire you to do so, it will provide a plan to examine and confront the very issues that are standing in the way. In fact, if you routinely practice the practical steps presented, your ability to live your greatness in every encounter every day will sharpen.

Until recently, living an emotionally healthy and intelligent life was more or less left to chance, but today people take steps to improve all different aspects of their lives. Many people build healthy bodies through exercise, diet, and vitamins. Others take classes, read books, and pursue knowledge to learn new skills. Many seek spiritual growth by attending religious services. Improving emotional intelligence is just one more avenue to living a healthy, productive life. If you integrate the steps presented in this book into your daily lives, it will prove to be a comprehensive plan for developing emotional intelligence and living your intentions. Although in the human experience perfection may not be achievable, improvement is. So, get ready to see more of your greatness. It's time to become unstuck.

One Saturday morning in early spring, as I was sipping coffee and peering out the window. I saw two turkeys in the woods along the fence line in my backyard. If you've never seen a wild turkey, suffice it to say that they are very large birds. Their wingspan is great. If they were any larger, they would probably put numbers on their wings and begin to haul passengers. And a bird that big needs lots of room to take off in flight. I watched as they came to the edge of the fence, turned around, and walked back the other way. They went several yards and sure enough they turned around and walked again along the same path they had walked before. They kept repeating this again and again, back and forth. It occurred to me that they were stuck because they didn't have enough room to expand those massive wings and fly away. Soon I was almost able to hear the dialogue between these two birds. "George, I told you to stop and ask for directions. You never stop and ask for directions. Now, we're lost. We're stuck. We'll probably never get out of here." "Ah, Harriet, if you'd just shut up and stop confusing me, we'd be home by now." And so it went. In fact, it went for forty-five minutes before I moved away from the window to get on with my Saturday morning chores. Two hours later I went back to the window and there were George and Harriet—still stuck. I finally roused Abby, my old sleeping bird dog, and asked him to lend a hand to George and Harriet. "Just point them in the right direction, Abby." As Abby approached, this time George and Harriet deliberately quickened the pace and kept on going. They were flushed into the open land, spread those amazing wings, and took off and soared into the open sky.

George and Harriet had all of the resources they needed to fly, but they were stuck. They needed help in breaking the cycle of going back and forth over the same old territory. Instead of using those resources, they bickered and blamed one another for their plight.

George and Harriet parallel the human experience. Most people have many resources within that could help them to soar to greater heights, but sometimes they are unable to access them. And out of frustration, they may argue, fuss, fight, become immobilized, or otherwise remain stuck, rather than use that energy to harness their resources and move forward.

Emotions can either fuel our actions toward true fulfillment or, like a car traveling on ice, cause us to spin while getting nowhere and accomplishing nothing except burning rubber. Managing this fuel, our emotions, is the essence of emotional intelligence. The focus of this book is to get you off the ground and into flight, just like my bird dog Abby did for George and Harriet. The book will help your inner bird dog develop into a self-coach that will help you to master the five areas of emotional intelligence and fully live your intentions, at home or at work.

Adele B. Lynn

ACKNOWLEDGMENTS

I express heartfelt thanks to the community of colleagues, friends, clients, interviewees, and family who wrote this book. There simply would be no book without them. They are Jacquie Flynn, Earl McDaniel, Char Kinder, Emily Schultheiss, Ben Leopold, Ben Butina, Sally Goodboy, Deborah Propes, Mike Boccia, Ralph Cain, Franky Johnson, Olwen Herron, Lindsay Shepheard, Ginia Polyzos, Bobbie Fetsko, Debbie Dix, Donna Kuhl, Hal Swart, Mary Butina, Olivia and Drew Ninchak, Dee Bergfelt, Deborah Bernstein, Robin Craig, Jane Duffy, Tim Switalski, Geoff Carroll, Laura Johnson, Sally Abrahms, Steve Aldrich, Geri Amori, Prinny Anderson, Janis Anderson, Clarence Bacher, Julie E. Benesh, Joy Barton, Sue Bicknell, Debbi Campisi, Jonnetta Chambers, Rita Coco, Leah K. Coffman, Tony Comella, Gary M. Cook, Jill Cooksey, Chris Davis, Filomena T. Day, Mariam de Samaniego, Maribeth Dockety, Lynn R. Dutton, Brenda D. Dykema, Roderick Ellen, Anita M. Eldridge, Sonja Eveslage, Glen Fahs, Julie Farschman, Marcia A. Fitzgibbons, Bob Foxworthy, C. A. Francke, Eusebio Franco, Mary Franklin, Suzanne E. Froehlich, Debbie Fulmer, Colleen Gallagher, Chris Gargoline, Melonie Garrett, Stacey R. Glover, Michelle Goodwine, Joy Gormley, Carol Grainger, Suzanne Haas, Vicki L. Harris, Gail Hart, Laverne Hibbett, Rick Hicks, Judy Hodgson, Carol Horner, Tara Huber, Rose Jones, Dave Kahle, Connie Komack, James Kinneer, Renita R. Kinney, Joanne Koopman, Tom Kopler, Patty Kreamer, Pat Krivonak, Francine Lanar, Terri Logan, Bruce Mabee, G. Marceau, Geraldine Markel, Tony Martin, Roberta Chinsky Matuson, Carol P. McCoy, James A. McCully, Deranda McDade, Larry McMullen, Kelly Meyer, Kathy Mills, Louise Miner, Lesley Morgan, Bob Morris, Karen Mosier, Erick Mowery, Lisa Neil, Agnes Newman, Vikki Newton, Jeanne Nicholson, Jeff Nixon, Brian O'Brien, Lynne Palazzolo, Marilyn Parente, Ardyth Pfaff, Howard Pratt, Mary Anne Robinson, Jack Roseman, Mark Rulle, Mary Saily, Bob Sandberg, Kacy Schwartz, Jane Seiling, Greg

Sigerson, Paul Spindel, Marilyn S. Steen, Faith Stipanovich, Jack Stucko, Barry Swanson, Pat Tangeman, Lawrence R. Taylor, Rich Taylor, Toby Thompson, Sharon Thorne, Nancy Thornton, Gladys Tillmon, Don Waterhouse, Shurli Wilkinson, Laura Wilson, and Christine Zust.

Lastly, Bill, Janele, Karl, mom, dad, Abby, and God.

Adele B. Lynn

PART I EMOTIONS
The Fuel of Life

CHAPTER 1

THE CONNECTION AMONG BEHAVIOR, FEELINGS, AND PERFORMANCE

Koppers Building
Conference Center, 9th Floor
Pittsburgh, PA
8:30AM, June 1999

(Group of 10 executives from various companies is seated around a large chestnut conference table. Two flip charts, each divided into three columns, are at opposite sides at the front of the room.)

ADELE: Tell me the characteristics of the best boss you have ever worked for, the boss that you'd do anything for, assuming that it was legal and moral. What characteristics describe him or her?

FRANK: A man of his word. High integrity.

JIM: Supports me to take risks.

HAROLD: Gives me the credit for the successes.

JORGE: He listened to my ideas.

MARTHA: She challenged me to reach higher.

JEFF: Cares about my development.

JANET: Respectful.

KIM: Open-minded.

NILL: My boss was very authentic.

ADELE: What else?

GROUP: (individually in turn) Easygoing. Genuine. Flexible. Recognized my efforts. Clearly stated expectations. Relentlessly looked for improvements.

ADELE: What else?

GROUP: Innovative. Creative. Self-directed. Inspiring. Compassionate. Sincere. Smart. Visionary. Decisive. Involved. Accessible. Organized. A mentor.

(Adele moves to the opposite side of the room to the first flip chart.)

ADELE: Now, tell me about the characteristics of a bad boss, someone who you wouldn't want to work for. We'll just assume that you've never experienced a bad boss, but perhaps heard about these characteristics through the grapevine. Oh, and no names please.

FRANK: Micromanager.

JORGE: Self-serving.

MARTHA: Poor communicator.

JANET: Unavailable.

JORGE: Judgmental.

HAROLD: Clueless.

ADELE: Wow, I don't need to prime you for this one.

GROUP: Self-centered. Inflexible. Negative. Belittling. Unapproachable. Secretive. Controlling. Insensitive. Temperamental. Irresponsible. Opinionated. Demanding.

ADELE: Anything else?

GROUP: Untrustworthy. Indecisive. Risk-adverse. Blaming. Dishonest. Demeaning. Poor planner. Wishy-washy.

(Adele walks to the second flipchart and directs the group's attention to Column 2.)

ADELE: Now, tell me how you **feel** when you work for this good boss. That's right I know it's not a word we usually use, but just go with it, please. Imagine it's Monday morning, and you're going to work, and here's what you find when you walk through the door. You find someone who has high integrity, is supportive, gives you credit, shows appreciation, listens, challenges you, is caring, who is easygoing and flexible, and cares about your development, and so on.

FRANK: I feel energized.

KIM: I feel confident.

JANET: I feel empowered.

GROUP: Happy. Appreciated. Trusted. Respected. Loyal. Creative. Competent. Independent. Productive. Motivated. Included.

ADELE: Anything else?

GROUP: Peaceful. Intelligent. Supportive. Supported. Inspired. Committed. Purposeful. Focused. Appreciated. Encouraged. Hopeful. Grateful.

(Adele walks back the first flip chart.)

ADELE: OK, now tell me how you **feel** when you work for someone who is a micromanager, who is also self-serving, a poor communicator, unavailable, judgmental, clueless, self-centered, inflexible, negative, clueless, unapproachable, secretive, controlling, insensitive, temperamental, irresponsible, opinionated, demanding, untrustworthy, indecisive, risk-adverse, blaming, dishonest, and of course, demeaning.

BILL: Anxious.

KIM: Frustrated.

MARTHA: Trapped.

JEFF: Tired.

GROUP: Sick. Stressed. Demoralized. Angry. Worthless. Stuck. Unproductive. Defensive. Hopeless. Abused. Smothered. Negative. Stagnant. Angry. Depressed. Annoyed. Revengeful. Stupid. Incompetent. Worthless. Sneaky. Indignant. Scared.

(Staying at this flip chart, Adele points to Column 3.)

ADELE: OK, so you're going into work. It's Monday morning, and you are feeling anxious, frustrated, trapped, tired, sick, stressed, demoralized, and angry. Not only on Monday, but you continue to feel worthless, stuck, unproductive, defensive, hopeless, abused, smothered, negative, and stagnant on Tuesday and Wednesday and even Friday afternoon. What does that cause you **to do or not do?** Try to be specific.

FRANK: Job hunt. (Laughter.)

HAROLD: Call in sick.

JEFF: Go home early.

GROUP: Take as little risk as possible. Cover my tracks with E-mail. Hide in my office. Keep my mouth shut in meetings. Don't offer ideas or opinions. Reciprocate by treating my peers this way. Treat customers poorly. Lash out at others. Look for what others are doing wrong. Be defensive.

ADELE: What else?

GROUP: Save memos. Sabotage. Dump on others. Not concentrate on work. Look for opportunities to prove my boss is a jerk. Isolate myself. As little as possible.

(Adele walks back to the second flip chart.)

ADELE: You're working for a person who is honest and caring, and supportive and gives you credit, shows appreciation, listens, challenges you, is easy going and flexible, and cares about your development. On Monday morning as well as Friday afternoon, you feel encouraged, inspired, empowered, competent, included, and so on. What does that make you want to **do or not do?**

KIM: Stay with the company.

BILL: Work harder.

HAROLD: Come in early because I want to.

FRANK: Stay late.

GROUP: Look for ways to improve my area. Deliver more. Volunteer. Take risks with ideas. Be creative. Offer ideas and opinions. Treat my staff well. Encourage others to come up with ideas.

ADELE: Anything else?

GROUP: Bring donuts. Speak well about the company on the outside. Recruit others to the company. Display a positive
attitude to others. Reciprocate with peers. Treat customers
well.

ADELE: Congratulations! You just made the business case for why
emotional intelligence is important in the workplace.
And a growing body of research confirms what you have
just said.

(Adele writes the word high performance in the final column on the
good boss chart, high trust in the middle column, and EQ (emotional intelligence) and IQ in the column on the left. See Figure 1.1.)

(Adele walks over to the bad boss chart. She writes the word low
performance in the final column, low trust in the middle column,
and poor skills and competency in the column on the left. See Figure 1.1.)

What are the lessons from this activity?

LESSON 1

Other People's Behaviors Can Affect Our Feelings.

Recognize that I use the word "can." Emotional intelligence is the
ability to manage ourselves and our relationships with others so that
we can live our intentions. Indeed, emotional intelligence is about
making choices. However, having said that, it is important to recognize that, other people's behavior can definitely influence your feelings. Just think about the last time someone jumped in front of you
at the deli counter or cut you off on the freeway. Those behaviors
could have caused you anything from mild irritation to road rage.
Or think about the last time at work that people expressed gratitude for your efforts. More than likely, those behaviors had some
positive effect on your feelings, causing you to feel happy or proud.
Granted the result may vary greatly depending on many things,
including the person, the circumstances, and even the mood you're
in. In fact, research has confirmed that emotions are contagious. In

Good Boss

Emotional Intelligence and IQ	High Trust Culture	High Performance
Characteristics	**Feelings**	**Actions / Do**
Integrity	Energized	Stay with the
Supportive	Confident	company
Gives credit	Empowered	Work harder
Listens	Happy	Come in early
Challenges me	Appreciated	because I want to
Cares about my	Trusted	Stay late
development	Respected	Look for ways to
Respectful	Loyal	improve my area
Open-minded	Creative	Deliver more
Genuine	Competent	Volunteer

Bad Boss

Poor Skills and Competencies	Low Trust Culture	Low Performance
Characteristics	**Feelings**	**Actions / Do**
Micro-manager	Anxious	Job hunt
Self-serving	Frustrated	Call in sick
Poor communicator	Trapped	Go home early
Unavailable	Tired	Take little risk
Judgmental	Sick	Hide in my office
Clueless	Stressed	Keep my mouth shut
Self-centered	Demoralized	Treat customers poorly
Inflexible	Angry	Lash out at others
Negative	Worthless	Be defensive
Belittling	Stuck	Save memos
Unapproachable	Unproductive	Sabotage
Secretive	Defensive	Dump on others
Controlling	Hopeless	Isolate myself

FIGURE 1.1

"The Ripple Effect," Sigal Barsade states that both outside observers' and participants' self-reports of mood were affected by the moods of others.[1] In that study, a trained person enacting positive mood conditions was able to affect others so much that they experienced improved cooperation, decreased conflict, and increased perceived task performance.

LESSON 2

Our Feelings Can Influence Our Performance.

Here again, recognize the word "can." As we saw in the discussion, emotions can affect performance. In fact, if you think about your own energy and motivation level, you'll recognize that whether at home or at work certain moods often dictate your pace, enthusiasm, and interactions with others. Nothing motivates me to clean the house or cook quite as much as the anticipated arrival of a welcome guest. What may have seemed like a chore in one state of mind suddenly becomes fun in another. The same holds true at work. If I'm feeling overwhelmed or defeated, a simple task may seem insurmountable. When my mood is lighter, I can breeze through the same task and even much more difficult ones without even noticing.

Take the emotion of anger. When feeling angry, you may quicken your pace. All of a sudden you experience an enormous energy boost fueled by your rage. So if we want to boost productivity, perhaps the answer lies in finding a way to keep people in a constant state of anger. Well, maybe not. The problems created by that strategy far outweigh the benefits. It's hard to predict just where that energy is going to manifest itself. The actions that result from anger could be higher productivity as the person works faster and with more determination, or they could be harassment, corporate sabotage, and workplace violence.[2] In reality, productivity suffers. Hendrie Weisinger in "Anger at Work: How Large Is the Problem?" states that

---

[1]Barsade, Sigal G. "The Ripple Effect: Emotional Contagion and Its Influence on Group Behavior." *Administrative Science Quarterly* 47 (December 2002):, 644.

[2]McShulskis, Elaine. "Workplace Anger: A Growing Problem." *HR Magazine* 41 (December 1996): 16.

"Anger in the workplace is the unseen source of many of the productivity problems that confront U.S. business today."[3]

Now think about depression. By mere definition, depression slows down one's actions. Motivation levels decrease so that the severely depressed person is unable to function well enough to accomplish daily chores. Even basic grooming becomes an insurmountable task. Imagine that depressed individual in the workplace with stacks of reports to run, lab tests to perform, or transactions to complete. In fact, a study reported in the *American Journal of Psychiatry* confirms that the likelihood of decreased performance on the job is seven times higher for depressed employees.[4] Another study, by AdvancePCS, revealed that U.S. workers with depressive disorders are nonproductive 14 percent of a standard hour workweek .[5]

Recognizing that some emotions do translate into action and others into inaction is an important foundation to understanding how emotions can be channeled in the workplace. The examples of anger turning to violence or depression rendering one incapable of simple tasks were illustrations to punctuate the point that emotion can cause action or inaction. Clearly, this book does not intend to provide answers to the problems of workplace violence or depression. Those serious issues require a more serious venue. But the vast majority of people can benefit from a general understanding of the effect of emotions on their abilities to function. Tips and suggestions on how to understand, interpret, and harness your emotional resources are invaluable. Besides, as you become more adept at influencing the emotional reactions you bring to your workplace, the more you can determine how your work will be affected. Each of you has within you the power to influence the emotional environment in your workplace. Why would you want to? For some, the appeal may be for greater productivity or higher quality, which will help to

---

[3] Weisinger, Hendrie. "Anger at Work: How Large Is the Problem?" *Executive Edge Newsletter* 27 (November 1996): 5.

[4] Martin, Melissa. "Depressed Employees Take Twice as Many Sick Days." *Occupational Hazards* 63 (July 2001): 16.

[5] ———— AdvancePCS. "Study Finds U.S. Workers with Depressive Disorders Cost Employers $44 Billion in Lost Productive Time." *Insurance Advocate* 114 (July 7, 2003): 30.

ensure the future. For others, it may be that managing the emotional environment in your workplace simply makes your work life better. You'll feel more like going to work. Let's face it; many of you are going to work because you have to. Why not make that "have to" more pleasant? Besides, understanding emotions will give you a sense of mastery that can increase satisfaction in all areas of your life.

LESSON 3

Performance Can Be Enhanced Through Positive Behaviors.

If we take the first two lessons a step further, we can see that behaviors, especially those of the leader, will have a direct effect on performance. Note the consistency of the findings in the published literature. The *Journal of Occupation and Organizational Psychology* examined the relationship between loyalty to one's supervisor and work performance. Results indicated that work performance on and beyond the job was directly affected by loyalty to one's supervisor.[6] Thus, a supervisor who behaved positively commanded greater loyalty from employees. In *First, Break All the Rules,* Marcus Buckingham and Curt Coffman present twelve core elements that are needed to attract, focus, and keep the most talented employees. All of the items point to positive feelings in the workplace that are directly attributable to the relationship with one's supervisor.[7] In addition, a survey by Personnel Decisions International reported in *HR Focus,* states that 37.3 percent of employees believe that interpersonal relationships are of high importance when deciding what makes a good boss. In addition, 19 percent of respondents cited the ability to understand employees' needs as one of the most important characteristics of a boss.[8] *Nation's Business* reports in "How to Be a

---

[6]Zhen Xiong, Tsui; Farh, Anne S.; Jiing-Lih Chen. "Loyalty to Supervisor vs. Organizational Commitment: Relationships to Employee Performance." *Journal of Occupational and Organizational Psychology* 75 (September 2002): 339.

[7]Buckingham, Marcus, and Coffman, Curt. *First, Break All the Rules. New York:* Simon and Schuster, 1999.

[8]———— "What Makes a Good Boss?" *HR Focus* 77 (March 2000): 10.

Great Boss" that when people feel good about the person they report to, they feel better about the company they work for—and everyone benefits.[9] Stan Beecham and Michael Grant in an article in *Supervision* write that the employee sees the company through the lens of the relationship he or she has with the supervisor. They further state that employees do not leave companies—they leave bosses.[10] *Organizational Science* reports that worker productivity increases because of a supportive social context defined as more support from supervisors and coworkers.[11]

LESSON 4

Emotional Intelligence Is Important, But It's by No Means the Only Factor That Leads to High Performance.

Intellect has proven invaluable to our success in business. Financial decisions based on analyzing details, sound strategies based on facts and data, and processes and procedures based on review and analysis are all critically important. Businesses could not survive without very smart people to run them. Engineering advancements, process improvements, automation, and supply-chain enhancements can create enormous wealth for company owners and shareholders, and smart bosses are always part of the mix. We are in no way insinuating that emotional intelligence is the only avenue of success; rather, we prefer to think about blending our knowledge and emotional intelligence so that our businesses or organizations can achieve the highest level of success. In fact, given the quality and productivity advances that have been made, it's more and more difficult to get big wins just from improving engineering efforts. However, in many ways, advances in emotional intelligence provide new borders that have yet to be expanded. Our gains in this area can be great.

---

[9]Maynard, R. "How to Be a Great Boss." *Nation's Business*79 (December 1991): 44.
[10]Beecham, Stan, and Grant, Michael, "Smart Leadership in Tough Times." *Supervision* 64 (June 2003): 3.
[11]Staw, Barry M.; Sutton, Robert I; and Pelled, Lisa H. "Employee Positive Emotion and Favorable Outcomes at the Workplace." *Organization Science—A Journal of the Institute of Management Sciences*. 5 (February 1994): 51.

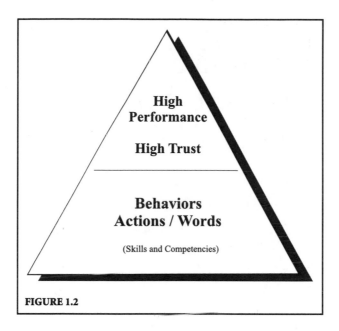

**High
Performance**

High Trust

**Behaviors
Actions / Words**

(Skills and Competencies)

FIGURE 1.2

With these lessons in mind, a prudent business decision would be to learn more about emotional intelligence and how it can help our business succeed. We can achieve this goal with a model in the shape of a triangle. Because we can safely assume that the output generated on the good boss chart is desirable, I placed high performance at the top of the triangle, supported by high trust. We place behaviors at the bottom of the triangle, because our opening discussion shows that high performance and high trust often grow out of the behaviors of the leader. These behaviors are sometimes referred to as skills or competencies. Therefore, the model begins to take shape, as shown in Figure 1.2.

CHAPTER 2

THE MYSTERY OF HUMAN BEHAVIOR

I have striven not to laugh at human actions,
not to weep at them, nor to hate them,
but to understand them.—Baruch Spinoza

Because behavior has such an important effect on performance, it would be worthwhile to understand the complicated factors leading to human behavior, especially our own. Family and societal values, laws and mores of church and state, personality, group influences, assumptions and beliefs, life experiences, and reinforcement and punishment all drive human behavior. These factors account for the vast differences among people. Some of those differences are easy to recognize, while others are subtler. Personality differences are among those sometimes easily identified. For example, some people are innately aggressive or assertive, while others are more passive. Others are outgoing by nature, while others are more withdrawn. We also understand that people who were raised with certain beliefs or values may apply those beliefs to their adult behavior. Similarly, we may recognize that to live in our society, certain behaviors, such as murder, are more than illegal; they are simply not acceptable and may also be against our values. Other behaviors are not only acceptable, but are also encouraged. Saying "thanks" and "please" and helping others—may be behaviors that you were taught. Parents, extended family, religious leaders, and community all mold our behaviors.

Yet, people sometimes behave differently when influenced by a group. Every teenager's parent wonders what peer pressure his or her child is experiencing when it comes to music, clothes, and behavior on social occasions, such as prom night.

But what do you know about your behavior? Probably a good deal. After all, you've been living with yourself for quite some time. However, no matter what your current knowledge, increasing that knowledge is a worthwhile and lifelong process. Also, what you do with that knowledge may be the difference between a life of mastery and one filled with repeated errors and struggles.

Personality and style have long been recognized as influencing behavior. Many companies have trained leaders and other staff to identify personality- and style-driven behavioral differences. We often teach people to adapt their styles to accommodate those of others. We encourage people to empathize, which is to see the world through the eyes of others. So, we know that the highly analytical person craves facts and figures and that the quick-driver types prefer quick summaries that do not bore them with details. Many in the workplace have studied the Myers–Briggs Personality Type Indicator and know that introverts and extroverts draw their energy from different sources that affect the way they work. Introverts derive energy from being alone and require private time to recharge. Extroverts derive their energy from being around others. Myers–Briggs also tells us that extroverts prefer discussing things with others and that they do their best thinking when engaged with other people. Further, those scoring in either the "thinking" or "feeling" preferences in Myers–Briggs have a different way of processing information.[1] Therefore, in addition to the factors mentioned earlier, personality accounts for differences in people's behaviors.

We also understand that values have an impact on workplace behaviors. Most major companies have eloquently written values statements describing themselves as places at which we'd all want to work. Because these values are expected to shape behaviors, they are

---

[1]Myers, Isabell, and Briggs, Katharine. *Myers–Briggs Type Indicator.* Palo Alto, CA: Consulting Psychologist Press, 1993.

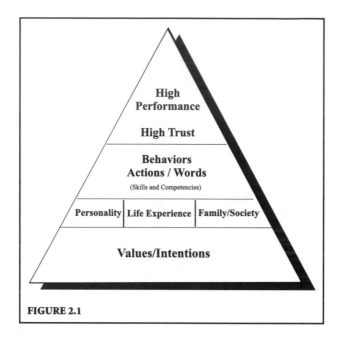

FIGURE 2.1

placed at the base of our triangle model (see Figure 2.1). If you have a well-written values statement, people (both leaders and employees) are supposed to understand how to behave, thereby creating a high-performing culture. Values certainly are an important piece of the puzzle. If people always behaved in the way they should, that would be the end of the story.

THE DANCE BETWEEN VALUES AND EMOTIONS

Assuming then that values drive our behavior, how do we explain the following scenario? Let's just say that if you interviewed me, I would tell you that there are two values that I hold dear. (Don't bother to decide if the values are right or wrong, just let the scenario unfold for the purpose of illustration.) First, I do not believe in beating children, and secondly, I do not believe in belittling people at any time—and especially not in public. So, I'm walking down a busy street with my two-year-old grandchild. I do not have him by the hand and suddenly he darts toward the street directly into the path

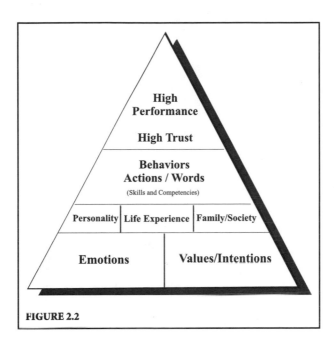

FIGURE 2.2

of a Mack truck. I rush to grab him and carry him to safety and then proceed to beat his behind as I scream in the crowded streets, "How could you be so stupid?" Given the values that I stated earlier, could this scenario occur? Sure it could. Why? It could occur because of the tremendous power of the emotion (terror) that I was experiencing as I witnessed my grandchild heading for danger. Thus, our emotions also drive our behavior (see Figure 2.2).

However, in this example, my intention was not to belittle or beat the child. In this instance, emotions overrode my values or intentions. When emotion overrides values or intention, it is called emotional hijacking (see Figure 2.3). Everyone has experienced emotional hijacking at some time. Daniel Goleman, who described the term emotional hijacking in *Emotional Intelligence,* compares emotional hijacking to an emergency signal sent to a part of our brain.[2]

Although the example was rather extreme and obvious, it's important to recognize that emotions can also play an important, although

---

[2] Goleman, Daniel. *Emotional Intelligence.*, New York: Bantam Books, 1995.

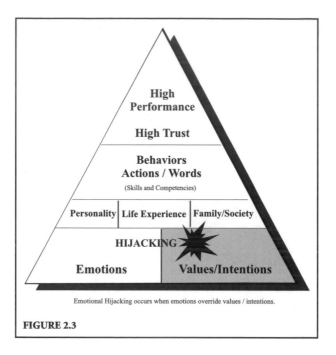

Emotional Hijacking occurs when emotions override values / intentions.

FIGURE 2.3

sometimes more subtle, role in influencing everyday behavior in the workplace. No doubt you've either contributed to or witnessed a hijacking when someone just happens to enter with the wrong message. Who hasn't had the urge to "shoot the messenger?" Some organizational cultures encourage the concept of placing blame and expressing mistrust. In those cultures, hijacking is an expected daily ritual. In one company, employees referred to the room where the morning production meeting was held as "the torture chamber." At a particular meeting, a review of the numbers proved painful—and that pain was spread to others. I'm referring to the way in which the conversation took place, not the fact that the issue of declining production numbers needed attention. In another company, one executive routinely broke and threw pencils when he was angry or frustrated in a meeting. With each outburst, the room fell into silence. Both of these companies, by the way, had beautifully written values statements that included treating others in a respectful manner. When I interviewed the leaders of the perceived attacks in the torture chamber and the pencil-breaking executive, all said they valued open discussion and didn't want "yes" people working for them. Yet, their actions did not contribute to the type of culture they said they valued. None of them realized the full negative impact of their actions.

Hijacking takes many different forms. Anger is one of the most obvious to identify. As said earlier, anger in the workplace sometimes takes on a more subtle tone. However, anger is not the only emotion that diverts us from our intentions. Hijacking has many other faces. Most of us have witnessed a time when peers, who moments before a meeting were loudly contesting an issue, are suddenly muted when the powers enter the room. Perhaps we could even count ourselves among those peers who lose their voices when a meeting begins. It is not unusual for people to be muted by some perceived fear of being labeled or sounding stupid. We have placed the mute button on our remote switches because it is perceived to protect us from something threatening. A study of employee silence in the *Journal of Management Studies* found that most employees who were concerned about an issue did not raise it with a supervisor because they felt uncomfortable speaking to those above them about their concerns.[3]

Inertia is another one of the more profound manifestations of repeated hijackings. When feeling overwhelmed or fearful, many people take no action at all. They just freeze. Although their intention might be to move the project along or reach some milestone on the pert chart, the emotional glue of inertia has their feet stuck to the ground. People are somehow distracted from their intentions, and they suffer greatly. The project constantly stares them in the face, yet they cannot break the bonds of this powerful adhesive. Over and over, they think about implementing their plans, but are unable to execute them. Whether their inertia is caused by fear of failure, self-imposed standards that are too high, or feeling overwhelmed by the enormity of the task, they are not living their intentions. This

---

[3]Milliken, Frances J.; Morrison, Elizabeth W.; Hewlin, Patricia F. "An Exploratory Study of Employee Silence: Issues That Employees Don't Communicate Upward and Why." *Journal of Management Studies* 40 (September 2003): 24.

pattern of inertia caused by repeated hijackings can become rooted in a person's behavior.

In each of these examples of hijacking—the routine tortures at the production meetings, the pencil-breaking executive, the muting at the meeting when issues were discussed, the inertia resulting from being overwhelmed—all have well entrenched roots that are difficult, but not impossible, to break. Each of these behaviors can be replaced with new behaviors and reactions, but changing requires effort. To break these patterns, new responses need to be created and then repeated, so that new habits can be formed.

HIJACKING CAN ALTER PERCEPTION

It's also important to understand that emotions can alter perceptions. Hijacking can cause you to confuse the facts, as illustrated in the following example. When my daughter was just three months old, we were involved in a horrific automobile accident that resulted in serious injuries and fatalities. A drunken driver struck us broadside on a beautiful sunny afternoon. Our car turned on its side trapping my daughter and me. As I became oriented, I found my daughter dangling in her car seat in the back seat of our twisted automobile. (Yes, thank God for car seats.) I reached for her and was struggling to release the clasp on the car seat when two things became apparent to me. One, I smelled gasoline, and two, I heard people outside screaming, "Get them out of there, it's going to blow." I finally freed my daughter from the constraints of her car seat and passed her safely to the arms of a brave Good Samaritan. After being helped out of the vehicle, someone handed my daughter back to me. I remember vividly walking along the side of the road to flee the threat of fire. I panicked as I looked down the side of the road and realized that I was walking along a drop off that must have been at least twenty-feet deep. All I could think was that we survived the crash only to be killed by a fall over this deep cliff.

A week after the crash, I went back to visit the scene of the accident. To my surprise, the twenty-foot cliff was no greater than two feet. That's right. I drastically overestimated the depth. My rational brain was rendered completely nonfunctional, as my emotional reaction to the accident distorted my perception and my ability to assess facts. In fact, I would have sworn in a court of law that that drop off was twenty feet or close to it, not two. This example shows how impaired perceptions caused by emotions affect decision-making. Emotions can likewise impair decision-making in the workplace, which can also have serious consequences.

CHAPTER 3

THE WAY
WE ARE WIRED

Habit is stronger than reason.—Santayana

A rudimentary understanding of the science of our brain is necessary to understand hijacking. Emotions are rooted in our brains and our biochemistry; they are not simply a matter of the heart. A growing body of research in many disciplines, including neuroscience, psychology, leadership, and medicine, has shed light on the make-up and role of emotions.

Emotional signals originate in the brain and are felt throughout the body.[1] Although unknown to us, some of the common language we use actually has a scientific basis. For example, when we talk about a gut reaction, or we say something makes our stomachs turn, or the words are stuck in our throat, or it's a pain in the neck, we're actually expressing how our emotions may manifest themselves physically. Every cell in our bodies has receptors that transmits messages from the brain to the body systems.[2] So that pain in the neck may actually have its origins in the brain. And those lumps in

---

[1]Ekman, Paul, and Davidson, Richard, eds. *Questions About Emotions.* New York: Oxford University Press, 1994.
[2]Cohen, M., and Stumwasser, F. *Comparative Neurobiology.* New York: John Wiley and Sons, 1985.

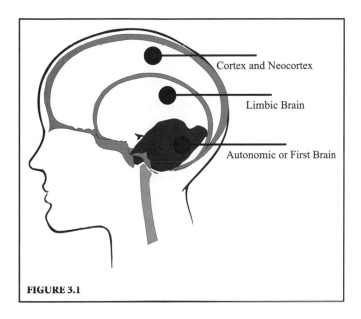

FIGURE 3.1

our throats have more to do with our emotions than with the physical structure of our throat.

THREE-BRAIN STRUCTURE

Autonomic Brain

Our brains consist of three fundamental areas (see Figure 3.1). One area is our autonomic, or first, brain. According to scientists, the autonomic brain is responsible for such important functions as breathing and the beating of our hearts. These functions occur automatically, without thought or input. They occur when we are asleep, as well as when we are awake. We have the ability to think about some of these functions, such as breathing, and call them into our awareness, but generally these functions occur completely without our conscious awareness. And it's a good thing. I can barely remember what to pick up at the grocery store, so I'm thankful that my autonomic brain can take care of those essential functions. These autonomic functions have evolved over time since early in our evolutionary history.

Limbic Brain

Another area of our brain structure is our emotional brain, or limbic system, which consists mainly of the amygdala and the hippocampus. On the evolutionary timeline, our limbic systems developed
after our autonomic brains. The limbic system is the storehouse
for emotional data and emotional memory. Everything that has
occurred in our lives is recorded in our limbic brains, and this information is essential for our survival. For example, the limbic system
records danger and fear, thereby giving us the basis for deciding
whether to instantly fight or run in particular circumstances. This
system of reaction gets us out of harm's way quickly. The database
of our limbic system constantly grows and provides us with more
and more information on which to base reactions. Our limbic system
can remember two things: (1) the actual incident, including the time
of day, what we were doing, or other details of some strong emotional event that are stored in the hippocampus, and (2) the feeling
created by the event that is stored in the amaydala.[3] For example,
most Americans can vividly recall where they were on September 11,
2001. The details of how they learned of the news, whom they were
with, what they were doing, and so on, are stored in the hippo-
camus. In addition, the amygdala has a permanent record of the
feelings associated with the event. This storehouse of feelings, rather
than the details, activates very quickly if an event with similar characteristics were to occur. For example, not long after September 11,
2001, news of a plane crash in the borough of Queens in New York
City created a wave of concern and fear that was magnified because
of September 11. That wave was the handiwork of the amygdala.
Because of the evolutionary context of our development, the amygdala reaction is quick and can reign supreme over our entire being.
We've all heard accounts of people who put their lives at risk to save
a child or otherwise performed some incredible feat for the sake of
life or death. Our amygdala has served us well and plays a role in our
species' survival.

---

[3] LeDoux, Joseph E. "Emotional Memory Systems in the Brain." *Behavioral and Brain Research,*
58 (1993): 111-116.

Within the limbic system, neurons transmit messages from the brain through an electrical and chemical system. Substances, called peptides, which are the chemical components of emotions, are carried to every cell of our body and are responsible for triggering emotional responses.[4] Therefore, the gut reaction, pain in the neck, or lump in our throats triggered by our limbic system is literally felt and remembered throughout our body so that the next event that triggers the amygdala is felt in the same way. In addition, evidence indicates that emotional pain, or hurt feelings, such as that experienced because of social rejection, activates the same pain center in our brains as does physical pain.[5] A study published in the *Journal of the American College of Cardiology* identified emotional turmoil as a risk factor for both heart attacks and long-term heart health.[6] So the connection between emotions and our bodies is strong.

Rational Brain

As our evolutionary development continued, the cortex and neocortex developed as the center for cognitive responses. The cortex is responsible for higher order rational thought. It is the seat of problem-solving and decision-making. It is here that data and information are stored and analyzed. For example, early in our educational experience, we learned that two plus two equals four. We've stored that fact, and each time we add a column of numbers, we recall that fact and incorporate it into our calculations. It is here that we interpret data and draw conclusions based on facts and figures.[7] As we study the steps to improve emotional intelligence, the rational brain can assist us in navigating the path to living our intentions and help us to avoid emotional hijacking.

[4]Ekman, Paul, and Davidson, Richard, e.ds. *Questions About Emotions,* New York: Oxford University Press, 1994.

[5]Eisenberger, Naomi. "The Pain of Social Rejection," *Science* 302 (October 10, 2003).

[6]Strik, Jacqueline; Donollet, Johan; and Lousberg, Richard. "High Anxiety May Warn of Future Problems for Heart Attack Patients." *Journal of the American College of Cardiology,* 42(10) (November 19, 2003): 42-48.

[7]Bloom, F. *Brain, Mind, and Behavior.* New York: W. H. Freeman, 1985.

WHY HIJACKING OCCURS

If I stick a match and put it close to your face, your limbic system will cause you to pull back to protect yourself from being burned. Without consulting your rational brain, your limbic system will take over and sound the danger alarm. Instantly, you will be at a safe distance from the match. It's important to know that your limbic system works really fast. In fact, your limbic system can react in milliseconds, as opposed to the seconds that it takes for your rational brain to respond. Depending on the circumstances, this response time has been measured at as between eighty and one hundred times faster than your rational brain. So quick, in fact, that your rational brain isn't even aware that a danger may exist; it is simply following the intense alarm put out by your limbic brain.[8] If your rational brain were consulted, it would have to process data such as the temperature of the match, the temperature at which skin burns, and the risk or injury that would likely result before it could devise a rational plan of action. Although your rational brain may process this information fairly quickly, it's not the sprinter that your limbic system is. Therefore, the limbic system would no doubt deliver you from danger sooner. So in a hijacking situation, your limbic system just takes over, and your rational brain is simply not consulted. Besides, your limbic brain is well positioned for hijacking. Located in the center between your rational and your autonomic brains, the limbic system readily controls your autonomic reactions and your rational patterns. Want to increase your heart rate? No problem. Keep your mouth shut in a meeting where a threat is perceived? No problem. The limbic system rules.

Thus, perceived threats have created well-ingrained pathways for reactions. But, the reality is that even though our physical survival is not usually threatened, our limbic system still sends signals of risk and danger. Why? Because it has created patterned responses that serve our needs. If screaming and yelling for a cookie at age two produced the desired result, we may still be using that method in pro-

---

[8]Angevine, J., and Cotman, C. *Principles of Neuroanatomy.* New York: Oxford University Press, 1981.

duction meetings to get something we want. At age two, before our rational processes and language were well developed, this mechanism served us well. Now, however, those pathways are still working as if nothing has changed. Thus, the pencil-breaking executive and the guillotine production meetings are serving some "flight or fight" syndrome that long ago became an established pattern of behavior. Likewise, the muting that occurs in many meetings is rooted in the limbic brain's signal to hush and lie low until the danger or threat passes. Inertia, too, has been carved by pathways that the limbic system devised over time, systems in which inaction is seen as contributing more to our safety than action. Those neuropathways contribute as much, if not more, to our behavior than rational thought.

CHAPTER 4

EMOTIONS: WHAT ARE THEY?

Let's not forget that the little emotions are
the great captains of our lives and we obey
them without realizing it.—Vincent Van Gogh

Generally in our society, we describe emotion in terms of feelings. You may feel happy that Friday afternoon is approaching. A coworker may feel angry that she received a poor performance review. Another coworker may feel nervous about making a presentation. In fact, this "feeling language" is present everywhere. And you'll notice that some people express themselves by describing feelings more frequently than others. So, for our discussion about emotional intelligence, we need to understand the three basic components of emotions: the cognitive component, the physiological component, and the behavioral component.

THE COGNITIVE COMPONENT

Consider Tom in the Information Technology department. Tom loves his job. He thinks nothing is more interesting, challenging, and stimulating than writing computer programs. No other career interests him. On the other hand, Karen, a landscape designer, would accept almost any work, as long as she can be outdoors. Karen can think of nothing more boring that sitting in front of a computer screen all day. Tom and Karen have completely different perceptions

[28]

or interpretations about the type of work they like. These perceptions, thoughts, beliefs, and expectations make up the cognitive component of our emotions. Or, as Shakespeare wrote in *Hamlet*, "There is nothing either good or bad, but thinking makes it so." Our thoughts, beliefs, and expectations, which are housed in our rational brain, definitely contribute to our emotions.

Consider John. John was an accountant in the accounts payable department at a large company. He enjoyed his job, considered himself reasonably well paid, and liked that he could walk out the door at a decent hour and have dinner with his family. For all intents and purposes, John was a picture of contentment. He never seriously considered applying for higher paying positions because he believed those positions came with headaches and that his time wouldn't be his own once he was promoted beyond a certain level. Then, along came Ann, John's new boss. Ann saw a great deal of potential in John, and she believed that he had what it took to be promoted well beyond his current position. She kept talking to John and, although well meaning, planted thoughts that he had outgrown his current position. She pointed to the lack of variety in his current position, the minimal opportunity to learn new things, and that, all in all, his current position was just not very satisfying. Again, Ann's intentions were never malicious. She believed that she was helping John by encouraging him to stretch and improve. So, John reluctantly began to apply for higher-level positions in different areas of the company, but he was rejected for posting after posting. After approximately two years, John found that he hated his current job. He was disgruntled about the company, and he frequently complained to coworkers. Why? Because John's thoughts had changed. His cognition, once positive, now had different expectations and beliefs about his work.

There's nothing inherently right or wrong about this situation or about the way John or Ann behaved. It's just an example of how thought, expectations, and beliefs can affect your emotional state. The most common example of this is the new employee, who is just delighted to have the position. She is filled with enthusiasm about the company, the pay, and the benefits, and is eager to learn the job. Then, six months down the road, this new-hire enthusiasm has turned sour. What once seemed like the world's greatest opportunity now looks like a prison term. Why? What happened? One thing for certain: this employee's expectations, beliefs, and thinking have changed. It could be because, indeed, she has been treated poorly, or that the picture painted by the recruiter was far from reality. It could also be that coworkers or others in the workplace focus on the company's shortcomings rather than its assets. If, each day, she goes to work and hears about all that is wrong with the company, her thinking and beliefs will soon begin to shift. No new employee orientation program can outweigh the cultural beliefs that are generated by the actual workforce. Therefore, genuine efforts to instill positive beliefs within our workforce have a positive multiplier effect on the emotional state of existing employees and new hires.

The Physiological Component

It's about 2:00 AM, and you are walking down the street in a dark and dangerous neighborhood. All of a sudden someone springs out of an alley and runs toward you. What emotion do you think you are experiencing? For most of us, it would be fear—fear that would cause an immediate physiological reaction, including rapid heartbeat, dry mouth, rapid or irregular breathing, trembling, dilated pupils, perspiration, and increased blood sugar. The automatic physiological reaction is controlled by our limbic system (in particular the hypothalamus and amygdala). As discussed earlier, it protects us and is responsible for controlling our actions, especially during times of attack, defense, or retreat. As a result, it is often called the "fight or flight" response[1] Thanks to flight or fight, our ancestors were able to deal with a dangerous world. When confronted by the saber-toothed tiger, the body instantly prepared itself either to defend itself or run. The body prepares itself by releasing powerful hormones that make the senses sharper, the muscles tighter, and the heart

---

[1]Cannon, W.B. *The Wisdom of the Body.* New York: W.W. Norton, 1932.

pound faster. These physical reactions still take place. The only thing missing is the saber-toothed tiger.

Now, imagine that you have been asked to stand up and make a presentation in front of the company board of directors that would justify your job. Depending on your presentation, you will either stay at your job or your job will be eliminated. Can you imagine your physical state right before and during the presentation? No doubt, most of us would have many of the same physical reactions described in the earlier example. Many of the situations that we respond to in the workplace are perceived threats that the limbic system will interpret and then address with immediate physiological reactions.

Of the two examples above, one poses a perceived threat on your life and the other a perceived threat on your livelihood, so you can see why your limbic system would respond by creating a physiological reaction. However, let's get realistic. Most of us are not working in situations in which either our lives or our jobs are at stake. (We certainly recognize that some people literally do put their lives on the line every day at work, such as police, fire, and other emergency personnel.) For the majority of us, surely our limbic system wouldn't be involved at the workplace, right? Wrong. Our limbic system goes to work with us every day. In every meeting, every customer interaction, every coworker encounter, our limbic system is hard at work scanning the environment for even the slightest perceived threat. That threat could come in the form of a raised voice from an irritated customer, an uncomfortable question at a staff meeting, a pronouncement of impending change at a department meeting, or a critical remark from a coworker. These more subtle "threats" are all significant to our limbic system. The more in tune you are with your physical reactions, the better you will be able to understand your emotions. Your physical reactions don't lie. They are a credible source of information regarding your feelings. I can still vividly remember that during my first performance appraisal nearly thirty years ago, my supervisor gave me a cup of coffee. My hands were trembling so badly that, as I lifted the cup to my lips, I missed my mouth and dribbled coffee down my chin. I have no recollection of what was said that day, but I sure do remember my trembling hands. I've kept in touch with that wonderful supervisor and we have laughed about that incident many times.

THE BEHAVIORAL COMPONENT

How do we express our joy? Our sadness? Our fear? Our anger? The behavioral component of emotions is how emotion is expressed. A simple example of this is joy or happiness. Most people smile when they feel joy. In fact, across cultures, a smile is a universal symbol of the emotion of happiness. In fact, nonverbal behaviors are the most common expression of emotions. Facial expression, gestures, body position, use of touch, position and expression of the eyes, and tone of voice are definite behavioral expressions of emotions. In our quest for greater emotional intelligence, nonverbal behavior is the most difficult to address.

Behavioral expression of emotions also includes words and actions. Just imagine the two-year-old in the grocery store in the throes of a temper tantrum. You can picture his body thrust against the floor, fists pounding, and his little voice straining at the top of his lungs, "I want a cookie, now!" Most adults have managed to get themselves up off the floor, so we longer expect to see this type of physical behavior. However, screams of "I want a cookie, now!" may have been replaced with, "I want that report, now!"

Most of us are capable of improvements in our behavioral expression of emotions in the workplace. Just take customer service as an example. Most of us can recall a customer transaction in which we have been treated rudely or insulted. Perhaps it was the repairperson who said, "What did you do to cause your TV to malfunction?" Or the deli counter person who said, "I can't read your mind. You didn't tell me that you wanted mustard instead of mayo." Or perhaps you told the computer help desk person that your computer was not working properly when you just booted up that morning, and she said, "Yeah, right. . . . That's what they all say." And of course, these behavioral faux pas are by no means confined to customer service. Leaders at all levels and coworkers and colleagues everywhere do things every day to express their frustration, disgust, anger, and fear that have a negative impact on others.

The cognitive and behavioral components of emotions are two areas on which we can focus our attention in emotional intelligence. And it is where we will focus much of our time and attention in the next chapters. The premise is, if we can change what we think and we can change how we behave in certain situations, we can positively influence our emotional intelligence.

CHAPTER 5

REWIRING FOR GREATER PERFORMANCE AND TO LIVE OUR INTENTIONS

To do good things in the world, first you must know
who you are and what gives meaning in your life.
—*Paula P. Brownlee*

Given our brain structure and the eons of evolution that have created our current human condition, is it possible to improve our level of emotional intelligence? If we look at that question in light of our working definition of emotional intelligence, the answer is yes. By thoughtfully applying what we know about the origins of behavior and the impact of emotions, each person can deliberately determine a path for greater emotional intelligence. For years, psychotherapy reconstructed our emotional pathways so that the results of traumatic events are lessened. Therefore, if people are able to learn ways to minimize trauma, people are certainly able to learn ways of addressing less severe emotional reactions that could be robbing or hijacking them of their intentions. In another context, some patients with disorders other than dealing with trauma are able to change destructive patterns of reaction through behavior therapy. New emotional learning can take place. This emotional learning, however, does not happen without intention and without method. In therapy, people are directed to reorder their emotional reactions to recover from trauma or other events with the help of a therapist. For those people motivated to improve their lives, not for therapeutic reasons, but for reasons of self-actualization, the news is good. By self-actualization, I mean the human desire for fulfillment, namely for a person to become everything he or she is capable of becoming, in essence our ideal selves. Emotional intelligence is an essential piece of this struggle. Those who have the desire and who work at it can definitely increase their emotional intelligence. In fact, for most people this is the ongoing process of emotional maturity. With thoughtful method, emotional maturity can be escalated to even greater emotional wisdom.

Also, unlike IQ, emotional intelligence is not a fixed capacity. The limits of IQ are quite well known. People either have the capacity to learn quadratic equations or not. Sure, there is some variance, but the variance is within a limited range. Even if someone has never been taught how to do the math that will solve the equations, it's certain that with the right teacher one either will be able to or not, depending on his or her mental capabilities. Emotional intelligence, however, is different; the limits are broader. The emotional capacity of an individual can increase with age and life experiences. This capacity certainly includes the ability to manage oneself and one's relationships.[1] For example, life experiences change not only the knowledge level but also the emotional wiring that contributes to people's maturity. Given the normal path of development, a toddler and a teenager learn how to control impulses. As a result, emotional outbursts lessen as they mature. That same toddler and teenager are also accumulating life experiences in the hippocampus and the amygdala that contribute to their development. So their capacity for emotional intelligence is actually increasing. Take another example. Many children have not experienced loss and its accompanying grief, so they may not fully understand these concepts. However, as we age and experience loss in our lives, we develop a greater capacity to understand our own experiences and to empathize with others who may be experiencing loss. In this way, our capacity increases

---

[1]Goleman, Daniel. *Emotional Intelligence.* New York: Bantam Books, 1995.

and adds to our emotional intelligence. However, without reflection and purposeful direction, some of that capacity will surely be lost.

Emotional intelligence harnesses and takes advantage of life experiences to add to our storehouse of emotional wisdom. At the same time, however, reflection and purposeful direction can also weed out of our limbic system reactions to life experiences that are detrimental to our evolving emotional intelligence. Behaviors resulting from fear, anger, and other negative responses to some life events may simply not be healthy or serve a purpose in our lives. Reflection on which behaviors are causing harm and inhibiting us from becoming who we intend to be serves an important purpose. None of this, however, can occur without thoughtful direction. Glimpses of insight must be cultivated so that these moments will result in lessons truly learned. If not, these moments will fade quickly, and we will repeat our errors in the next encounter.

Thoughtful and purposeful reflection can produce new learning. This new learning will eventually rewire our limbic system so that our emotional reactions are more in line with our intentions. That's not to say that we will never experience emotional hijacking, but rather that we will often be able to redirect a hijacking before it takes over en route to a land we don't care to visit. Most of us have experienced a time when we were proud that we avoided losing our temper or overcame some fear that interfered with our intentions. Capitalizing on that experience opens the path to greater emotional intelligence. Accumulating these experiences creates new pathways for our limbic system and reinforces behaviors that are more in line with our intentions.

EMOTIONAL INTELLIGENCE IS A PARTNERSHIP

Emotional intelligence can best be viewed as a partnership between our rational brain and limbic brain. By blending the thoughts offered by our rational brain with the rich information from our limbic brain, we can direct our own actions and behaviors. Otherwise, we will end up in an emotional alley that does not serve us well. Our rational brain can be an important partner that will help us make sense of the emotional memory and storehouse of data collected by our limbic brain. In addition, our rational brain can help our limbic system differentiate the real emergencies that threaten life and limb from those false alarms that our limbic system may be programmed to sound. Partnership, however, implies exchange. Indeed, our limbic brains have a wealth of information to share as well. Emotional intelligence isn't about extinguishing our emotions as may be implied if the rational brain rules; instead it's about understanding when our emotions can help us live our intentions and when our emotions may be getting in the way. It's about channeling our emotions in a fashion that works to our advantage. All emotion is useful. It's how we experience and behave as a result of our emotions that can cause peace or distress in our lives. I like to think of emotional intelligence as a radio to which we can tune in and then turn the volume on our emotions up or turn down to enjoy the desired music in our lives.

The music I'm referring to is living our intentions. What do we intend to do? What is our purpose? Emotional intelligence allows us to harness our emotions so that we can honor our intentions. It isn't that emotions are positive or negative. They just exist. Their existence lends information and energy to our lives. And because they exist, it's essential to understand how they influence behavior and how to interpret and master them so that our intentions are honored rather than corrupted. As in the earlier example of my grandchild running into the street, living my intention means finding a way to deal with the emotions that prevail, while still honoring my values. In that example, terror overrode my intentions. Imagining my grandchild in harm's way hijacked me from my intentions, which were not to beat or belittle the child. My actions violated my intentions. In this scenario, would it be possible to save the child from danger, while maintaining the integrity of my values? Most people can easily recognize that, in fact, both could have been accomplished. Instantly grabbing the child and hugging him while expressing my obvious fear and strongly stating my objection to his behavior would have accomplished both objectives. Emotional intelligence allows for that kind of mastery.

INTRODUCING YOUR SELF-COACH

It would be great if we all had someone who could follow us around during the day and help us know exactly what, when, and how to interact with others, but in reality, we're generally left to our own devices. Surely many methods exist to achieve mastery in the area of emotional intelligence. In this book, I am proposing the notion of a self-coach to help improve our emotional intelligence. By creating a self-coach, we would have someone to consult, someone to whisper in our ear, and someone to advise us about the sometimes treacherous path of human interaction. The self-coach I'm proposing lives within each of us, because I believe that we each have a higher capacity that we could tap into examine our behaviors and determine if we are acting in line with our intentions.

CHAPTER 6

THE FIVE AREAS OF EMOTIONAL INTELLIGENCE

Knowing others is wisdom, knowing yourself is enlightenment.—Lao Tzu

The definition of emotional intelligence introduced in Chapter 1 is simple and straightforward. Very often, however, emotional intelligence is misunderstood. In fact, many people think that emotional intelligence is equivalent to social skills. That, however, is like thinking that a car is a steering wheel. You're simply missing a huge part of the picture. Social skills define our relationship to the external world, how we interact with others. Although this is part of emotional intelligence, much of emotional intelligence is about our internal world. And it is our internal world that will drive how we interact and respond to the external world. Emotional intelligence, therefore, includes skills that drive our internal world, as well as our response to the external world.

Our model for emotional intelligence contains the following five components (see Figure 6.1):

1. *Self-Awareness and Self-Control:* The ability to fully understand oneself and to use that information to manage emotions productively.

2. *Empathy:* The ability to understand the perspectives of others.

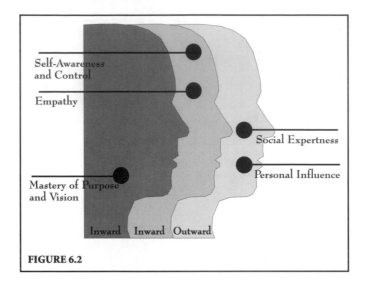

FIGURE 6.2

3. *Social Expertness:* The ability to build genuine relationships and bonds and to express caring, concern, and conflict in healthy ways.

4. *Personal Influence:* The ability to positively lead and inspire others, as well as oneself.

5. *Mastery of Purpose and Vision:* The ability to bring authenticity to one's life and live out one's intentions and values.

As you can see in the model depicted in Figure 6.1, three of the components of emotional intelligence relate to our internal world (self-awareness and control, empathy, and mastery of purpose and vision); the other two form our relations to the external world (social expertness and personal influence.) However, it is important to recognize that all are interrelated and that one component builds on the next. Self-awareness and self-control open the door to emotional intelligence. In essence, the seven steps in Part 2 of this book are about improving self-awareness and control. Without self-awareness and control, it is difficult, if not impossible, to improve one's relationship with the outside world. For example, if I am not aware of my actions, thoughts, and words, I have no basis for self-understanding. If I have some awareness and self-understanding, then I can ask, What is my impact on others in my current state? If I find that impact to be negative and detracting from my life goals, I may choose to change my actions, thoughts, or words. In emotional intelligence, this change is what we call self-control. It is about knowing and then determining the appropriate volume level and expression for our emotions. How can these emotions enhance our relationships with others and our life goals? How can they detract from them? Thus, self-awareness and self-control are intertwined, as self-awareness alone will be of little service without self-control.

Beyond self-awareness and control is empathy, which is also listed as an internal function on our model. Empathy must be felt inside before it can be reflected in our relationships with people in our external world. Therefore, empathy is a turning point or transition in our emotional intelligence as it plays out in the outside world. Also, without empathy, we are incapable of comprehending the impact of our actions or words on others. We may have been told that a particular behavior or word affects others in a negative way, but empathy enables us to experience it. Once experienced, the likelihood of change is much greater.

Next in our model is social expertness. Few of us can work or live in isolation. People are generally part of the equation. Social expertness has a few dimensions because it allows us to build genuine social bonds with others. Social expertness allows us to know people in a way beyond name, rank, and serial number. It allows us to connect with them honorably. The best analogy I can offer is that it's not about the number of people in your Roll-a-dex®, but rather the reaction that those people have when you're on the other end of the phone. Are they delighted that you called or would they rather be talking to the long distance carrier trying to sell phone services? Beyond honorable social bonds, social expertness calls on us to invite those within our social bonds to collaborate in achieving our intentions. How well are we able to collaborate with others and blend thoughts and ideas to achieve goals or live out intentions? But remember that once we have invited people to collaborate, conflict is inevitable as different ideas will emerge. How will we resolve those differences? Social expertness demands high levels of conflict resolution skills that work to preserve social bonds and trust.

Personal influence is the next area of our model of emotional intelligence. Personal influence is where true leadership emerges. Before this, we relate peer to peer; it is here that we intend to influence others toward goals or missions. However we cannot influence others if we have not created strong bonds, invited others to collaborate, or lack the ability to resolve conflict in healthy ways. Leadership is not reserved for positional leaders; all people are leaders. Even if we think about leadership in terms of influencing our children, this area of emotional intelligence is essential for a rich life and calls on us to influence others. But equally important is our ability to influence ourselves. It is within the walls of our own soul that the most of the work must be done. As we influence ourselves to change, we can be an instrument of influence on others.

Finally, the model includes mastery of purpose and vision. It is the most internally seated of all the facets of emotional intelligence, as it is foundation on which a more emotionally intelligent life can be built. It is, in essence, both the reason we strive for emotional intelligence and the driver that keeps us anchored. If we know our purpose, it is much easier to determine what type of emotional reactions will serve that purpose and which will defeat it. Mastery of purpose makes it easy to know why we should even bother. We place it last because it is sometimes the most difficult to know and conceptualize. Yet it is fundamental, even though it is certainly possible to make great improvements in all other areas of emotional intelligence without discovering true purpose. But once true purpose is discovered, emotional intelligence will be easier to improve.

To build emotional intelligence, this model requires that we work from the inside out. For example, we can't influence others until we have mastered self-awareness and self-control. Therefore, the next section of this book is a seven-step process designed to help us become more emotionally intelligent. With the help of a self-coach, these seven steps will help you develop greater understanding.

PART 2

TRAINING YOUR SELF-COACH

"Ah! If only there were two of me," she thought,
"one who spoke and the other who listened,
one who lived and the other who watched,
how I would love myself! I'd envy no one."
—*Simone de Beauvoir*

CHAPTER 7

THE DOORWAY
TO EMOTIONAL
INTELLIGENCE

The key to understanding others is
to understand oneself.—Helen Williams

Assuming that you are interested in improving your emotional
intelligence, just where do you begin? The doorway to emotional intelligence opens with self-awareness. Self-awareness is our
ability to understand ourselves and then to use that information to
fully live our intentions.

If you are interested in buying a home, you first see that home
from the curb. You may admire what you see, or you may not be sure
if it's for you. To find out more, you'll walk inside and poke around.
If you've done any house hunting, I'm sure that you've sometimes
been pleasantly surprised when you open the door. Other times, I'm
sure you've been disappointed by an appealing exterior that wrapped
around a rundown interior. Self-awareness helps us to align the curb
view with the interior view so we achieve authenticity.

SELF-AWARENESS IS CIRCULAR

Because self-awareness is such an important component of emotional intelligence, we will spend much of our time discussing it.
Later, as we discuss other aspects of emotional intelligence, self-

awareness will be a part of each of those discussions, because it is simply impossible to gain emotional intelligence without it. In your quest for greater emotional intelligence, you will find that self-awareness is a circular and cumulative process that is never fully achieved. Each day, new experiences and new challenges will present new opportunities to learn something about yourself. As you progress through life, each of these learning opportunities can build on each other. This cumulative learning is important. I'm sure you know people who go through life and never seem to learn from their mistakes, or they don't see how one experience is connected to another. Self-awareness will help prevent this from happening to you, but only if you keep building on your lessons. This linking of life experiences into ever-increasing lessons is the foundation of wisdom. It is the quintessential difference in living one year of experience thirty times versus thirty years of experience.

THE SELF-COACH: YOUR SELF-AWARENESS PARTNER

Earlier we introduced the concept of a self-coach, who could sit on your shoulder and provide guidance, wisdom, and monitoring as you go through life. Your self-coach could help you maneuver through those difficult situations with ease. Your self-coach can whisper in your ear when you're heading for trouble or sabotaging your intentions. If you've ever worked with a real coach, whether in sports, business, or some other venue, think about the value the coach brought to your activities. A coach offers tips, suggestions, praise, and techniques—all so you can achieve success. A true coach cares deeply about your performance and success. A true coach believes in you and commits time and energy to making you better. It might be great if all of us could have a real coach following us around through life—cheering us on, offering us advice, helping us reach our goals, and otherwise supporting our success. But, in fact, most people don't have that luxury. And even if you work with an outside coach, you are the one who will ultimately decide how to interact and behave, what choices to make and what paths to take.

So, we suggest that you call on the resources of a self-coach. This self-coach will be accessible 24/7 and can greatly enhance your emotional intelligence. Why? Because the self-coach is to self-awareness what the steering wheel and navigation system are to the car. If you want to go in a certain direction, the self-coach can be your means to get there. You're the one who is driving, but without a functioning steering wheel, your car can go out of control. Your self-coach can also serve as a navigation system, helping you find the way to your final destination. If you have a well-developed self-coach, your needs won't outpace your coach. He or she will always be there. As you gain more and more self-awareness, your self-coach will become more and more sophisticated. In fact, we suggest you give him or her a name because this partner can serve you for a lifetime.

So what exactly is the role of your self-coach? First, let me distinguish your self-coach from your conscience. Your self-coach isn't there to tell you right from wrong. The self-coach isn't there to impose guilt when you've done something wrong, but rather to help you learn from your experiences. In fact, a large part of the role of the self-coach is to help you learn from your experiences, both good and bad, so that you can fully live your intentions. Your self-coach is there to help you monitor your progress; to be a clearinghouse for lessons learned; to offer tips, suggestions, and advice based on your experiences; and to celebrate your successes. Your self-coach will keep you from getting stuck like those turkeys George and Harriet.

So, as you become familiar with your self-coach, the first thing you'll begin to notice is his attitude. You won't find him sarcastic or belittling or demeaning. He knows that wouldn't serve you well. Instead, he's supportive. Because he wants you to achieve your intentions, he often challenges you to be your best. He knows your ideal self, and he is strongly bent on helping you live that ideal. As you become more and more familiar with your self-coach, I hope you'll also find him to have a sense of humor, not laughing at you, but rather with you, regarding your follies and mistakes, as the two of you integrate these and deepen your awareness and mastery.

How do you prepare your self-coach for these important duties? Without your willingness, you can't improve your emotional intelligence. The fact that you are reading this book suggests that you are willing to learn more. Therefore, if you follow the steps outlined in

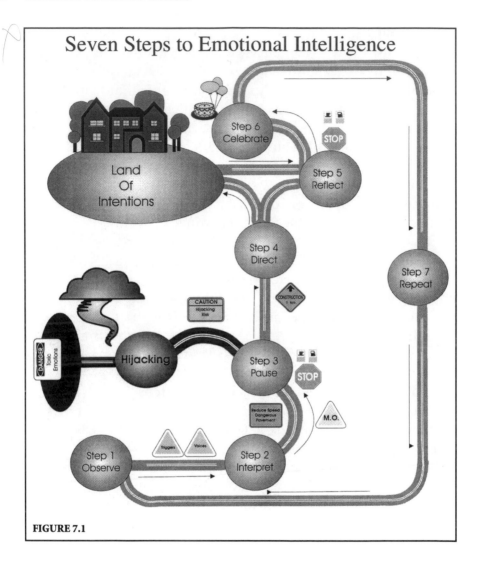

Seven Steps to Emotional Intelligence

Land Of Intentions

Step 6 Celebrate

STOP

Step 5 Reflect

Step 4 Direct

Step 7 Repeat

CAUTION Hijacking Risk

CONSTRUCTION 1 km

DANGER Toxic Emotions

Hijacking

Step 3 Pause

STOP

Reduce Speed Dangerous Pavement

M.O.

Triggers   Voices

Step 1 Observe

Step 2 Interpret

FIGURE 7.1

this book, your self-coach will be ready, willing, and able to assist you on your path to greater emotional intelligence.

SEVEN STEPS TO EMOTIONAL INTELLIGENCE FOR THE SELF-COACH

The Seven Steps to Emotional Intelligence for the self-coach to master are (1) Observe, (2) Interpret, (3) Pause, (4) Direct, (5) Reflect,

(6) Celebrate and (7) Repeat. By mastering these steps, the self-coach can direct and guide you to live in a more emotionally intelligent way. With continued practice and patience, you'll find your self-coach an invaluable partner in your daily experiences, both at home and at work. Let's begin to enhance our emotional intelligence (see Figure 7.1).

CHAPTER 8

STEP 1: OBSERVE

*When a man gains knowledge through
the observation of his truth, his view
of the world changes.—Kilindi Iyi*

Every great coach, regardless of the sport or discipline, observes. Coaches watch and analyze each movement of their players. They are able to detect even the slightest change. Therefore, the power of observation is the first essential skill that your self-coach must master. You already have experience related to observation, so it's a matter of sharpening this skill rather than building it from scratch. For example, I'm sure you can recall a time when you were in a situation that you knew was going downhill. Perhaps you could hear words coming out of your mouth and instantly thought: That wasn't exactly the right thing to say. Or perhaps you didn't speak up, and you heard yourself thinking: Why am I not speaking up? Perhaps you could feel yourself getting tense or frustrated. One leader explained that she was sitting in a meeting with her staff, and it was as if she could see two videos in her head. In one video, she saw her present behavior. She had lost her temper and was telling the group that she was tired of having to nag them for results. In this video, she saw herself doing all the wrong things and saying all the wrong words. Then, she said, she saw another video that showed her calmly addressing her staff and asking for solutions to her frustration over missed deadlines and other lackluster results. Unfortunately, she said, she continued her present behavior and even in the moment found herself regretting her words and actions.

In another instance, someone described his ability to observe his behavior as if he were looking through a two-way mirror. He could see himself in the middle of the scene, a scene that he wasn't particularly proud of, yet, he wasn't sure what to do to get to the other side of the glass. These individuals already have keen observation skills that will assist the self-coach in improving their emotional intelligence. Your similar experiences will also be valuable in this step. For example, you probably already have a way of observing yourself. Think about ways you now observe your behavior.

GET OUT MORE

How can you strengthen the power of observation? For starters, your self-coach needs to get out more. No, I'm not talking about going out to dinner, although dinner might be a fine place to begin. I'm talking about allowing your self-coach to distance himself or herself from you by climbing above your head and hanging out. Imagine him just watching, perhaps perched on a ledge and observing you from ten feet away or so. Not only can he see and hear you, but he can also see and hear others in the room. He can sense your mood, your body language, your breathing, and your voice intonations. He can also observe these things in other people around you.

You can practice this technique when you are seated someplace and not interacting with others. You could be in the waiting room at a doctor's office or at an airport or in a park. Just allow your self-coach to drift above your head and pay attention. Where are you seated? How are you seated? Where are your arms? Your legs? What are your hands doing? Are you seated straight? Are you slumped? No judgments please, just observation. What is the expression on your face? Are you smiling? Frowning? Ask your self-coach to observe your mood. Does he see you as happy? Sad? Peaceful? Determined? Impatient? Relaxed? Perplexed? As your self-coach gathers information through observation, his coaching skills begin to take shape.

After you have practiced observing yourself while alone, ask your self-coach to watch you interact with people. To begin, select situations that are relaxed and comfortable, perhaps as you walk down the hall to your workstation. Ask your coach to gauge the expression on your face. Are you smiling? How are you holding your head? What is your pace? If a coworker passes, what do you say? What was your tone of voice? For example, if you said "Good morning," did it sound enthusiastic? Rote? Did you speak loudly or softly? Did you enunciate clearly? Or did you mumble? Did you make eye contact? Did you call the person by name? What are you thinking about?

Now ask your self-coach to observe others with whom you are interacting. Remember, emotional intelligence has two dimensions: understanding ourselves and understanding our relationships with others. During that same walk down the hall, how were your co-workers dressed? What were their facial expressions? Were they smiling? Frowning? Did they appear hurried? Or leisurely? Who spoke first? What were the tones of their voices? Encourage your self-coach to keep practicing in relaxed or comfortable situations, such as lunch with your friends.

OBSERVE IN THE MOMENT

The trick is for the self-coach to be observing *in the moment.* By that, I mean for the coach to be able to determine as the action occurs just what is happening. This will be her greatest value to you in conflict and high-stress situations. That's why it's important to begin to sharpen this skill in low-stress situations. Pleasant encounters allow you to practice until observation becomes part of your routine. Observation in the moment also has side benefits. As you practice your observation skills in the moment, you will find that you are more present to the other person. Observation alone will improve your self-awareness. Even if you take no other steps, your emotional intelligence will likely improve. Yes, it's that important. Mastering observation will also help you later, because you will be accustomed to picturing yourself in different situations. You'll use this skill in later steps.

OBSERVE IN CONFLICT SITUATIONS

After you practice observing in pleasant situations, you're ready to assume the challenge of observing yourself during conflict or high-stress situations. In fact, this will occur automatically as your observation skills become ingrained in your repertoire. You'll find yourself observing all the time. In conflict situations, watch for changes in your heart rate, your breathing, your nonverbal behavior, and your tone of voice. What happens to your muscles? I can always tell when I don't agree with something because the first thing I do is clench my teeth. My jaw muscles tighten as if to warn me to "keep my mouth shut." In conflict situations, at first, try to pay particular attention to your physical reactions. Your physical reactions may well be the first indicators of trouble. Remember the limbic brain? It's working eighty to one hundred times faster than your rational brain. It's sending signals to all parts of your body. So, the likelihood that those muscles will tense, those jaws will clench, your breathing pattern will change, or your face will feel flushed will offer your self-coach the first clues that conflict is imminent.

As you cue into your physical reactions, you'll also want to observe other things about yourself. Here again, observe your mood. What are you feeling? Attacked? Worried? Tense? Angry? Scared? Think about your facial expression and look at your body language. Observe your tone of voice. As if you were a courtroom illustrator, capture the picture that is you. This picture should be as accurate, complete, and as objective as possible. While your self-coach is in training, it might be helpful to ask a trusted colleague or friend to help you with this observation process. After a high-stress or conflict situation, ask a trusted friend or adviser to tell you what he or she has observed. It's particularly difficult to see your own nonverbal behavior. Therefore, characteristics such as facial expression and body language, especially in a conflict situation, may take some time to master. But with persistence and, perhaps, the help of someone else, your self-coach will begin to see clearly.

TURNING YOUR OBSERVATION OUTWARD

Thus far in conflict situations, you've been training your self-coach to observe you and your reactions. Eventually, your observation should take into account the actions, words, nonverbal behaviors, and moods of others. By assessing tone of voice, facial expressions, body language, and other cues, you will gain important information regarding your interactions with others. Also, upon close observation, you may find, as we learned earlier, that your perceptions about a particular interaction might be different from what you assume to be true.

SCANNING

Scanning, a technique widely taught in law enforcement to sharpen and broaden officers' perceptions in high-stress situations, could be useful in improving emotional intelligence. Officers are taught in tense situations to keep their heads moving left and right to scan their environment.[1] For example, if an officer is focused on apprehending a suspect, he needs to scan his environment or he may miss the fact that two other suspects are approaching to the right. By focusing on just one factor or piece of information, the officer could miss important data that could cost him his life. Also, because scanning allows a look at the whole picture rather than at only one detail, it enhances the officer's problem-solving and decision-making skills. Many other professionals are also taught scanning techniques to enhance performance. In a study of airline pilots reported in *Aviation, Space, and Environmental Medicine,* those who used visual scanning performed better than those who did not.[2] Lifeguards too, as reported in *Parks and Recreation,* who were taught a five-minute scanning strategy improved their attention and concentration.[3]

Because scanning can be a useful tool in improving emotional intelligence, your self-coach should become accustomed to using it. Scanning engages your rational brain to help you think and interpret signals from your limbic system. Scanning plays an important role in expanding the partnership between your limbic and rational brains. Both systems are giving you data; scanning ensures that you

---

[1]Harney, John. "Officer Scanning Techniques." *Law Enforcement Journal* 8 (September 2000): 34.

[2]Bellenkes, A.H.; Wickens, C.D.; and Kramer, A.F. Visual Scanning and Pilot Expertise: The Role of Attention Flexibility and Mental Model Development." *Aviation, Space, and Environmental Medicine* 68(July 1997): 569–579.

[3]Vogelsong, Hans; Griffiths, Tom; and Steel, Donald. "Reducing Risk at Aquatic Facilities Through Lifeguard Training." *Parks & Recreation* 35 (November 2000): 66.

are accessing both systems equally. Scanning can build a far more realistic picture of the whole situation.

For example, we all know that employee or coworker who tends to grate on our nerves. Perhaps she is obsessively negative or whining. Sure enough, she approaches, and the first thing you hear from her is a gripe or complaint. Unfortunately, it's easy to fixate on this aspect of your interactions with her and perhaps miss some things of value she may contribute. If you scan the whole person, perhaps you could see that she is a perfectionist who deeply cares about doing a good job. Or perhaps embedded in her negative comments are some real pearls about how to do things differently. Scanning in this case means looking at the whole rather than fixating on the constant flow of negative comments. In another case, scanning can help you broaden your reactions in a meeting. When you're in a meeting and you've made a comment that wasn't received very well, you may fixate on the comment, perhaps trying to find opportunities to redeem yourself or further prove your point. Instead, try scanning. It can help you focus more broadly. Rather than fixate only on your comment, scan the room to think about others. How does the group react to other people? You may find that the group dynamics are negative, or that one person's dominant view is the only opinion tolerated. Or perhaps you find that only one person seemed to react negatively to your comment, not the whole group, as you first perceived. Or perhaps you find that, indeed, the group's negative reaction is limited to you. In any event, scanning can give you a broader source of data that you can later incorporate in your relationships with others.

In one-to-one encounters, scanning can also prove invaluable. Let's say you enter your boss's office to ask for a raise. Usually when this occurs, you're focusing on what you're going to say to convince the boss that you deserve the raise. You're thinking about all of your accomplishments. Perhaps you've even done your homework and have data to support your claims regarding similar jobs in similar industries. So, you're ready to make your case. Besides, just yesterday, the boss complimented you on how well you had handled a recent assignment. Your timing is obviously right. But when you go in to deliver your pitch, it blows up in your face. How can this be possible?

How could you have avoided this situation? For starters, if your self-coach had scanned, he would have told you to notice the look on your boss's face when you entered her office. She had a disgusted frown. Her brow was wrinkled as if in deep concerned thought. Her desk, usually neat and orderly, was scattered with papers. She reached for her PDA to check her schedule. The beeping sound of incoming mail kept coming from her computer. Her eyes wandered to her computer screen to check her inbox. The information that you gleaned from scanning would have told you all you needed to know: Not now.

In a verbal exchange, many people fixate on the words. Surely words are important, but there's more to the message than meets the ear. Let's say you're concerned about a particular project you've been working on. You need help from Jim, your coworker, to get some data for the project. When you see Jim in the elevator and ask about the number, he tells you that he will have it by the end of the day. The end of the day comes and goes—no data. You're falling hopelessly behind on your project. Is Jim just unreliable? Could this situation have been avoided? Perhaps. If your self-coach had been scanning for you, you might have noticed several things about your encounter with Jim. Jim's tone of voice indicated disgust. His body language was rushed and hurried. He seemed distracted. He failed to make eye contact with you when he said he could get you the data by the end of the day. As your self-coach becomes adept at reading situations like this, you will gain a wealth of information that will prove invaluable for managing your relationships with others. Later we'll discuss how to integrate the information for more effective relationships.

A Scanning Checklist for the Self-Coach

In any workplace situation, but especially in conflict or high-stress encounters, train your self-coach to consider two perspectives: (1) Self—your reaction to the situation and (2) Others—the reactions of others. The following checklist can help you quickly assess both reactions to broaden your perspective. Remember to practice scanning in non-stress situations so that your skills will be well developed when a conflict occurs. Also, for scanning to be most effective, your self-coach should toggle back and forth between performing a self-scan and performing a scan of the others involved in the situation. Another way to look at this skill is to think about the lens of a camera. You can adjust easily between a wide-angle and a close-up shot with the press of a button. As your self-coach becomes more adept, you'll be able to easily shift your focus from assessing your reactions to assessing those of others.

Self-Scan

1. What is my physical body telling me?
   Heart rate? Dry mouth? Breathing? Sweaty palms?

2. What am I feeling?
   Attacked? Worried? Defensive? Angry? Challenged? Scared?

3. On what is my thinking fixated?
   Defending my position? Discrediting others? Redeeming myself?

4. How do I appear to others?
   Tone of voice? Body language? Facial expression?

Scan with others

1. What are they conveying through their words?

2. What are their nonverbal behaviors?
   Facial expressions? Eye contact? Body language?

3. What are their moods?
   Pleased? Tense? Encouraging? Agitated?

4. What other signs are in the physical environment?
   Phones ringing? E-mail? Schedulers?

OBSERVING MOOD AND EMOTION

Throughout the discussion thus far, the self-coach has had an obvious role in observation. Because mood and emotion are critical to a higher functioning emotional intelligence, more information may help your self-coach be more astute. It will also help your self-coach to distinguish some of the triggers (which we'll discuss later) that may be important to you. Mood is the underlying effect you experience. It sets the framework for how you may assess a particular event or situation. Emotion is the reaction to a particular stimulus. For instance, if you are in a good mood and you spill a cup of coffee, you may laugh and joke about being a klutz. Spilling a cup of coffee when you are in a bad mood may cause you to become angry, lash out, and blame your spouse for purchasing cups with handles too small for your fingers. Moods tend to be more a state of mind, and certain moods may tend to characterize your personality. Some people are characterized as generally sullen; others are more jovial. Mood can be looked on as a more long-lasting characteristic, although moods can certainly change. Mood, then, sets the stage for how you may react. More and more research suggests that a positive mood makes people more helpful and cooperative in the workplace. It also reduces aggressive behavior.[4] In addition, research (George and Bettenhausen, 1991) determined that mood, both on an individual level and group level, influences positive behaviors toward both coworkers and customers.[5]

So, your mood may certainly affect your performance on the job. Your emotional reaction often depends on your mood; therefore, your mood may predict your emotional reaction to certain events. This information is critical for your self-coach. The more predictive your self-coach can be, the more effective you will become in engaging techniques that can diffuse negative situations. Imagine the challenge of assisting customers or patients when your mood is negative. A simple request could be the proverbial straw that breaks the camel's back. Obviously your career could suffer if you are not in tune with your mood and the emotional reactions your mood can trigger and if you do not find ways to mitigate negative reactions.

---

[4] Isen, A.M., and Baron, R.A. "Positive Affect as a Factor in Organizational Behavior." *Research in Organizational Behavior* 13 (1991): 1–53.

[5] George, J.M., and Bettenhausen, K. "Understanding Prosocial Behavior, Sales Performance, and Turnover: A Group Level Analysis in a Service Context. *Journal of Applied Psychology* 75 (1990): 698–709.

The Six Families of Emotion					
Happy	Depressed	Surprised	Anxious	Angry	Creative
Content	Sad	Shocked	Fearful	Enraged	Imaginative
Ecstatic	Suicidal	Dumbfounded	Worried	Sarcastic	Resourceful
Joyous	Melancholy	Startled	Concerned	Annoyed	Artistic
Pleased	Grieving	Astonished	Nervous	Furious	Inspired
Cheerful	Gloomy	Amazed	Uneasy	Irritated	Innovative
Blissful	Miserable	Stunned	Restless	Irate	Ingenious
Exultant	Heartbroken	Flabbergasted	Fretful	Livid	Inquisitive
Delighted	Distressed	Astounded	Frightened	Incensed	Playful
Jovial	Poignant	Taken Aback	Panicky	Cross	Pioneering

FIGURE 8.1

RANGE /FAMILIES OF EMOTIONS AND MOODS

Besides recognizing the difference between mood and emotion, you already know that moods and emotions fall within continuums. Depending on your mood, someone cutting in front of you on the freeway may cause you to be mildly annoyed or filled with rage. So these different degrees, or flavors, are important to recognize. Your self-coach should become more and more adept at identifying your emotions and the degree to which you are experiencing them, as well as the underlying moods and events that may trigger them.

To assist your self-coach to become more discerning, think about what each word on the following list means to you. I've loosely grouped some emotions together in families. Picture yourself with each of these emotions or in these moods. Can you imagine that your actions may be slightly or grossly different, depending on how you are feeling? Help your self-coach become skilled at recognizing the variations these words represent (see Figure 8.1).

Just as your self-coach is learning to distinguish your range of emotions, you should also begin noticing differences in the emotions of others. The skill of observation is always moving from self to others, so the more your self-coach practices noticing these differences, the more your self-coach can help you proceed on your path to greater emotional intelligence. The goal of all observation techniques is to strengthen your self-awareness. As you become more familiar with your moods and emotions, you should become better able to key in to the moods and emotions of others. The next step in self-awareness is to assess how others' moods and emotions affect you. Self-awareness involves predicting your possible reactions to a given situation so that you can decide how you wish to react.

OBSERVING YOUR REACTIONS TO OTHERS

By now, your self-coach practiced observing you in a variety of situations and has also been observing others. The key is to link your reactions to both the actions and moods of others. For example, when your boss, who is predictably critical, calls you into his office, what is your usual reaction? How can anticipation of this event affect you? Or, let's say that your coworker Sasha always walks through the door with a smile on her face. What is your reaction? Susan, on the other hand, is always frowning. What is your reaction? Perhaps you've been noticing at every staff meeting that your boss does not make eye contact with you. How do you react to her behavior? Or perhaps you've noticed that Esther and Lu always have the floor at your weekly meetings. What do you find yourself thinking in each of these situations? And what happens to you as you anticipate future meetings? What are your thoughts? Feelings? Eventually patterns will emerge. You will find that there is a predictable manner to how you think about and react to these events and to how you anticipate these events. This predictive quality will be useful later when we talk about self-control.

SELF-TALK: OBSERVING YOUR INTERNAL DIALOGUE

So, as you realize that tomorrow morning you have to sit through yet another one of those meetings in which Esther and Lu always have the floor and your boss rarely makes eye contact with you, what's going on inside your head? Perhaps you're saying, "I can't believe I have to sit through another one of these meetings. I'm wasting my time. I have a million other things I can be doing, but I need to go and hear Esther and Lu go on endlessly about things I don't even care about." Or perhaps your internal voice says, "Here we go again. I am so tired of being ignored in these meetings. I just wish Esther and Lu would shut up and realize how disgusting they are. I'm so sick of their self-important attitude." Or maybe, you have a different take on the situation, "They do talk a lot, but I learn so much from Esther's and Lu's discussion. When I pay attention, I find their experiences useful. I'm so glad they are willing to share them." You can see that whatever internal dialogue or self-talk is going on inside you may affect your behavior in the meeting. Therefore, the more your self-coach can tune in to your self-talk, the greater your self-awareness. In fact, being aware of self-talk and later controlling your self-talk is fundamental to improving your emotional intelligence.

One way to practice this is to ask your self-coach to interview you throughout the day. As you walk toward your place of employment, what's going on with your internal dialogue? As each coworker approaches, what does your internal voice have to say? How about at the lunch table? Or sitting in a meeting? Keep track of your internal voice. This concept is certainly not unusual; the expression, "I said to myself . . ." is widespread because we all recognize that there is a constant internal dialogue going on. Now, if your self-coach conducts these interviews aloud, you might get some strange glares, but otherwise, it is a useful and productive exercise to increase self-awareness. Your internal dialogue will also enable you to further define your moods and your emotions. Later you will see that your internal dialogue will be an important concept as you work on mastering your emotions and living your intentions.

VOICES

As you become more and more familiar with your internal dialogue, you will also notice that certain voices appear over and over again. In fact, you will find that these voices may dominate the landscape of your mind. For example, in my mind, one voice rings loudest: my self-doubt voice. I can usually hear her above the rest. In fact, she colors my thinking, and if I'm not careful, she can also influence my behavior. To give you a feel for her handiwork, I relate the following story. When I had finished one of my earlier books, I sent it for comment and review to Ken Blanchard, a much-respected authority on leadership who had authored numerous books. I had always admired Blanchard's work and found him to be somewhat of a mentor even though we had never met. His prolific contributions to the field of leadership had shaped my thinking. As I nervously anticipated a response, my self-doubt voice emerged. "Why did you send it to him? You can't possibly believe that he would take time to read your work. And besides, if he would, you'll just embarrass yourself. You can't possibly think that he would have anything positive to say." And so the internal dialogue dominated by the Self-Doubt Queen, as I had dubbed this familiar voice, went on and on. Out of the blue one day I got a call from a person who identified herself as Margret McBride, Ken Blanchard's literary agent. My self-doubt voice just raged, "Oh my gosh, what have you done? She must be calling to reprimand you for taking his ideas." Now, I knew absolutely that I had not ever taken his ideas, but my self-doubt voice instinctively berated me. Finally I gained control of this all too familiar voice and said. "Shut up, so I can hear what this lady has to say." As it turned out, to my delight, Margret McBride asked if she could represent my book.

Others may find that their sarcasm voice reigns or perhaps their pessimist influence dominates. Whatever the case, these voices have a powerful influence over our moods and our actions. We're not interested in a pop psychology approach to analyzing what childhood traumas may be responsible for your internal choir. Our only goal is to help you become aware of these voices so that you can understand how they may influence your behavior. They can help you reach your potential and live your intentions, or they can rob you of them. For example, let's assume that your internal voice often reflects sarcasm. In fact, this powerful voice is at work behind the scenes looking at every fact, every suggestion, every action to determine just the appropriate taunt or gibe. He is hard at work spending your energy in this pursuit. Have you ever heard this voice in one of your coworkers or perhaps your boss? Have you heard his voice in your internal dialogue? How about your pessimist voice? This voice is an expert at the glass-half-empty phenomenon. A quick study, this voice can always find ways to help you see what's going wrong.

In fact, it is often the first to speak. And it speaks with authority. After you hear its voice, you'll be convinced that, indeed, life is filled with gloom.

Getting a handle on the voices that speak most often in your inner dialogue is an important grasp for your self-coach. As he becomes aware of your tendency toward a particular voice, your coach will be able to quickly recognize the voice and determine how it affects behavior. If you just think about the workplace for a moment and the people you know there, can you readily recognize someone who is often pessimistic? How about someone who tends toward sarcasm? Self-doubt? The trouble is that these voices are often easy to recognize in others but more difficult to recognize in ourselves. However, even recognizing them in others proves fruitful. So, get your self-coach and take him for a walk around the workplace and see if he can point out some of these voices in others. Now, turn your attention inward. Can you identify any of these voices within yourself?

Here's a list that may prove useful to help you identify these voices. Which ones seem like old friends? If they seem familiar, chances are you've spent some time with them. In fact, you may know them so well that you choose to name them. Sometimes I tell myself that I'm hearing from the Self-Doubt Queen or that the Control Troll is visiting. These techniques help me to keep in touch with my inner dialogue and understand how this self-talk influences my behavior. Although I refer to some below by gender, please recognize that these voices know no gender.

- The Victim Voice: The victim voice reminds you that it's never your fault. She makes sure you don't take any responsibility for your life. After all, you're just a poor victim. The victim voice claims that you are a victim of anything and everything. Her hopelessness and despair are overshadowed only by her creativity in finding things to blame for your failure.

- The Failure Voice: Your failure voice is always there to remind you that you are indeed a failure. In fact, he reminds you that you are a failure at just about anything you try. Should you forget and try to accomplish something, he'll stay up late to quickly remind you of all of your past failures. He focuses on the past.

■ The Voice of Revenge: Just beneath the surface, the voice of revenge mutters the constant rumble of "just wait." He is bent on revenge, and he's collecting examples until he's ready to pounce.

■ The Self-Doubt Voice: The job of the self-doubt voice is to plant the seeds of doubt and fertilize them daily. She is great at projecting into the future and making sure that no confidence seeds take hold in her garden. She is always handy with a watering can for proper nourishment of her flowers of doubt. She's a future-focused pessimist waiting to kill your tomorrow.

■ Egregious Injustice Voice: Your injustice voice likes to help you see where you have been wronged. He has a great knack for dwelling on injustice. He points it out at work, at home, in social settings, and at the supermarket. You can always count on him to show what isn't fair.

■ The Famine Voice: This voice always reminds you that there is never enough and there will never be enough. She makes sure you live in a constant state of panic over resources. She may do her work as it relates to money, time, or physical attributes, such as beauty or good health. Whatever her canvas, she's skilled at creating a sparse picture.

■ The "Ain't it Awful" Voice: This voice looks for evidence (and finds it) to let you know that your fate will always prove awful. This voice makes everything a catastrophe. This voice even has an amazing knack for stringing three unrelated events together to prove that life comes with a master catastrophe plan.

■ The Hide Voice: He constantly tells you to lie low. Just duck out of sight and the situation will pass. Don't take any action. Avoid the situation. This voice reminds you that you'll only get in trouble if you try to act.

- The Wallflower Voice: This voice scans the room to find a place where you can hide. He works to make sure you aren't noticed. He is particularly adept at doing this in social situations.

- The Panic/Drama Voice: This voice helps in a crisis because she always is in a state of panic. You won't have to wonder how to panic because she'll do it for you. The trouble, though, is that she panics over everything, including broken fingernails.

- The Pleaser Voice: Your pleaser voices wants everyone to be happy. He's constantly at work to get you to please others. In fact, he stays up late and worries that someone somewhere may have been overlooked. He reminds you to please everyone and he will impose guilt if you haven't taken gigantic steps to do so.

- The Rabbit Voice: Your rabbit voice always smells the air for danger. She is keenly aware of risk and will run for safety in her comfortable rabbit hole at the slightest whiff of conflict. She protects you from conflict by running away.

- The Critical Voice: This voice has a knack for seeing the worst in everyone and everything. He is a connoisseur of perfection and, therefore finds it simple to find fault in the world. He encourages you to criticize others. He loves to point out to you just how others have failed to perform or failed to keep their word or failed to have nice hair.

- The Should Voice: The should voice lets you know everything you should do. She searches the world and keeps long lists of "shoulds" for you to adhere to. She compares you against some impossible standard and lets you know how you are falling short. She also keeps track of others to see what they should be doing.

- The Comparison Voice: This voice keeps score for you. She compares everything—the kind of car you drive, the schools your children go to, your clothes, your job title, your office size, your bank account, and even the color of your teeth— with what someone else has. She may be pleased or displeased with what she observes. But make no doubt; she'll be there to let you know how you rank.

■ The Sky Is Falling Voice: This voice finds ways to create catastrophes out of everything. He's there to remind you that no matter what is happening, it's bad. In fact, it's so bad, that you probably won't be able to recover. This voice prohibits you from being in a rational, problem-solving state of mind.

■ The Fix-It Voice: The fix-it voice claims that it is your responsibility to fix everything. Somehow this voice thinks that you should take an active role in all of life's problems, and she encourages you to jump in and fix things. Ms. Fix-It is busy not only in your life, but also in everyone else's life.

■ The I Have All The Luck Voice: This voice reminds you that the world revolves around luck and you don't have any. He constantly points out that everyone else gets all the breaks and you don't. His motto is, "If I didn't have bad luck, I wouldn't have any luck at all."

■ The Control Voice: Your control voice reminds you that the only way to live in the world is to control it. He helps you realize that true power comes from a fierce grip on things.

■ The Possessiveness Voice: A cousin of your control voice, your possessiveness voice says, "It's mine and I don't really want to share it." In fact, this voice will declare things as yours that you have no right to possess, such as another person.

■ The Envy Voice: Your envy voice spends her time comparing, just as the comparison voice does, and then becomes upset that you don't have what others have. The envy voice can find many reasons to be jealous, including professional accomplishments, material possessions, interpersonal relationships, and social status. With the help of the comparison voice to keep score, the envy voice dislikes anyone whose score comes out higher than yours.

■ The Perfectionist Voice: The perfectionist voice makes sure you are absolutely perfect. She likes things done right, and she lets you know when things don't meet her standards, which is generally all the time.

- The Good Seeker: The perspective of this voice is that there is good in just about everything. He sees good in you, in others, in bad situations. He's the one who, even in the face of disaster, will search for the kernel of goodness.

- The Abundance Voice: Opposite of the famine voice, the abundance voice proclaims that, indeed, life's riches are plentiful. She believes that somehow there will always be enough, and she refuses to be ruled by thoughts of scarcity. She can convince you that a crumb of bread, when served with a smile, is indeed a feast.

- The Hope Voice: Hope assures you that tomorrow will be bright. The hope voice is your internal optimist that applies its sunshine to the future. Your hope voice is filled with positive expectations of the future and of other people.

- The Humor Voice: This voice sees fun in every corner of life. He points out the silly, the absurd, and the ridiculous and encourages laughter to cure all that ails you. He is a constant reminder not to take life too seriously. His light, easy way is characterized by the sounds of mirth.

- The Optimist Voice: The optimist voice reminds you that, of course, it can be done. Of course it will work out. Of course things will be good tomorrow. The optimist is a companion of hope and abundance. They make a great trio to drown out doubt and fear.

- The Gratitude Voice: Constant gratitude fills the air as this voice finds new ways to look at a blade of grass and express her thanks. She focuses your attention on giving thanks and thinking thankful thoughts, even in difficult situations. She's the one who points out after losing your job, how fortunate you are to have this opportunity to reexamine your work preferences.

- The Creative Voice: "Imagine" and "innovate" are the two words that drive this voice. His mind is always spinning with new ways to approach life. This imagination and drive permeate work life, home life, and community life.

- The Forgiveness Voice: Your forgiveness voice encourages you to let go of your grudges, to release your anger, and to accept others despite their shortcomings. She guides you to judge less and accept more of your fellow people, often reminding you that no one is perfect.

- What Role Did I Play Voice: This voice asks you to look at situations to determine how you may have contributed to the negative event or occurrence. This voice isn't intending to blame you, only to inquire so that you may not experience the same negative event again. A powerful opposite of the Victim voice, the What Role Did I Play voice will help you decide your culpability in life's problems, not for the sake of blame, but rather to help you decide how to improve.

- The Faith Voice: The Faith voice knows that whatever life holds, you will be okay. This voice represents a sense of assurance and calm deep within. This voice carries a feeling that you can survive. The Faith Voice draws on a spiritual knowing that permeates all aspects of life.

- The Perspective Voice: Perspective talks to you about reality and asks you to get a grip. He reminds you of the facts. He keeps track of history for you so that you can recall events that were worse.

- The Honor Voice: The honor voice reminds you to admire others. This voice not only asks you to see the good in others, but also to let them know that you see it. Honor helps you to demonstrate respect.

TRIGGERS

Another important concept for your self-coach is to understand your triggers. Triggers are those factors that influence emotional reactions. Those emotional reactions can be either positive emotional reactions or negative emotional reactions, depending on the trigger.

In discussing emotional intelligence, triggers are important because the more you are of aware your triggers, the better prepared you are to react effectively based on your desired outcomes. Therefore, those individuals who exhibit strong self-awareness are able to understand the state of mind, situations, and other factors that are likely to foreshadow certain behavior. Triggers arise from many sources. Some are inward; others are related to our surroundings. Therefore, your self-coach must be adept at observing a variety of things. Again, he or she must also be able to switch focus quickly, going from an inward to an outward perspective, scanning self, others, situations, and surroundings.

So what are some of the potential triggers that your self-coach may need to consider? Here's a list of some possible triggers that could escalate an emotional reaction. Although we'll consider them from the perspective of causing a negative reaction, later we'll look at how the self-coach can help you identify triggers that influence your behaviors in a positive way.

Mood

Obviously, your mood can be a trigger and can escalate an emotional reaction that may result in negative behavior, including behavior that will hijack you from your intentions. We've already talked about the need for your self-coach to observe your moods. As he is tuning in to your moods, he should become more and more aware of how those moods can result in unwanted behaviors. In which moods are you most at risk for being hijacked, and what have you observed to indicate that mood is present? When I'm feeling overwhelmed, I am definitely at risk. I've come to observe several things about this state of being. First, my mind is jumpy. I jump from one thought or task to the next and have a hard time staying focused. Also, my face begins to burn. My breathing is not deep and relaxed, but shallow. I also know that if these periods are extended, my sleep is more restless. For me, being overwhelmed is an invitation to being hijacked. My ideal self who espouses wonderful values about how I intend to treat others is at risk of vanishing when I'm feeling overwhelmed. In what mood are you most at risk?

Moods and Attitudes of Others

Similarly, the moods of others can also influence you. As we saw earlier in the research, moods are contagious.[6] Therefore, your self-coach will need to understand just how the moods of others affect you. In the workplace, is there a particular coworker whose constant whining grates on your nerves? Or perhaps it's your coworker Kristin's arrogance that rubs you the wrong way. Or maybe it's your boss, Calvin, whose constant critical eye disturbs you. Or perhaps it's none of the people at work but your significant other whose pessimism sends you off to work loaded for bear. In any event, your self-coach should be gathering information about the moods or attitudes of others and how they serve as triggers that may hijack your intentions.

Prethinking or Foreshadowing

Imagine that you had asked a certain individual at work to have some important data in your in-basket in the morning so you could finish a pressing report. You have already extended the deadline for when the data were needed. As you are driving into work, you keep telling yourself, "I'm up the creek if I don't have those data in my in-basket. I remember the last time I needed information and I didn't get it. I was the one who was blamed for not having the report done. I'm going to be so upset if this happens again." In this example, you have already decided to be hijacked. Even before you take off your coat, you enter your office and frantically search your in-basket; you discover that, sure enough, there are no data. With the charm of a pit bull, you approach your coworker. She hands the data to you with an indignant "tskk," saying that she thought it might be lost in your overflowing in-basket, so she tried to be nice and make your life easy by planning to give it to you directly. She resolves never to try to be nice again. If you analyze your prethinking or foreshadowing, you realize you could have predicted this mess and avoided it. And

---

[6]Barsade, Sigal G. "The Ripple Effect: Emotional Contagion and Its Influence on Group Behavior" *Administrative Science Quarterly* 47 (December 2002): 644.

yet I realize that sometimes foreshadowing occurs because sometimes others have been unreliable. However, even if that is indeed the case, it doesn't solve anything. It just serves as a trigger to hijack you from an effective resolution. In fact, it may compound the situation, because now your negative behavior has further entrenched your coworker's negative behavior. Pay attention to any foreshadowing that you may be practicing.

Dwelling

A close cousin of foreshadowing is dwelling. Dwelling, however, lasts longer. Dwelling can set the stage for a variety of unwanted behaviors. Dwelling also entrenches our voices. Let's say I dwell on a particular injustice. Over and over again, I focus on and speak about how I was wronged. It consumes my thoughts and causes my "Egregious Injustice Voice" to speak louder and louder. Now, if some minor injustice occurs, such as being skipped at the deli counter, all of a sudden I am hijacked. Do you find yourself dwelling on things that could influence behaviors that take you away from your intentions? In fact, this dwelling may cause you to expand the situation beyond your concerns. Another example of dwelling may occur in grief. Through the mask of grief, it is difficult to see or experience joy, yet the more we dwell on the loss, the more we experience the loss. Experiencing loss is a healthy and important rite of passage, and it takes time to heal, but the difference is in remembering the loss for the joy and satisfaction that we gained, not just for the sorrow that it brings. In the workplace, if we dwell on a loss of status or position or lament the way things used to be, we will be trapped into comparing everything that occurs unfavorably to the past. We will be confined to a joyless work life.

Personality

The more you understand your personality traits, the better equipped your self-coach will be to determine potential triggers. For example, the common personality characteristics of introversion and extroversion are important considerations. If you are introverted, you realize that you need private time to recharge your batteries. If your schedule, both at work and at home, denies you private time, this may be a trigger for unwanted behavior. Also, if you have a strong need for order and your workplace is in constant chaos or change, this may trigger an emotional reaction. Information about The Type A personality is characterized by always moving, walking, and eating rapidly; feeling impatient with the rate at which most events take place; striving to think or do two or more things at once; an inability to cope with leisure time; and being obsessed with numbers and measures. Having to wait in line or having little to show for their time will trigger very negative reactions. Type Bs, on the other hand, are characterized by little sense of time urgency; little or no need for measures of achievements or accomplishments; an ability to play for fun and relaxation; and an ability to relax without guilt.[7] For these persons, measures, comparisons, too much to do, or strict accounting for time may trigger negative reactions. Your self-coach should understand and recognize your personality. The idea is for your self-coach to understand how your personality may trigger reactions if situations compromise certain basic attributes.

Hot Words/Hot Buttons

Other triggers stem from the perception that our values may be under attack. Teaching your self-coach to scan your reaction to various words or phrases that may trigger emotional reactions is another important technique. What words make your hairs bristle? What behavior do you find intolerable in the workplace? I know of one manager who was so offended by swearing that she was incapable of being open-minded in getting at the truth in conflict situations. Any swear word she heard served as a trigger, making her judgmental before she heard the facts. Swearing violated her strict moral values. I recall a woman who got into blows with a male coworker who was criticizing "working mothers." Any negative comment containing the words "working mothers" was guaranteed to end

---

[7] Robbins, Stephen. *Organizational Behavior, 9th ed.* Upper Saddle River, NJ: Prentice Hall, 2001.

in a conflict. Again, this was perceived as an attack on her values. In another instance, I recall a man who would become incensed when someone attributed his accomplishments to "luck." This man worked very hard and he viewed the "luck" comment as an affront to a value he held dear: his work ethic.

Perceived Criticism

For many people, criticism triggers an emotional reaction. The reaction varies depending on the individual, but could range from anger to defeat to self-doubt to revenge to inspiration. Ask your self-coach to identify how you react to criticism. Sure, it depends on who is delivering the criticism and how, but in general, become familiar with your reactions. Pay attention to your physiological reactions for clues. One study published in *Occupational Hazards* found that workers who are subjected to criticism when executing physical tasks may be more prone to injury. The participants of the study were subjected to criticism during lifting. Changes were measured in blood pressure, heart rate, and spinal compression, thus leaving them more vulnerable to injury.[8] Physical reactions to criticism are an interesting area of research. If our physical bodies react to criticism, it's triggered by our limbic system. But physical reactions aside, think about your limbic system's messages and subsequent emotional responses to better equip you in advance to deal with criticism or perceived criticism so that you are less likely to be hijacked.

Physical Environment

Triggers could also be prompted by your physical environment. Don't underestimate the power of something as simple as the weather. I live in the North and find that after sliding my car off an icy bridge several years ago, my limbic system still pumps massive doses of adrenalin into my body at the mere mention of the word "snow" in the forecast. In fact, my limbic hijacking is so severe that

---

[8]Martin, Melissa. "Workplace Criticism May Injure Backs." *Occupational Hazards* 63 (January 2001): 20.

it can interrupt my sleep if I know that I have to drive a long distance the next morning. Other physical factors—such as temperature, physical space, crowds, lightness, and darkness—can also trigger emotional reactions. Assess yourself to determine under what physical situations you are at your finest and when might you be at risk.

Illness/Physical Conditions

Another potential trigger is illness. When you are not feeling well, things that would normally be harmless can suddenly create a negative emotional response. Perhaps you can recall a time when, feeling under the weather, you spoke some harsh words. Or perhaps you had the opposite reaction. You simply resigned yourself to any criticism because you weren't feeling well enough to deal with it. Scan your physical state for indicators that you may become hijacked. Something as simple as a lack of sleep can also cause negative emotional reactions.

Situations

Triggers can also arise from certain situations that you associate with negative experiences. For example, I am an avid computer user. My business depends on computers, and I'm relatively adept at using a few software packages. However, the key word here is "using." I know how to use the software, not troubleshoot systems that go down because of system incompatibility problems caused by new equipment, driver conflicts, viruses, and the like. I find these situations particularly frustrating. For some people, getting a new piece of computer hardware may be a joy. For me, I know this situation could trigger a negative reaction should a problem arise. Your self-coach will be all the wiser when he or she is aware of those situations that serve as your triggers.

BEWARE OF MULTIPLE TRIGGERS

Awareness of multiple triggers could save you from the disaster of emotional hijacking. The old adage, "It's the straw that broke the camel's back," certainly holds true for hijacking. When multiple triggers strike, your self-coach will need to be working overtime. Let's say it's Monday morning and I'm feeling overwhelmed because several deadlines are pressing, my computer system fails, and I had to drive in the snow. My self-coach goes to Code Red Alert. For me, this is a deadly combination of triggers, and I have to be extra careful to manage my reactions or I'm headed directly down the path for a hijacking. For you, this combination may have absolutely no impact. Your combination will likely be quite different from mine. That's why your self-coach is so important. He or she is a personal adviser, who is monitoring and observing you and your situation. Ultimately, only you and your self-coach can truly advise and direct you.

The first stage is to recognize that, in fact, you are experiencing multiple triggers. Later we'll discuss how your self-coach will intervene to effectively manage your emotional reactions. But for now, awareness is key. For learning purposes, begin to record the triggers you experience during the course of the day; some of those triggers will be very mild, others will be more intense.

OBSERVING BIAS, PREJUDICE, AND FILTERS

Observing hot buttons will give you some insight into your biases and prejudices. However, because it is easy to have blind spots in this area, it's important to consciously stretch your observation skills to include these areas. They can certainly hijack your intentions if you are not aware that they are influencing your emotional reactions. One of my friends who is African-American taught me to observe how white women often pull their handbags closer to their bodies in the presence of African-American males on a busy city street. These same women will tell you that they do not prejudge, but their body language suggests otherwise. Are these women being hijacked by some unconscious fear that causes them to act differently than they intend in the presence of African-Americans? Perhaps. The point is that limbic reactions can be so subtle and so unconscious, especially when connected to prejudice and bias, that your self-coach may need some help to see clearly just where your prejudices lie. Keep in mind that as you open yourself to growth, all of these areas merit further exploration.

One way to become more sensitive to your biases and prejudices is to monitor your self-talk regarding various groups. What is your inner dialogue saying about African-Americans, Hispanics, the elderly, or other groups? Also, are there repeated inner voices that emerge when you are in the presence of these groups? If so, pay attention for prejudice that may be creeping into your thoughts and your actions. The more you can monitor yourself, the more you will be able to mitigate these thoughts with contrary evidence. However, much of this thinking may be invisible to you because you may be painfully unaware of how your thinking has been corrupted in these matters. Franky Johnson, an expert on diversity from Johnson and Lee Consulting, says, "The mind has a different place for different types of people and it works hard to keep people in that place. If you want to overcome prejudice, you have to help your mind think differently. If not, prejudice becomes a self-fulfilling prophecy." To overcome prejudice, Johnson suggests spending time with people and getting to know them. "You need to open your mind; but more importantly look in your heart to overcome prejudice," Johnson says. "You need to allow for a different attitude when you spend time together. Your attitude should help you confront your stereotypes and spend time with others to prove your stereotypes wrong, not to prove them right," said Johnson. Especially look for ways that you are filtering information with your rational brain. Chances are you are working on a completely false set of facts that your rational brain isn't even aware is false. That false set of facts is affecting your behavior in subtle ways that may be sending messages of exclusivity to others. Challenge your rational brain to think more inclusively. Your self-coach can play a powerful role if it poses questions to you: "How might I be excluding others? How might I be sending subtle messages of bias or prejudice? How might I open my heart to others who don't look or act like me?" I'd also suggest asking a person who is a member of another group to be your mentor. Mentoring can be a powerful experience to overcome your biases and prejudices. But be forewarned, you "risk" forming lifelong friendships and bonds with this mentor as well as changing your assumptions and "facts" about others.

OBSERVATION SUMMARY

Throughout this step, we've focused on the self-coach as a trained and astute observer. That observation takes in those things you are feeling, as well as those things in your environment. We've stressed the fact that the self-coach must constantly scan the picture so she can create an accurate assessment. In addition, we have talked about the need for the self-coach to constantly switch lenses, going from a wide view to an inner view. We've also stressed that the self-coach consider a wide variety of elements, including mood, physical environment, and the voices that present themselves in your inner talk. The purpose of all of this observation is to encourage greater self-awareness. As we said earlier, self-awareness is the doorway to emotional intelligence, and by opening the door you will instantly gain insights into yourself. By paying attention, you'll learn more about the conditions that prompt you to be hijacked from your intentions. So, through observation you will take the first steps that will serve you well in living your intentions.

Observation, however, is never-ending. You're not finished with this step. As we said, self-awareness is a circular process; so observation is constant. You'll build more and more information through observation that will increase your self-awareness throughout life. Therefore, your self-coach will serve as a constant set of eyes, seeing things about you and others that you will integrate into your emotional intelligence. Just imagine how much factual information you've gained from the time you completed high school, such as how to manage your money, how to maneuver through city traffic, how to apply for a mortgage, how to get the best deal at the supermarket, how to use a cell phone, and how to start the snow blower. All of those facts have added to your competence as a fully functioning adult. Just as the facts you have encountered in your life experiences keep improving your knowledge level; the facts that you accumulate through observation will improve your emotional intelligence. The difference, however, is that now you are acquiring more facts through observation that will improve your emotional intelligence. As we said earlier, your capacity is actually improving. But it will improve only if your observation skills are honed and if you integrate those observations into your daily life.

CHAPTER 9

STEP 2: INTERPRET

The trick is to accept what makes you good.
—*James Baldwin*

Step 1 focused on training the self-coach to be an astute observer. So what do we do with all the data garnered through observation? Here again, you need to ask your rational brain for some assistance. One of the things your rational brain does best is analyze information. As the main character in *Dragnet* used to say, "Just the facts, ma'am." The purpose of analysis is to determine stimuli and patterns that are uniquely yours and to determine just how these stimuli and patterns affect you at the moment.

SELF-COACH DATA BANK

Your self-coach should be collecting data to be stored in a master data bank that can be quickly accessed so that the information can be integrated into your behavior. The data bank would contain all the information collected about you, including your reaction to others, your triggers, your moods, your environment, and the other information discussed in Chapter 8. In addition, your self-coach must be intimately familiar with your intentions and values, a subject addressed later. The purpose of the data will be to help you quickly draw conclusions about events occurring in the moment so you can take necessary action to modify or correct your behavior. Accumulating data is the perfect way to engage your rational brain in the process, thereby slowing your limbic reactions. Remember, the goal is to partner the information from both parts of your brain so that you can react in accordance with your wishes and live out your intentions.

As in any database, your data must be organized and easily retrievable. If you are like most people, your observation skills have been intact for a long time. However, it's sometimes difficult to remember just what you've already learned through experience. I often ask myself, "Just how many times, do I have to learn this lesson before it actually sticks?" For example, I know that technology problems can hijack me. I know that when my self-coach runs up the red flag, I need to pay attention. I have come a long way in mastering my emotional reactions when dealing with technology problems. I have come to expect technology problems when I buy new equipment, add software, or otherwise change my system. I've also learned the magic of good back-up systems that save hours of hard-earned data. To learn this lesson, I had to pay attention to my limbic reactions and my rational thoughts. I had to identify the triggers, determine how I wanted to act (what my intention was in these situations), and devise a method for living out those intentions. But I couldn't have done it without data, organized and retrievable data provided by my self-coach. Do I still get hijacked? Occasionally. But not nearly as often as I would have in the past.

MODUS OPERANDI

One of the most useful concepts for assimilating and interpreting information is modus operandi (M.O.), or method of operation. The idea is that each person has a unique pattern of behavior that repeats as circumstances repeat. Just as the FBI analyzes criminal behavior for preferred methods of operation, which are akin to a behavioral fingerprint, your self-coach should look for your preferred behavioral fingerprints. For example, what happens when you get angry? Most of the time, your reaction will be the same or at least have similar characteristics. This predictable nature of your emotional reaction will help your self-coach immensely on your path to greater

JOY	
Emotional M.O.	**Typical Behavior Exhibited**
The Verbal Exuberant	The exuberant lets everyone see the joy he experiences. This person experiences joy loudly and demonstrably. Typical behaviors would include smiling, laughing, and verbalizing joy. Rapid speech and excitement characterize expression.
Stonefaced Joy	This person may be experiencing joy, but her outward expression is stonefaced. She doesn't exhibit outward reactions. She does not express joy verbally. Her poker face gives little clue that she is joyful.
The Quiet Grin	The typical M.O. for this person when experiencing joy will be at most a quiet grin or smile. No wild expression here, only a subtle grin that indicates happiness.
The Physical Exuberant	Hugging, giving someone a handshake or a high five are physical behaviors that indicate joy for this person. He or she uses the body to demonstrate joy.
Tearful Joy	Tears of joy serve as an outward expression for this M.O. Wet eyes are the indicator of happiness.

FIGURE 9.1

emotional intelligence. Also, by assimilating information into a predictable emotional reaction, your self-coach can more readily catalogue important data about you.

To start your self-coach, we've listed a few typical M.O.s for a few emotions. As you consider these M.O.s, do you see yourself in any listed here? If not, think about your patterns and create your own M.O. for various emotions you frequently experience. Ask: "How do I typically behave when I experience a particular emotion?" Or "What is the impact of a particular emotion on my behavior?" See Figures 9.1 through Figure 9.5.

ANGER	
Emotional M.O.	**Typical Behavior Exhibited**
The Verbally Explosive	The typical M.O. for the verbally explosive would include angry outbursts filled with explosive language. When this person gets angry, everyone around him or her will hear it.
The Door Slammer	Stomping, slamming, throwing, and other physical expression characterize this anger monger.
The Sarcasm Thrower	Biting sarcasm is the hallmark of this M.O. The sarcasm thrower is skilled at knowing just the right remark to cut and penetrate the target.
The Pouter	Pouting and withdrawing and feeling sorry for himself, the pouter sulks and appears aloof and miserable to others.
The Machine Gunner	Get out of the line of fire when the machine gunner is angry, because even if you are not the target of her rage, you'll probably be hit. This person spills anger in all directions, regardless of the person who prompted the initial reaction.
The Grudge Holder	Some people will seemingly be unaffected by a situation, however, they are holding onto it for later. They store up and keep score of their anger. Later, they cash in in a variety of ways.

FIGURE 9.2

The M.O.s in the figures only scratch the surface. They help your self-coach realize that patterns do exist. Train your self-coach to think about the wide number of emotions and the emotional reactions you most commonly experience. Get a handle on whether you wallow or explode or withdraw in emotional situations. Don't forget the very common nonreaction M.O. Many people have become masters at suppressing their emotional reactions. Instead of experiencing the

OVERWHELMED	
Emotional M.O.	**Typical Behavior Exhibited**
Oh, Woe is Me	Poor, poor, miserable me. Typical behavior would include ruminating about how bad life is. The aim may be to evoke sympathy or attention, but the focus is all about being a victim.
I Can't Take It Anymore	This person lets others know that the situation is intolerable by verbally expressing his stress. However, what you hear is just a statement of the mood as if to let off steam. It's not about putting energy toward the situation in hopes of resolving it.
Anger Busy	Resentful and angry that somehow it "all falls on my shoulders." This person is in a constant rage and the to-do list gets the focus.
Defeated Busy	"I might as well give up," she says. "I'm so overwhelmed and behind that I'll never catch up. It's hopeless, it's useless to try."

FIGURE 9.3

emotion, they use various methods to numb themselves to the emotions of everyday life, including empty glaring into the television set.

Some may even go as far as destructive addictive behaviors. In a *CareerOne* Jobs Poll, 15.78 percent of respondents said they turn to alcohol as a way to cope with job stress.[1] Glen Hanson, director of the National Institute on Drug Abuse, in *USA Today* said that nearly 2 million more Americans used illicit drugs and alcohol in 2001 than in 2000 according to a major government survey.[2] In addition, in *Alcoholism and Drug Abuse Weekly,* researchers at the Australia

---

[1]CareerOne Jobs Poll. *The Australian* (October 4, 2003): 1.
[2]Kolchik, Svetlana. "More Americans Used Illegal Drugs in 2001, U.S. Study Says." *Alcoholism and Drug Abuse Weekly* 14 (September 6, 2002): 2a.

Proud	
Emotional M.O.	**Typical Behavior Exhibited**
Tell it on the mountain	This person tells everyone about his pride. He wears it on his T-shirts. He invites others to celebrations. These people carry pictures for the world to share in his pride. This is the proverbial proud grandpa (or grandma) behavior. In the workplace, he sends e-mails and letters and speaks up in meetings about his accomplishments or the accomplishments of others that he is proud of.
Humble Pride	This person downplays any attention or acknowledgement regarding her accomplishment. She finds it difficult to talk about her victories. Instead, she usually diverts the attention or acknowledgement to others or dismisses it altogether.
Choked up	Some people tend to tear easily when they feel a sense of pride. The reaction renders them somewhat incapable of immediate verbal expression because they can't get past the lump in their throat.

FIGURE 9.4

Institute have concluded that a third of Australians rely on alcohol, prescription medicine, and illegal drugs to cope with stress.[3] "White-collar Addiction on the Rise," an article in *USA Today,* reports that white-collar addiction plagues professional business ranks and costs companies billions of dollars a year in lost productivity.[4] *Women's Health Weekly* reports that more than ninety percent of the 681 people who completed their Web-based survey described the level of

---

[3]——— "In Case You Haven't Heard." *Alcoholism and Drug Abuse Weekly* 15 (June 30, 2003): 8.
[4]Armour, Stephanie. "White-Collar Addiction on the Rise Since Sept. 11." *USA Today* (June 03, 2002): Money, 1.

Self-Doubt	
Emotional M.O.	**Typical Behavior Exhibited**
Extrapolator	The extrapolator is quite skilled at extending one set of events into an entire lifetime vision. The extrapolator will quickly conclude, "If I am unable to do A, then obviously I am unable to do B. If I cannot do A or B, then I am obviously a complete and total failure." A and B may be completely unrelated, but not to the extrapolator. His doubt in one area will naturally cast huge shadows about his ability to perform in another area regardless of truth.
Paralyzed	This person's self-doubt simply leaves him or her paralyzed to try anything. Failing is to be avoided and the best way to accomplish that is by simply standing like a deer caught in the headlights.
Defeat Through Observation	By observing the failures of others, he concludes that most everything is impossible. He is skilled at finding numerous examples that support his claim.
Prove Myself Wrong	This person keeps working frantically to prove himself wrong and is caught in a never-ending cycle of trying to gain proof of accomplishment.

FIGURE 9.5

stress in their daily life as moderate to high. Fewer than half said they always felt capable of coping with their stress.[5]

Leading an emotionally intelligent life isn't about suppressing emotions, but about experiencing and expressing a full range of emotions in a way that allows you to live your intentions. It is about

---

[5]____ "Not Unusual for Women to Cope by Engaging in Unhealthy Behaviors." *Women's Health Weekly* (July 24, 2003): 67.

not submitting to stress to the point of practicing destructive behaviors. Your self-coach can help you understand your emotions and your emotional responses to stressful situations. Allow your self-coach to label you. It serves as a way of categorizing your behaviors so your self-coach will have data readily available when he needs it most. Granted, the human experience is diverse, and you will no doubt have experienced many of the M.O.s listed above rather than just one. However, patterns are helpful because they can give you insight into your most predictable behavior.

COMBINING M.O.S WITH TRIGGERS

The next task in assimilating and interpreting data is to combine what you know about your M.O. with the knowledge you gained about your triggers through observation. When your self-coach is capable of quickly determining what triggers cause what type of emotional reaction in you, you will be on your way to greater emotional intelligence. So you're interpreting not only what triggers hijack you, but also how you react when you're hijacked.

Let's say that at your next staff meeting, multiple triggers threaten you: you are feeling sick, you are feeling overwhelmed because of a new assignment, and you have been dwelling on the fact that no one seems to notice that you are doing most of the work. Just then, your supervisor asks you for an update on your projects and expresses disappointment that you aren't further along. Let's also assume that your M.O. when you become angry is to make sarcastic and cutting remarks, which, by the way, has not enhanced your career in the past. Your self-coach is on the verge of a gold mine if he can retrieve all of this data *in the moment*. If your self-coach can catch you before you open your mouth and blurt out just the right—or wrong—sarcastic comment, you may have an opportunity to save yourself. Otherwise, you may suffer by being labeled as a chronic sarcasm thrower. With some practice and with the help of your self-coach, you can avoid this career dead end. Always look for the patterns created by triggers and M.O.s. Also, look for differences in your M.O. at home and at work. Certain patterns of behavior may be different depending on where you are and who's present. The reasons for this are many, including the cultural influences in certain work environments that create norms for acceptable and unacceptable behavior. In addition, our self-control may be better at work because we're on our best behavior; when we're at home we may feel freer and less restrained, or vice versa. Circumstances also may be more or less stressful in one situation or the other. So attention to our environment and situations will shed further light on our M.O.s.

VOICE INTERPRETATION

Now your self-coach should add another data point. He should interpret any inner voices that may fuel a particular situation. For example, if you are concerned that a coworker is dumping an unfair share of the work on you, tune in to those inner voices. It's possible that your injustice voice may be blowing things out of proportion. Your voices can escalate situations quickly. It's important at this point for your self-coach to distinguish between a voice and a thought. A voice is a pattern that repeats in your thoughts, which may or may not be based in reality. For example, my self-doubt voice is a constant companion, but much of what she has to say is simply not true when I compare her proclamations to my abilities and accomplishments. That's not to say that her voice doesn't occasionally speak the truth. For example, if I thought I could climb Mt. Everest this weekend, I'd probably hear her proclaim, "What are you, crazy? You can't do that!" The fact is she'd be right. I'm in no condition to climb Mt. Everest. I haven't had the proper training nor do I have the equipment. Besides, it's Friday, and I'm nowhere near Tibet. It would take a few days just to get there. During this step of assimilation and interpretation, we're searching for *relevant* data. Your self-coach will need to filter your thoughts and voices through reality. Ask your rational brain to step in and look for evidence. This is a tricky step because, as stated earlier, emotions and perceptions can get in the way of rational thinking.

IMPACT ON OTHERS

The next data point your self-coach will need is information regarding your impact on other people. As you observe others, you'll find that your behavior affects them in different ways. Some people will bristle when you get angry. Others will cower. Distinguishing the impact you have on others will help you know how to adjust your behavior. Besides, just understanding that you have an impact on others is a huge accomplishment in self-awareness.

Let's say that you are at work and a coworker forgets to tell you about an important development that will affect one of your projects. Suppose some other triggers are present and you lose your cool. From experience, you know that this coworker is likely to get upset when this happens and will run to the boss to report your behavior. Your database is growing. You have lots of information to assimilate and predict that the outcome will more than likely result in a situation that is not what you would intend or desire.

BEWARE THE PITFALLS OF INTERPRETATION

If you've done a good job at observation, you should be able to keep bias and judgments at bay as you interpret and analyze your findings. Right? Wrong.

Each of us has an enormous capacity to interpret incorrectly based on some common erroneous beliefs. The problem is compounded because our rational brain has been fooled to think that these beliefs are actually facts. For example, if your rational brain thought that two plus two equals five, then no matter how many times you added a list of these numbers, you'd come up with the wrong answer. Something similar happens when we ask our rational brain to interpret data if the "facts" are incorrect. The facts I'm referring to here are erroneous beliefs and prejudices that creep into our thinking. Without discernment, they can delude our thinking, and we can base actions on these falsehoods and generalizations. However, the rational brain can take in data and reanalyze the "facts" if we permit and engage the rational brain in such activity. Therefore, if the rational brain is retrained to understand that two plus two equals four, our math computations will no longer be inaccurate. Likewise, if our rational brain is retrained to understand facts that were erroneous regarding our prejudices, then our output, including our behaviors and emotional reactions, will be different.

Let's examine these erroneous beliefs so that your self-coach will be able to detect when they invade your thinking. These beliefs are the based on the work of Dr. Albert Ellis, who developed Rational-Emotive Behavioral Therapy (REBT), which is an action-oriented therapeutic approach that stimulates emotional growth by teaching people to replace their self-defeating thoughts, feelings, and actions with new and more effective ones.[9] REBT teaches individuals to be responsible for their own emotions and gives them the power to change and overcome unhealthy behaviors that interfere with their ability to function and enjoy life. Further clarity of cognitive theory is provided by Judith Beck.[7] These 12 most common false beliefs, which I've interpreted in terms of how they may sound in the business world, I call the Dirty Dozen.

Needing Approval

"Everyone I work with must approve of me at all times." This belief will inhibit your ability to speak the truth. Because you seek others' approval, you'll find yourself wanting to please. Although wanting to please is not necessarily a problem, you should not sacrifice your own intentions and values in order to please others. You may find that others begin to view you as indecisive because, in an effort to please, you will find it difficult to take a stand. Also, in a leadership role, it's unrealistic to have everyone's approval. You will need, at times, to make difficult decisions that some people may not like.

Some voices that support this belief are The Self-Doubt Voice, The Pleaser Voice, The Should Voice, and The Rabbit Voice.

Common phrases that support this belief are: "I don't want him to be upset with me." "My needs aren't important. What do you want?" "I can't possibly be good at that."

---

[6]Ellis, Albert. *Overcoming Destructive Beliefs, Feelings, and Behaviors: New Directions for Rational Emotive Behavior Therapy.* New York: Prometheus Books, 2001.

[7]Beck, Judith. *Cognitive Therapy: Basics and Beyond.* New York: Guilford Press, 1995.

Making Mistakes

"I must prove thoroughly competent, adequate, and achieving at all times." On the surface, this sounds like a great belief for any employee. But if you probe a bit under the surface, you'll find that this belief causes our negative emotional reaction to change. It also causes us to hide our mistakes. Also, if we believe this, we find it difficult to ask for help or take advice. We are also overly sensitive to criticism.

Some voices that support this belief include The Self-Doubt Voice, The Perfectionist Voice, The Failure Voice, and The Should Voice.

Common phrases that support this belief are: "I'm sure I did it the way I was told." "We have this running smoothly, so why change it?"

Changing Others

"I have an obligation to change others who act unfairly or obnoxiously." The problem with this belief is that you will see unfairness and obnoxious behavior everywhere. If you follow through with this belief, you will spend your day doing nothing but pointing out these injustices, and all of your energy will be depleted. More than likely, the time and energy you are spending will frustrate you, and that frustration will hijack you to the point of insulting or belittling co-workers. You'll find customers, too, who will be obnoxious and unfair, and this belief will no doubt sabotage your success.

Some voices that support this belief are The Egregious Injustice Voice, The Revenge Voice, and The Critical Voice.

Common phrases that support this belief are: "You should be more considerate of others." "Don't you see how you are causing problems?" "I told you about this before."

Catastrophize

"When I get very frustrated, treated unfairly, or rejected, I have to view things as awful, terrible, horrible, and catastrophic." Every day you're likely to be frustrated, treated unfairly, or rejected to some degree or another. You may be rejected for a job posting. You may get an assignment you don't want. You may think your supervisor favors another employee over you. If you tend to "catastrophize" over these events, then you will spend your life in a constant state of "ain't it awful."

Some voices that support this belief are The Ain't-it-Awful Voice, The Famine Voice, The Sky-Is-Falling Voice, and The Panic / Drama Voice.

Common phrases that support this belief are: "Oh, no. What am I going to do?" " This is the worst thing that ever happened." "I'll never get through this."

Others Cause Misery

"My emotional misery comes from external pressures that I have little ability to change." My job demands are overwhelming; my supervisor is an ogre; my department is going to be moved; my computer system failed. The list goes on and on. The world will no doubt continue to present a list of external pressures. If you believe your emotional misery comes from outside sources, you will always have an endless supply of reasons to be miserable.

Some voices that support this belief are The Victim Voice, The I-Have-All-the-Luck Voice, and The Ain't-it-Awful Voice.

Common phrases that support this belief are: "What am I to do?" "I always have to put up with these awful people/ circumstances." "Why me?"

Worry, Fret, and Fear

"If something seems dangerous or fearsome, I must preoccupy myself with it and make myself anxious about it." So it may seem frightening to stand before a large audience and make a presentation. This belief says that you should just dwell on it and keep yourself anxious and stirred. In reality, we all know that it does no good to worry, but this belief will not permit us to let go. Remember the anxiety I described about driving in the snow? I held on to this belief and dwelt on something fearsome to me. In fact, my anxiety didn't take away my fear; it perpetuated it. Besides, this is an uncomfortable state of mind to be in all day long.

Some voices that support this belief are The Failure Voice, The Famine Voice, and The Sky-Is-Falling Voice.

Common phrases that support this belief are: "I'm so worried about. . . ." "I can't think of anything but this presentation tomorrow." "I'm so concerned about. . . ."

Avoidance

"It's easier to avoid facing difficulties and self-responsibilities than to do something about them." It may indeed be easier, but this belief puts you on the path of a victim. It sets you up for not only blaming others, but also for feeling helpless regarding your own destiny. Ultimately, this belief requires you to abdicate your role and responsibility in your own life. To get the next promotion, you may be required to go to school to learn something new. Or taking on the next level of responsibility may require you to dedicate more hours to the job. In either case, if you follow this belief, you have no chance of success other than what luck throws your way. Are you really willing to turn over your entire future into the hands of Lady Luck?

Some voices that support this belief are The Victim Voice, The Hide Voice, and The Wallflower Voice.

Common phrases that support this belief are: "Well, I'll just wait and see. . . ." "I don't know what they will do with me." "There's nothing I can do. . . ."

The Past

"My past remains all-important and, because something once strongly influenced my life, it has to keep determining my feelings and behavior today." This kind of thinking will definitely get you into trouble. In essence, it says that because you were passed over for a promotion twenty-five years ago, you should still be upset about it. In fact, holding onto that bitterness defines the way you think. Take another situation. Let's say you were downsized from an executive position that fed your pride. Since then, you've not been able to regain the same position or status. Given this flaw in your thinking, you would never be able to recover from this blow.

Some voices that support this belief are The Failure Voice, The Self-Doubt Voice, and The Should Voice.

Common phrases that support this belief are: "I remember when they did this to me. . . ." "Let me tell you about the way it's been around here." "I don't know. I tried it once and it didn't work."

Unrealistic Expectations

"People and things should turn out better than they do, and I must fix them." If you really stop and think about this belief, you're setting yourself up to have all of the answers, even to the most difficult situations. Also, you're not only expecting yourself to have the answers, you're also going to blame yourself if you can't come up with solutions to everything. I'm not sure about you, but some things are just outside my grasp. And, I'm not responsible for other people's choices. I can give them the information, the training, and so on, but I can't control what they do with them. If you're a leader, you will feel responsible for every employee who fails. I'm not suggesting that you shouldn't have a sense of responsibility for others, but there's a line between a responsibility to help and a responsibility to fix. You'll condemn yourself to a life of guilt if you don't let go of this one. Also, with this assumption, collaboration isn't a part of your mindset because you should know the answers and have the fix already.

Some voices that support this belief include The Failure Voice, The Self-Doubt Voice, The Fix-It Voice, and The Control Voice.

Common phrases that support this belief are: "I don't want him to be upset with me." "I don't care. What do you want?" "I can't possibly be good at that."

Competition

"My worth can be measured by competitive situations." Our society embraces winners. Since childhood, we have been engaged in a competitive mindset. We are obsessed with getting the best grades, making the most baskets on the basketball court, being the best dressed, or winning the biggest bonus. Trouble is, however, that this very mindset is counter to the culture of teamwork and collaboration that many companies are trying to foster in the workplace. If we are still entrenched in this belief, then it may be difficult to share information or ideas or resources if someone else may take the credit or gain from it. Also, competition implies a quest for winning. For you to win, someone else has to lose. Competition sets a frame of mind of deciding who is better than whom.

Some voices that support this belief are The Comparison Voice, The Control Voice, The Possessiveness Voice, and The Envy Voice.

Common phrases that support this belief are: "I can't believe Tom got the promotion. What has he ever done?" "I have to score better than Jane." "I don't care what kind of raise I get as long as it's better than Sue's."

Source of Problems

"The people and conditions in my life are the source of my problems." If only the people in my life were not all turkeys; if only I worked at a better place; if only people understood the business; if only people could see my strengths; if only. . . . This constant belief that other people or the circumstances are to blame for all of our problems is a wonderful comfort. As long as we hold onto this belief, we have no reason to take any responsibility for any of our problems. This belief permanently stunts our personal growth. This belief sets another trap. If somehow we fix or control the people or conditions in our lives, then our lives would be better. Either position blocks us from looking at ourselves as a potential source of our own problems.

Some voices that support this position are The Victim Voice, The Control Voice, The Fix-It Voice, and The Critical Voice.

Common phrases that support this belief are: "If John would just stop doing. . . . my life would be better." "John, you're the reason I can't. . . ." "If HR would hire the right people. . . ."

Negativity

"Certain occurrences or events are negative by nature." This belief, grounded in the absolute, means that you can't possibly see something positive in a particular situation or event. For example, if you lose your job, you may see only the negative. But no event is singularly positive or singularly negative. Certainly there could be at least one positive thing about losing your job. If nothing else, you'll get to sleep in tomorrow morning. This belief prohibits you from looking at a situation or event objectively. You are capable of seeing only the negative. This belief will affect your ability to solve problems, as well as deal with change. If, for example, you see change as negative by nature, then no matter what happens, you will see only the negatives associated with a change and none of the positive possibilities.

Some voices that support this belief are The Sky-Is-Falling Voice, The Famine Voice, and The Ain't-It-Awful Voice.

Common phrases that support this belief are: "There is nothing about this situation that is good." "No good will ever come out of this." "He'll never recover from this blow."

BEWARE OF CONFIRMATION BIAS AND SUGGESTION

Another obstacle to rational thinking is confirmation bias, which occurs when you look only for information to confirm your position and ignore any conflicting data. Let's say you are shopping for a car, and you're already leaning toward a particular brand. You will tend to focus on all of the positive information you hear or read about that brand and filter negative information that does not support your leaning. This concept is even truer if you have a particular loyalty to a certain brand. In fact, according to a marketing research study done by Dick Wittink and M. Guah, automobile brand loyal consumers will pay anywhere from $1,051 to $7,410 more than nonbrand loyal customers because their confirmation bias discounts facts and interferes with their rational processing, even on something as concrete as price.[8]

The same bias occurs in our relationships with others. If we have already decided we like a particular person or coworker, we do not judge his or her behaviors as harshly as we may someone we like less.

---

[8] Wittink, Dick, and Guah, M.. Marketing research done for Cornerstone Research, Cambridge, MA, 1997.

Managers have been taught for years to be concerned with "the halo effect" when preparing employee ratings. The halo effect tends to filter perceptions so that the manager perceives only positive information because he or she had a positive bias toward the employee. No wonder claims of favoritism arise. Likewise, if you view a particular coworker in a negative light sometimes called "the horns effect," you will look for information that confirms your bias.[9] From an emotional intelligence point of view, this information can have an important impact that will set the stage for your encounters with that person. Each encounter is an opportunity to prove our bias. So, because we think Louise is a whiner, we search her words for complaints and ignore any positive comments she may make. Conversely, our favorable opinion of Harry allows us to overlook his negative behaviors. And more often than not, this information will be based on first impressions that are difficult to overcome.

Another popular bias that influences our interactions with others is the power of suggestion. Consider the following research as it influences decision-making.[10] A group of professional real estate appraisers were asked to look at a piece of property and estimate its appraised value. Each agent was given a tour of the house and a ten-page packet of information about the house, including a list price of $65,900. Another randomly selected group of professional appraisers was given the same tour and the same ten-page packet of information about the house, but these agents were given a list price of $83,900. The first group's average appraisal was $67,811; the second group's average appraisal was $75,190. Preconceived suggestions influenced the outcome in this strictly financial decision. The impact of suggestion on relationships is likewise interesting. In a study conducted by Robert Steinberg in *Group Intelligence,* incoming freshman were told by their resident assistant that certain residents on their dorm floor were particularly friendly and helpful,

---

[9] Ilgen, D.R., and Klein, H.J. "Organizational Behavior." In M.R. Rosenzweig and L.W. Porter (Eds), *Annual Review of Psychology,* vol. 40. Palo Alto, CA: Annual Reviews, 1989.
[10] Northcraft, J, and Neale, S. Study done on power of suggestion and decision making at University of Arizona, 1987.

while others were less friendly and helpful.[11] After one month of dormitory living, the freshman were asked to rate their dorm mates in terms of overall helpfulness and friendliness toward freshmen. In fact, the freshmen rated the group suggested by the resident assistant as friendly and helpful 42 percent more friendly and helpful than the other group. Well-meaning others inform us to "watch out for Debbie," or that "George will never let you down." These powerful suggestions then bias our ability to take in the whole picture, and we fixate on either the positive or negative behaviors of Debbie or George to validate the suggestion. The concept of scanning should apply here as well. Your self-coach should be scanning to assess the accuracy of the data that you've collected and to look for contrary evidence. Particularly when a relationship isn't working well, looking for contrary evidence can save you from being hijacked. Therefore, searching your rational brain for irrational bias will serve you well as you interact with others. So much of the bias and prejudice results from a malfunctioning rational brain who somehow has accumulated the wrong "facts."

DECISION TIME

At this point, your self-coach has assimilated important information for you. He understands your M.O. and your triggers. He knows your impact on others and has checked in with your voices to see what's going on. He has checked all of this data against potential confirmation bias and suggestion. Now, it is decision time. *In the moment*—and frankly that will always be the tricky part—your self-coach will have to make the call. If you continue on your present path at this particular meeting or encounter, are you at risk for being hijacked? Could you become angry and say something that you may later regret? Are you on the verge of cutting sarcasm? Could you become fearful and lack the courage to speak the truth? Are you going along with a plan that you know won't work just to please

---

[11] Steinberg, Robert. "Group Intelligence." *Intelligence* (July 1988): 16.

others? Any of these emotions could result in hijacking. If so, the red flag should be waving and the whistle blowing. From this point, your self-coach needs some techniques that will change the emotional reaction and the outcome to more closely align with your intentions.

CHAPTER 10

STEP 3: PAUSE

Always being in a hurry does not prevent death,
neither does going slowly prevent living.—Ibo

If you've ever watched a classic old movie, you'll remember that scene in the flick when the star, confronted with some difficult moment, takes a long drag on his or her cigarette before responding. Then, after a long and pronounced exhale, he or she delivers the most memorable line in the movie. Just imagine Humphrey Bogart, or Betty Davis, or Spencer Tracy as they deliver that one great line with smoke still lingering in the air. Somehow, they always had it right.

Well, I'm certainly not advocating cigarette smoking for improved emotional intelligence, but there's something about that pause that would be useful to re-create. That pause serves as a cooling-down period. It allows you to put on the brakes, shift gears, and, eventually, regroup. Without it, your limbic system rushes ahead, controlling the situation without any help from your rational brain.

How many times have you made a comment that you instantly regretted? With the words still fresh in the air, you realize that those words serve no good purpose, but rather further deteriorate an already shaky situation. Alas, once they are spoken, even a team of oxen does not have the power to pull them back. I once witnessed negotiations turn on a quick anger-induced statement by the CEO that cost the company three months of down time because of a labor stoppage. And to think, all it would have taken to change the course of those negotiations and the company's profits for the year was a ten-second pause.

Daily in the workplace, those pauses that don't occur cost us time, money, and untold anxiety. I recently spent nine hours consulting with a senior executive and a member of his senior staff. The executive had made a flippant comment that sent an unintended, yet serious, message that he had lost confidence in the ability of this staff member. "Unintended" is a critical word here. Remember, the definition of emotional intelligence is the ability to manage myself and my relationships with others so that I can live my intentions. In addition to my time, the staff member spent at least 28 hours of his work time proving that he was indeed productive. He also engaged the help of the finance department to run some special reports to prove that his area had indeed been producing at a rate equal to or exceeding those of other departments. When another department head got wind of what his peer was doing, he was concerned that his numbers might look bad in comparison, so he wrote a special report justifying the additional expenses that his area had incurred that quarter. All told, when you add up staff time, consulting charges, computer time, and the like, I estimate the cost to the company of this one flippant remark to be at least $32,500. And that doesn't include the most important cost of all—the cost of missed opportunity as all concerned focused on proving their positions rather than generating new business or seeking creative solutions to other problems. Nor does it consider any damage that may have been done from an employee-relations point of view that, no doubt, had a ripple effect on the morale of others in the organization who witnessed this incident. Mind you, this was one thoughtless remark made by one person.

Make no mistake, as I look around, I see similar situations daily at all levels of organizations. Some will tend to trivialize the impact of emotions. They will point to Susie in the mailroom as being overly sensitive to a comment by a coworker. This is not about being overly sensitive. This is about real impact at all levels, across all aspects of business. The dollars lost are huge, and they are not confined to a particular area or level. And yet, if our self-coach had just been taught the art of the thoughtful pause, much of this could be avoided.

So, how do you engage that moment of pause? Well, remember in Step 2 that your self-coach had been called on to assimilate and interpret for you. There is that moment when your self-coach decides that if you continue on your present path, you are at risk of being hijacked and not living your intentions. Instantly, whenever that flash of insight occurs, your self-coach needs to have a planned and practiced technique for pausing. There should be some practiced ritual that you engage that should include three components.

First, breathe. The technique, according to Linda Jones in *Heart and Soul*, is to close your mouth and count to eight while breathing in slowly and deeply through your nose. Take your breath all the way down to your belly. Place your hand on your belly and feel it expand like a balloon. Gently let the air out through your mouth. Repeat at least ten times.[1]

Second, there should be some physical movement that you immediately can revert to as you breathe. Examples include taking a long sip of coffee, removing your eyeglasses, adjusting your tie, getting up and stretching, or consciously shifting your body weight. A dear friend said to me that if only he would have taken a long sip of coffee before speaking, his career would probably have taken a different path.

Third, you should have a mantra that you recite while breathing and performing the physical movement. That mantra should be uniquely yours and should be something that helps you shift your thoughts and gain perspective. For example, one school principal I worked with who was prone to angry outbursts decided on a mantra that her mentor had planted. Her mentor suggested that before she speaks, she should ask herself, "Would you say that in front of a school board member?" My own mantra is, "In the overall scheme of life, is this really significant?" Over the years, I've found that those words help me to gain perspective and remain calm when otherwise I would

---

[1]Jones, Linda. "The Art of Pause." *Heart and Soul* 10 (January 2003): 3.

have been hijacked. My mentor's favorite line was, "Choose your battles wisely." Another colleague asks himself, "Is this the hill you are willing to die on?" As a young child, my shy daughter was prone not to anger, but more to fear. For courage in those moments of fear, she engaged the help of Spot, her favorite stuffed animal and constant companion. Spot's comfort line consisted of two words: "It's okay." I remember her first day of kindergarten, where stuffed animals were forbidden; she taped a picture of Spot inside her pencil box and bravely headed for the bus stop. Nearly twenty years later, we joke about Spot's wisdom. His worn and tattered body still collects dust on her bedroom shelf. Whatever your risk, whether it be anger or fear or some other emotion that holds you back from living your intentions, having a well-thought-out mantra will get you through some very difficult moments.

The three simple actions make up this step called "Pause," a deep long breath, a shift in your physical movement, and a mantra, should be practiced and rehearsed until you can instantly revert to this pattern. Begin practicing by visualizing. Decide on your mantra and your physical movement. Try to select a physical movement that you can perform whether sitting or standing, such as shifting your body weight to another side or running your hands through your hair. Visualize yourself doing all three things simultaneously. Now, actually do them. You can practice right now if you like. The idea is to have these steps become natural and easy for you and to be able to do them without consciously thinking of the steps.

Your self-coach should begin practicing in nonstress situations. Just before you are about to make a comment, practice the three simple actions until they become a natural part of your repertoire. Besides, I learned that once I began to practice even in nonstress situations, I found that if I kept my mouth shut and allowed for that pause, the other person would volunteer additional information or take our conversation in a direction that it would not have traveled had I not kept quiet. Conversations often took on a new richness and depth. This technique is particularly useful if you tend to be extroverted and you are speaking to your introverted counterparts; you'll find they volunteer much more information if given the luxury of that pause.

After a while, your self-coach will graduate to doing this in stressful or conflict situations. Obviously in these situations, you will reap the greatest rewards. This step allows for a cool-down period that enables the rational brain to catch up with your limbic system. It sets the stage for the thoughtful rather than reactionary behavior. Thoughtful behavior is the essence of emotional intelligence. It allows you to decide and manage your behaviors so that the chances of your intended outcome are improved. Without thoughtful behavior, your outcomes will have a much greater variance. Even with thoughtful behavior on your part, it is certainly possible that you will still not attain the outcome you seek, but your chances are improved.

For example, let's say you have a rather timid employee working for you whom you would like to inspire to become more creative and take more risks. If you are prone to angry outbursts, you may be creating an environment of fear. Creativity and fear are not good partners. According to A.D. Amar in *Managing Knowledge Workers,* "Managing by fear may manage employees' low-grade senses; it will not manage their higher order faculties, which are essential to attain innovation and gain productivity in knowledge organizations."[2] Amar further states that, "A manager should know that, with few exceptions, everyone looking for a decision from others has one's own alternative decision, which one may not accept for many reasons, such as the lack of confidence, a hesitation caused by the fear of rejection, a need for help in implementation, and a need for approval by others." If your self-awareness has been honed to the point of understanding this impact you have on others, especially those who are timid, you would most likely decide that your behavior is not going to give you the desired result. Therefore, this moment of pause can create thoughtful behavior that can save your intentions, thereby improving your likelihood of gaining greater creativity from your employee. Although this won't guarantee greater creativity from your employee, the other path would more than likely have killed any chances of it occurring.

---

[2]Amar, A.D. *Managing Knowledge Workers.* Westport, CT: Quorum Books, 2002.

Thoughtful pause allows you to change the channel. Rather than watch a predictable ending, you can look for a new show. It offers alternatives to a tired and worn plot. Changing the channel isn't about extinguishing the emotion that you are experiencing, but rather allowing for another form of expression of that emotion, a form of expression that will ultimately serve you better.

CHAPTER 11

STEP 4: DIRECT

The only thing that will stop you from
fulfilling your dreams is you.—Tom Bradley

Through observation, assimilating important data, and thoughtful pause, your self-coach has already proven himself an invaluable partner. But, you haven't seen anything yet. It is this step, which
we call "Direct," that makes the difference between a self-aware
person and one who lives in mastery. You may know someone who
exhibits great self-awareness, yet doesn't seem to act in a way that
reflects that knowledge.

Consider Robert. Robert is the plant manager of a 1,500-employee
manufacturing operation. Robert called me because he thought that
some of his senior leadership team were not always candid with
their opinions. Robert values honesty, and he believes that the best
decisions emanate from open discussion and an honest exploration
of the issues. Robert genuinely believes this. In fact, Robert led the
leadership team in defining values to live by, and honesty and open
communications topped the list. Further, he and his leadership team
worked to define each value that should govern their interactions
with one another and defined specific behaviors related to these
values. In particular, Robert was concerned that one behavior was
not being adhered to: speaking up whenever people disagreed with
a course of action. On more than one occasion, Robert found good

evidence that indeed his staff were "yes men (and women)" who were not offering their opinions when they disagreed with a particular decision or action. This created all kinds of problems for Robert and the plant, because he would find himself going down a particular path only to discover that his leadership team did not really support him. Robert was getting increasingly frustrated with this behavior. In fact, he had lost his temper at more than one staff meeting regarding this issue. Robert was indeed a very passionate leader.

I interviewed the senior management staff and discover that Robert was right. His staff often did not speak the truth on pertinent issues. However, they gave me example after example of two things that occurred whenever they attempted to speak the truth:

1. Robert would engage them in fierce debate in what they perceived as an effort to prove them wrong.

2. Robert would get angry whenever they didn't see his point of view. His anger sometimes even resulted in insulting statements, such as "You're just not a big-picture person," "You're just not thinking logically," or "You're just proving to me that you don't really understand our business."

When I asked Robert about this possibility, he immediately acknowledged that, indeed, that did occur frequently. But he explained that he had told his staff numerous times that debate was a healthy thing. He chalked up his anger to his passion and immediately dismissed any impact that it could possibly have. He explained that if he really meant any of those things, the people wouldn't be serving on his senior staff. Robert knew that his behavior had caused his staff to be close-mouthed, but he thought that his staff members were the ones with the problem. He believed they needed to get over it. (Certainly, the staff did have work to do in this regard.) Robert's self-awareness was quite strong. He believed that by just telling people to accept his behavior, they should do just that and shouldn't let it affect their behavior.

Guess what? Robert was wrong.

On many occasions, I have administered *The Index for Emotional Intelligence,* a 360-degree assessment of emotional intelligence that informs leaders of areas of strength and weakness in their emotional intelligence.[1] It turns out that many leaders were well aware of their strengths and, in particular, their weaknesses. In fact, they were so aware that they didn't really need to take the assessment. I had one executive who scored very low on self-control tell me that if it had come out any other way, he would have seriously doubted the validity of the survey. So, the point is that self-awareness is a wonderful thing; it is fundamental to emotional intelligence, but unless we do something with this awareness, it's useless in helping us manage our relationships with others—and that makes up half the definition of emotional intelligence.

So, first and foremost, the leader must have the desire to understand. Only then can the leader take great strides to direct his or her emotional impact to gain the desired results. If you look at the situation with Robert and his senior staff, Robert was not getting the results he desired, so he hired me to "fix" his staff. It took some time for him to realize that the results were all within his reach, but that the required change needed to begin with him.

Step 4 is all about acting or behaving in a way that will increase your likelihood of living your intentions and advancing your purpose in life. It's about careful selection of your words and behaviors so they are congruent with your values. In a very practical way, it's about knowing techniques so that when you are at risk of being hijacked, you know precisely how to rein in your emotional expression. It consists of three parts: visualizing, strategizing, and implementing. In this step, your self-coach first reminds you of your intentions, then acts as a strategic partner to determine the best approach for helping you live those intentions. Finally, he provides invaluable assistance and techniques to help you know how to behave.

VISUALIZE THE END RESULT

Have you ever thought about something in such vivid detail that it seemed as though your entire being was actually experiencing this

[1] Lynn, Adele B. "Index for Emotional Intelligence." Boulder, CO: The Booth Company, 2002.

thought? It could be either positive or negative. For example, any parent with a teenage child who is out late at night with the family car can generally conjure up images of twisted metal, cracked windshields, and the ditch where Johnny lies helpless. Generally that image quickly vanishes at the sound of the garage door opener, and they breathe a sigh of relief. That visualization, complete with the sigh of relief, speaks to the power our thoughts have to induce emotional reactions. When visualizing, the greater the detail, the more opportunity for the reaction to take hold.

Research and information about visualization from the world of sports have provided insights that can be directly applied to emotional intelligence. Athletes with the most stellar performances routinely practice visualization. In one study conducted by the Elite Athlete Project at the Olympic Training Center in Colorado Springs, Colorado, top-ranked downhill skiers visualized a specific course on which they had competed. While the skiers pictured themselves going down the course, electrodes on their legs monitored muscle activity. The muscle activity recorded on the skiers corresponded to the exact muscle activity they would have experienced as they traveled down the course.[2] These athletes, by using recurring visualization, developed neurological patterns that led to muscular responses. The recurring neurological patterns strengthened the probability of the muscular response in the actual situation. Marie Dalloway, Ph.D. who is a renowned expert on sports performance, refers to this phenomenon as a neurological blueprint, or template, created by visualization. Dr. Dalloway further states that visualization practice strengthens the neurological patterns and increases the probability of performance outcomes that have been visualized.[3]

Remember our discussion of physiological component of emotions, how our bodies respond directly to our emotional states with changes in heart rates, breathing, and other bodily reactions. We also talked about training our self-coach to observe these physical cues.

---

[2]Teichand, M., and Dodeles, L. Study at the Elite Athlete Project at the Olympic Training Center in Colorado Springs, CO, 1987.
[3]Dalloway, Marie. *Visualizaion: The Master Skill in Mental Training.* Phoenix: Performance Media, 1992.

Now imagine taking this one step further. Not only is your self-coach able to observe your physiologic emotional reactions, but he would also be able to influence them. At the beginning of this book, we talked about your ideal self: the self that does things just right, the self you are most proud of. Throughout this book we have also talked about living your intentions. These two thoughts are central because they force you to answer these questions: "What do you stand for? What are the values you would like to live each day?" In each interaction, if these questions are central in guiding you, then you can indeed do as Stephen Covey suggests, which is to begin with the end in mind.[4]

Let's look at a practical example. Let's say you've just missed your flight, and you are now standing at the ticket counter hoping to get a seat on the next available flight to your destination. Imagine that, to say the least, you are a little more than ticked. If it weren't for the long lines at the security checkpoint, you would have had plenty of time. Not only were the lines long, but you were rerouted in the security line to another checkpoint a great distance from your gate. Even with the long lines, you would probably have caught your flight if not for the personnel issue, so you're furious that security checkpoint was understaffed. So, at this point, you are standing in front of the ticket agent, and your self-coach says that all the systems are go for a hijacking (not of an airplane to get you to your destination, although you may have considered this option, but rather a hijacking of the limbic type). If you proceed with the limbic hijacking, what may occur? Chances are you'll take out all that frustration on the ticket agent. Trouble is, who's the one person who can help you get to your destination? Right. The ticket agent.

So, let's go back to what values do you hold dear. Most people would probably not state that one of their values is to belittle people or express anger in a demeaning way. Even if you believe in accountability, you probably don't believe in holding accountable someone who has absolutely nothing to do with a problem. That's about as

---

[4]Covey, Stephen; Merrill, Roger; and Merrill, Rebecca. *First Things First: To Live, to Love, to Learn a Legacy.* New York: Free Press, 1996.

irrational as calling a phone number at random to yell and scream at whoever answers about your bad day. So, more than likely you are not living your values if you become hijacked with the ticket agent. Next, what is your intended outcome in this situation? You want to get on the next flight home so that you can spend time with your family. It's the ticket agent who can help you with your desired outcome. So on two counts, living your values and gaining the desired outcome, your hijacking would serve no purpose but to immediately let off some steam. If you take Covey's advice and begin with the end in mind, you would definitely see that one set of actions on your part would probably serve your intentions much better than another set of actions.

Now you could take the actual hijacking route. That's right, you could literally hijack a plane. That action would probably get you to your destination. But in that case, I'm not so sure you'd be spending time with your family, unless your family is housed at a federal penitentiary. In scenario after scenario, your self-coach can name the actions either to take or to avoid that would serve you well. However, you have to train your self-coach to think in those terms. Get your self-coach to think outcomes **and** values. What outcomes do you want, **and** in what manner do you want to achieve those outcomes?

In the workplace, we can often get outcomes at the expense of values. More and more companies and organizations are recognizing the value of both and are even restructuring reward and compensation programs and performance measures to reflect both of these important components. The leader who generates tremendous profits through tyrannical behavior is no longer acceptable in many companies. However, those tyrant behaviors are often the result of a leader who doesn't understand how to control his emotional energy. The passion that drives his results is often the same passion, turned frustration, that foils his interpersonal relationships.

Some companies use this concept to rate their employees, and any employee who scores high in results but low in values is put in an at-risk category, and their raises suffer. In addition, if they remain in that category for three rating periods, they are terminated, regardless of how high their productivity is. It takes courage and commitment on the part of a company to institute this kind of policy. High producers translate to higher profits. However, many companies realize that when these higher profits come with compromised values, profitability can decline in the long run. These companies are taking steps to integrate the way in which they do business with the results.

So Step 4, Direct, begins with training your self-coach to keep in mind the outcome **and** the values that you want to achieve and to visual those outcomes in your interactions with others.

STRATEGIZING TECHNIQUES

After your self-coach has successfully reminded you of the intentions and values you hold dear, you should engage your self-coach as a strategist to help you. To advise you on a particular strategy, your self-coach will need many tools and techniques at his fingertips. Without them, your self-coach will be ill-prepared to advise. Just imagine, in the scenario with the ticket agent, that your self-coach had only two ideas on how to approach the situation: yell and scream at the ticket agent or hijack an airplane. If that's the best your self-coach could come up with, you're in trouble. Most of us are already much more astute and have several ideas on how to approach the situation that would probably result in a better outcome. In fact, if we brainstormed some alternative approaches, we would more than likely come up with something ideal. What we may lack is familiarity and practice with the techniques that can hold our emotional reactions at bay. So for your self-coach to be truly adept as a strategic partner, he'll have to be well versed on a variety of techniques.

The Basic Formula

For your self-coach to help you choose techniques that will keep you from being hijacked, you need to understand a common basic formula[5] In an unwanted emotional response, A (activating event or circumstance) + B (belief about the activating event fueled by our

---

[5]Ellis, Albert. *How to Stubbornly Refuse to Make Yourself Miserable About Anything – Yes Anything.* New York, Lyle Stuart, 1988.

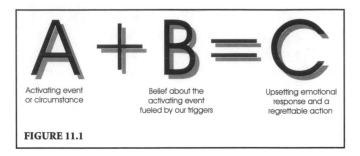

FIGURE 11.1

triggers) = C (upsetting emotional response and a regrettable action). See Figure 11.1.

Here's an example of what this might look like in the workplace:

A: Your boss fails to recognize your contribution on the Miller account at today's staff meeting.

+B: You believe that you worked harder than anyone else on this project and that your boss's lack of recognition is an injustice (belief). Besides, you are overwhelmed because you have four other accounts (trigger).

=C: You are angry (emotional response.) You burst into the boss' office with your resignation (action).

This is the typical formula that drives emotional hijacking. If, however, you could insert just one more step, you could drastically change the situation. Let's change the formula to A (activating event or circumstance) + B (belief about the activating event fueled by triggers) + C (redirect beliefs and thoughts) = D (new emotional response and action.). See Figure 11.2.

Example:

A: Your boss fails to recognize your contribution on the Miller account at today's staff meeting.

+B: You believe that you worked harder than anyone else on this project and that your boss's lack of recognition is an injustice

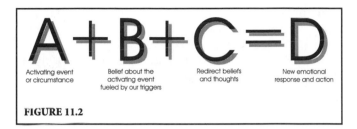

A+B+C=D

Activating event or circumstance

Belief about the activating event fueled by our triggers

Redirect beliefs and thoughts

New emotional response and action

FIGURE 11.2

(belief). You're also highly competitive (belief). Besides, you are overwhelmed because you have four other accounts (trigger).

+C (redirect beliefs and thoughts): Find a way to redirect your emotional response so that you are not hijacked.

This step can entail many possibilities, and it will be up to your self-coach to decide. Here are some possibilities:

- I don't really believe my boss meant to slight me.

- Maybe my boss was planning to talk to me later.

- He did say something last week in support of my work on the Miller account.

- So my boss probably forgot. He isn't perfect.

- I don't need my boss to tell me that I did a good job on that account. I know I did.

- Maybe I didn't do as good a job as I thought I did.

- I will talk to my boss and ask him to give me some feedback on the Miller account.

- I will tell my boss that his positive feedback is important to me.

- My boss knows that I did a good job; otherwise, he wouldn't have assigned me the Gonzalez account.

- Whether my boss thinks I did a good job is irrelevant because I have already decided to look for a job in which I can market my analytical skills. That is what I like to do best.

=D: You shrug it off, decide to choose your battles wisely, and determine that this doesn't seem like a big deal (new emotional response and action).

Using Rational Thought to Mitigate Negative Beliefs

Remember the Dirty Dozen that we discussed earlier? Those false beliefs can lead us to emotional hijacking and thwart our intentions. If we are afflicted by any of those beliefs, we may be stuck like the turkeys George and Harriet. One useful technique in freeing us is to mitigate the beliefs that could be the problem. To mitigate these beliefs, your self-coach should engage in some self-talk that will help you to view things more realistically. In this situation, the purpose of the self-talk is to determine if you are being objective. The most important question to ask is, "Where is the evidence that this belief is true and rational?" Other key questions that can further engage your rational brain are listed below for each of the Dirty Dozen.

1. **Needing Approval: "Everyone I work with must approve of me at all times."** Voices that support this belief are The Self-Doubt Voice, The Pleaser Voice, The Should Voice, and The Rabbit Voice.

   To mitigate this belief, your self-coach should ask the following:

   - Do you really need this person's approval?

   - Will your life go on if you do not get this person's approval?

   - Who/what makes this person's approval so important?

   - What would be the worst that could happen if you don't get this person's approval?

   - How exactly will your life change without this person's approval?

   - How will it change with this person's approval?

- What is the cost of gaining this person's approval?

- How have you not lived your intentions because you've been so focused on pleasing this person?

2. **Making Mistakes: "I must prove thoroughly competent, adequate, and achieving at all times."** Voices that support this belief include The Self-Doubt Voice, The Perfectionist Voice, The Failure Voice, and The Should Voice.

   To mitigate this belief, your self-coach should ask the following:

   - What exactly is the worst that could happen if you make a mistake or do not know something in this situation?

   - How will your life change if you make a mistake or do not know something in this situation?

   - How can you learn from making a mistake in this situation?

   - What is the cost of your fear of making a mistake or not knowing something?

   - What can you learn if you admit that you don't know something?

   - How have you not lived your intentions because you've been so focused on being right or knowing something?

3. **Changing Others: "I have an obligation to change others who act unfairly or obnoxiously."** Voices that support this belief are Egregious-Injustice Voice, The Revenge Voice, and The Critical Voice.

   To mitigate this belief, your self-coach should ask the following:

   - How would your life be different if you stopped trying to change others?

   - What would happen if you accepted the fact that life isn't fair?

- What would be different if you decided not to let others know they were wrong?

- How do you know that you are right and they are wrong?

- What is this belief costing you?

- How is this belief affecting your relationship with others?

- How have you not lived your intentions because you've been so focused on letting others know they are wrong?

4. **Catastrophize: "When I get frustrated, treated unfairly, or rejected, I have to view things as awful, terrible, horrible and catastrophic."** Voices that support this belief are The Ain't-It-Awful Voice, The Famine Voice, The Sky-Is-Falling Voice, and The Panic/Drama Voice.

To mitigate this belief, your self-coach should ask the following:

- What is really the worst thing that could happen in this situation?

- How would your life be different if the worst that could happen in this situation actually did?

- How is this belief affecting your energy toward other things?

- How is this belief affecting your relationship with others?

- Why does being rejected by someone have to be so dire?

- What is this belief costing you?

- How have you not lived your intentions because you've been so distracted by thinking that everything is a disaster or catastrophe?

5. **Others Cause Misery: "Emotional misery comes from external pressures that I have little ability to change."** Voices that support this belief are The Victim Voice, The I-Have-All-the-Luck Voice, and The Ain't-It-Awful Voice.

To mitigate this belief, your self-coach should ask the following:

- Do you have absolutely no choice in how you react to this situation?

- What do you gain from giving your power away?

- What can you do to change the situation?

- What would happen if you decided that you could change the situation?

- How have you made this situation occur?

- What role have you played in this situation?

- What is this belief costing you?

- How have you not lived your intentions because you believe this?

6. **Worry, Fret, and Fear: "If something seems dangerous or fearsome, I must preoccupy myself with it and make myself anxious about it."** Voices that support this belief are The Failure Voice, The Famine Voice, and The Sky-Is-Falling Voice.

To mitigate this belief, your self-coach should ask the following:

- What is the worst that could happen in this situation?

- Is worry, fret, or fear going to change the outcome of this?

- Would some action on your part ensure a different outcome?

- Could you have avoided this situation?

- What positive outcome may result from this situation?

- What would happen if you focused on the positive outcome instead of worrying about the situation?

- What is your worry, fretting, or fear costing you?

- How have you not lived your intentions because you've been so consumed by worry, fret or fear?

7. **Avoidance: "It's easier to avoid facing difficulties and self-responsibilities than to do something about them."** Voices that support this belief are The Victim Voice, The Hide Voice, and The Wallflower Voice.

   To mitigate this belief, your self-coach should ask the following:

   - How is avoidance making your life easy?

   - How is avoidance making your life difficult?

   - How has this caused you to not live your intentions or values?

   - What is avoidance costing you?

   - How have you been victimized?

   - What responsibility do you have for this situation?

   - How could taking responsibility change your situation?

8. **The Past: "My past remains all important and, because something once strongly influenced my life, it has to keep determining my feelings and behavior today."** Voices that support this belief are The Failure Voice, The Self-Doubt Voice, and The Should Voice.

   To mitigate this belief, your self-coach should ask the following:

   - What about your past says that it must dictate how you feel today?

   - What is it costing you to hang onto your past?

   - How have you not lived your intentions because you've been so focused on your past?

   - What would happen if you had no past?

   - How would it change your perspective if everything about your past was perfect?

- What would happen if you thought only about the future and the present and never thought about the past?

- How is the past defining you?

- How is the past restraining you?

9. **Unrealistic Expectations: "People and things should turn out better than they do, so I must fix them."** Voices that support this belief include The Failure Voice, The Self-Doubt Voice, The Fix-It Voice, and The Control Voice.

To mitigate this belief, your self-coach should ask the following:

- Who gave you the ultimate power to control and fix things?

- What does it cost you to think that everyone should live up to your expectations?

- How have you not lived your intentions because you've been so focused on others not living up to your expectations?

- What would happen if you stopped viewing it as your problem or your responsibility to fix things or control things?

- How can your view that it is your responsibility hold others back?

- How would your life be different if you didn't believe it was your responsibility to fix things?

10. **Competition: "My worth can be measured by competitive situations."** Voices that support this belief are The Comparison Voice, The Control Voice, The Possessiveness Voice, and The Envy Voice.

To mitigate this belief, your self-coach should ask the following:

- Do you really need to be better than others?

- What is this need to win costing you?

- How have you not lived your intentions because you've been so focused on winning?

- What do you really need to win?

- Who cares if you're not No. 1?

- Can you still contribute without being the best?

- How can comparison hurt your relationships with others?

- What would happen if you were last?

11. **Source of Problems: "The people and conditions in my life are the source of my problems."** Voices that support this position are The Victim Voice, The Control Voice, The Fix-It Voice, and The Critical Voice.

To mitigate this belief, your self-coach should ask the following:

- What part of your life is your responsibility?

- How would your life be different without the people or conditions in your life?

- Is it possible that you would find the same types of people and conditions elsewhere?

- How are you contributing to the people and events in your life?

- What behaviors on your part fuel the events in your life?

- What is this belief costing you?

- How have you not lived your intentions because you've been so focused on believing that others are responsible?

12. **Negativity: "Certain occurrences or events are negative by nature."** Voices that support this belief are The Sky-Is-Falling Voice, The Famine Voice, and The Ain't-It-Awful Voice.

To mitigate this belief, your self-coach should ask the following:

- What possibly could be good about this situation?

- What can I learn from this situation?

- What would it be like to be free of this thinking?

- What humor can you see in this situation?

- What is this belief costing you?

- How have you not lived your intentions because you've been so focused on the negative?

Humor as a Mitigating Force

Persons being treated for cancer at the Memorial Sloan-Kettering Cancer Center are prescribed a daily dose of *I Love Lucy, The Red Skelton Show, Late Night with David Letterman,* the Three Stooges movies, or some other comedy series of their choice. Why? Although the research is still quite limited, preliminary studies suggest that humor may change moods that produce changes in the body chemistry that promote healing.[6] According to the *American Journal of Medical Science,* neuroendocrine and stress hormone changes occur during mirthful laughter. In *Pain,* humor is reported to be a cognitive technique for increasing pain tolerance.[7] According to Allan Reiss of Stanford University, a new study reported in *Neuron* suggests that humor activates brain mechanisms involved in reward.[8] In fact, humor activates the same reward areas of the brain as do amphetamines and cocaine. Despite the fact that research is still in the early stages, most do see humor as a powerful force for changing perceptions, mood, and emotional reactions. Developing a sense of humor about yourself and life's situations can help redirect your emotional response. "No one is immune to taking him- or herself

---

[6]Berk, L.S.; Tan, S.A.; Fry, W.F., et al. "Neuroendocrine and Stress Hormone Changes During Mirthful Laughter." *American Journal Medical Science* 298 (1989): 390–396.
[7]Weisenberg, M; Tepper, I; and Schwarzwald, J. "Humor as a Cognitive Technique for Increasing Pain Tolerance." *Pain* 1995; 63: 207–212.
[8]Reiss, Allan L. "Humor Activates Reward System." *Neuron* 2003, 40: 1041–1048.

too seriously," states Lawrence Mintz, Ph.D., of the American Humor Studies Association in an article on the American Cancer Society Web site.[9] Taking yourself too seriously sets the stage for a variety of emotional responses that may be detrimental to your daily functioning. In the *American Humor and Interdisciplinary Newsletter*, Dr. Mintz says, "People use humor to separate the truly threatening from what's not truly threatening. You learn to laugh at the day-to-day things and reserve seriousness for what is really tragic. We tend to blow things out of proportion."[10]

For example, how often is something in the workplace truly tragic? Yes, there have been serious and tragic incidences of workplace violence. But I'm talking about everyday incidents that people react to in a way that suggests disaster. Yes, you may be late for lunch because a coworker didn't give you the paperwork for the order that you were shipping, but just how much energy are you willing to invest in this emotional reaction? Too many people spend a dollar's worth of energy on a situation that is worth about a penny. If you could look at the light side, find something humorous about your reaction, you may find that life is just easier.

Mike Boccia, Ph.D, a cognitive therapist, has learned to use humor to quell his own anger when driving down the freeway. If someone cuts in front of him, rather than become angry, Dr. Boccia uses humor to put the situation in perspective. Dr. Boccia reported to me in an interview that he tells himself, "Look, that person must have gotten his driver's license in a cereal box." Dr. Boccia looks for ways to laugh at himself and the situation. By changing his thinking or his cognitive response in these situations, he can avert a negative emotional reaction. He finds driving much more pleasurable, and he doesn't have to worry about being arrested for an incident of road rage.

Every day in the workplace, we can allow humor to shed light on our shortcomings. And you must admit that sometimes our shortcomings and mistakes are downright hilarious. If we could just look

---

[9]Mintz, Lawrence. "Humor and Healing" 2004 (*www.Cancer.org*).
[10]Mintz, Lawrence. *American Humor and Interdisciplinary Newsletter*. December 2001.

from afar with a playful heart, we would see that at times we are truly ridiculous. Sometimes, we are the most ridiculous when trying to be the most serious. Step back and appreciate the humor of you. Read the comics section in the newspaper, watch the latest TV sitcom, or go to the movies. Laugh. Identify with the characters. Where can you see yourself? Which cartoon character exemplifies you at your most absurd? Where can you laugh at yourself? The ability to laugh at our shortcomings and mistakes makes our spirit light. In lightness we can dance to greater heights.

One day I finally saw myself rushing like the White Rabbit in *Alice in Wonderland.* My vision was complete with theme music, "You're late, you're late—for a very important date." Finally it dawned on me that when I am in this frenzied state, it's funny and enormously unproductive. I also identify with Wile E. Coyote, in that I am resilient and do not give up. That's a positive quality, but sometimes I take it to the extreme. Have you ever seen Wile E. emerging after one of his encounters all tattered and torn? Sometimes I feel that way, and it could serve as a trigger to a negative emotional response. Or I could laugh at myself for being so ridiculous and allowing myself to get there in the first place. I paste up cartoon characters in my office to poke fun of myself and to serve as a reminder not to take myself too seriously. Have your self-coach look for some cartoon characters that exemplify you in some of your best "moments." Enjoy. You're a riot.

Your self-coach could use humor as a way to redirect your thinking and to divert your potential hijacking. It's fun and harmless. Remember, the humor should be directed at you or at the situation that you find yourself in, not at someone else. In fact, Frank Prerost, Ph.D., psychotherapist from Western Illinois University, has noted that people who attain this ability to laugh at themselves actually feel a greater sense of control of their lives, and when they feel this greater sense of control, they are able to take responsibility.[11] The workplace is filled with great fodder for humor. Just imagine humor

---

[11]Prerost, Frank J. "Presentation of Humor and Facilitation of a Relaxation Response among Internal and External Scores on Rotter's Scale." *Psychological Reports* 72 (1993): 1248–1250.

as private jokes between you and your self-coach. Just be sure they stay within the confines of your head.

Voices as a Mitigating Force

Besides humor, you have at your disposal other tools that could help you mitigate negative emotional reactions. But, just like everything else, if you aren't aware that you have these tools or you don't know how to use them, they serve little value. Earlier, I listed voices that could come in handy. That list included items such as The Forgiveness Voice, The Creative Voice, The Gratitude Voice, The Abundance Voice, The Good Seeker Voice, and The Humor Voice. However, sometimes these voices have been lost. In fact, one of my colleagues said that she's not sure where these voices are anymore. She thinks they might be bound with duct tape and riding in the trunk of her car.

For example, at the end of the work day, it is easy for me to look at everything that has yet to be completed. If I choose, I can quickly and effortlessly list all the things that we didn't do or didn't do very well. Yes, that's my Critical Voice coming through loud and clear. If I listen to this voice, I can convince myself that our work efforts have been below par today. Also, if I let this voice dominate, it will inform me of everything that is wrong with my staff. All of their shortcomings will suddenly come to the forefront, thanks to my Critical Voice. However, if I use humor and prod myself to use some other voices, I find that what this voice is suggesting is absurd. Yes, not everything was finished by day's end. So would we have been better off if everyone had just stayed home? Perhaps I should have given everyone a paid holiday since we accomplished nothing anyway. When we take our thinking to the extreme, we can see how silly it is. Now, I'm not suggesting that you lower your standards to accept poor performance. I'm asking instead that you be reasonable and objective in your assessment of the situation. For me, being reasonable means that I must engage some other voices. For example, I need to ask my Good Seeker Voice to tell me what my staff does right. I also need to consult my Gratitude Voice to help me see their accomplishments with a grateful eye. Also, it would help if I tuned into my Abundance Voice so that I could see how much work we have and what a good situation that creates.

Using your voices to change your emotional reaction is a very powerful tool to enhance your emotional intelligence. When we gain control over which voice is dominating our inner dialogue and make some decisions about which voice would serve us best, we are beginning to master the intricacies of emotional intelligence.

Self-Coach as Choir Director

An important technique for greater emotional intelligence is to think of your self-coach as a choir director conducting the many voices that can dominate our thinking. Getting to know that inner talk and which voices are most frequently heard is an important step in observation. Now in this step, your self-coach will want to direct the volume of those voices. Perhaps the self-critic is just too vocal, and your self-coach, acting as choir director, will want to tell him to hush a bit. More *pianissimo,* if you will. Your self-coach may find that sweeter voices that carry a beautiful melody need more volume. More *forte* please, your choir director would direct. However, expressing those voices may take practice. In fact, sometimes it even takes time to discover these voices. Your self-coach should seek out the voices that reflect gratitude, hope, joy, calm, forgiveness, reassurance, strength, and humor, and coach them to take a more prominent place in the choir in your head. These voices will redirect your emotional responses and help you to find a way to channel your energies in a direction that maintains your integrity of purpose. So next time you find that you are close to a hijacking, practice turning up the volume on those voices that can do you good versus harm.

Creating New Assumptions

Thus far, the entire point of this step called directing has been about creating new assumptions. These new assumptions are about replacing the Dirty Dozen irrational beliefs that draw us toward negative emotional responses. If you practice the techniques presented thus far, you will no doubt form healthy new assumptions that will serve you well. As you become more skilled at challenging your irrational beliefs, adding humor to your thought processes, amplifying the voices that will serve your intentions, and hushing voices that escalate negative emotional reactions, you'll find new assumptions forming. Your self-coach should be assisting you in forming new assumptions that will be uniquely yours. Here are a few examples that might help.

OTHERS WANT TO SEE YOU SUCCEED, NOT FAIL

Assuming others are on your side and care about your success will abate many negative thoughts about how the world views you. If you believe that people would rather see you fail than succeed, then you are forced to be suspicious, overly averse to risk, and otherwise self-conscious. With this new assumption, comments by a supervisor who may indeed have your best interests in mind are not viewed as condemnations but rather as useful mentoring. You can see immediately that if you would adopt this assumption, you would be less inclined to a hijacking the next time your boss says something about your performance.

OTHERS' INTENTIONS ARE NOT TO HARM YOU

As we master our assumptions related to the motives of others, this new assumption helps us to believe the best about others rather than the worst. This new assumption helps us to feel trust and safety and frees us to take risks and express ourselves. You still may want to avoid dark lonely alleys late at night, but this new assumption will help you gain a healthy perspective about others.

MOST INCONSIDERATE ACTS ARE NOT AIMED AT YOU PERSONALLY

Most of us give way too much credit to the motives of others. Most people are not aiming their inconsiderate acts at you. Instead, they simply may be misinformed, misguided, or just not paying attention, and you happen to be on the receiving end of behaviors in these situations. More people are simply thoughtless rather than motive driven in creating a bad day for you. If you hang on to the belief that motives lie behind every action, you'll spend your work day trying to figure out the grand scheme when none exists.

YOU ARE WORTHY

This might be an assumption worth cultivating. Too often people experience the opposite and, therefore, assume that others think the same. Low self-worth can leave us feeling defensive and hurt. In the workplace, as you practice feeling worthy, you give yourself the power and freedom to perform at your top level. As long as you believe that you are not worthy, you will have difficulty achieving your full potential.

PEOPLE WILL COME THROUGH

As you shift your assumptions about other people and their performances, you'll find that a shift will occur in their performances. This is partly the result of what you're expecting to find, but it's also coming from the notion that people will perform better when we believe they will. If you think objectively about the number of people that you encounter in the workplace, most do their jobs. Most do come through. It's just that we may tend to focus on the times and the people who do not. This assumption is powerful for leaders and for coworkers.

IT'S PROBABLY NOT AS BAD AS I THINK

You've got that right. Put your rational brain to work, and I'm sure you can come up with many scenarios that could be worse. This new assumption will get you through many difficult moments. Besides, it will help you to move from your disaster-thinking to true problem-solving. If we are overcome by catastrophizing over a situation, our limbic systems render our rational brains incapable of doing their best work. And if indeed this is a problem, your rational brain is most needed.

I WILL SURVIVE

I can't help but think of this one with theme music. Just imagine Gloria Gaynor singing the words "I will survive" in a powerful voice, and you'll be inspired to believe that, indeed, you will survive, even in the face of adversity. Assuming that you are strong will make you stronger. The power behind this assumption is in knowing that your spirit is strong. We act what we believe.

TODAY WILL BE A GOOD DAY

Facing each day with this assumption will statistically improve your reality. In fact, according to an article by M. F. Scheier in the *Journal of Personality and Social Psychology,* optimism may also improve your life expectancy. In a five-year follow-up with patients in this heart surgery study, optimists, as compared to pessimists, were more likely to adhere to healthier habits such as using vitamins, eating less fatty foods, and enrolling in a cardiac rehabilitation program. The optimists had increased life expectancy because of these actions.[12] Therefore, this assumption will provide you with a new direction for your energy. Why? Because when you make this assumption, you suddenly have a renewed sense of how to spend your time and you enhance your sense of commitment to your tasks.

THIS IS TEMPORARY

Recognizing that most problem situations are temporary makes it much easier to recover. If we believe that our distress will be forever, then coping with the problem may seem overwhelming. Assume, instead, that our problems will pass. This creates an entirely different mindset regarding both the problem at hand and the future. People in the middle of organizational change often become para-

---

[12]Scheier, M.F., et. al. "Dispositional Optimism and Recovery from Coronary Artery Bypass Surgery: The Beneficial Effects on Physical and Psychological Well-Being," *Journal of Personality and Social Psychology* 57 (1989): 1024–1040.

lyzed because of the chaos they experience. Their chaos is probably temporary, but depending on their mindsets or assumptions, they may not be able to see it that way, which can cause greater anxiety.

I HAVE POWER TO CHANGE MANY THINGS

When we assume power, our position changes from one of helplessness to one of control. Sure, some things we can't control, but, for the most part, situations at work are among the things we can improve. The outcome may depend on the methods we use to initiate and execute that action, but, for the most part, people respond positively to others who take action to improve situations. Career satisfaction in particular is stronger when people take responsibility for their situations. In the *Pursuit of Happiness,* David Myers, Ph.D., writes that one of the traits of happy people is personal control. Happy people believe they choose their destinies.[13]

Our Worldview/Workview

Assumptions form our worldview. Let's say my assumptions include the following: I have little or no power to change things; today is going to be a bad day; and people rarely come through. Then my worldview is going to be bleak. In fact, I may have difficulty getting up in the morning. Yet if people checked their assumptions, many of them would find that those are the kinds of thoughts they are carrying around. No wonder why they get hijacked. Imagine the difference in someone's attitude who has the assumptions listed above versus these assumptions:

- People, including my supervisor and coworkers, want to see me succeed.

- Today is going to be a great day at work.

- People really want to do a good job and come through.

---

[13] Myer, David. *Pursuit of Happiness.* New York: Avon Books, 1992.

"Workview" Assumptions	
I work at this company because I have to.	I choose to work at this company.
Work is just a part of existence that I must bear in order to survive.	Work is a productive part of my day that allows me to live all of my life to the fullest.
The people that I work with are stupid and insensitive.	The people that I work with are competent, caring, and helpful.
Management doesn't care about us.	Management wants to make the company successful so we all prosper.

FIGURE 11.3

Their entire worldview about work would be completely different. In fact, I believe that people carry sets of assumptions about work, which I label their "workview." Of course these people probably carry the same assumptions in the rest of their lives, as well. Consider the following examples of assumptions that could change our workview (see Figure 11.3).

But wait. Isn't it true that sometimes management doesn't care that some people are insensitive, and that we have to work to survive? Sure. Any of the items listed in the left column can be true. And, I've certainly seen many examples that would support those assumptions. But, as I have seen in many examples, the items on the right can be equally true. So, it's not about which is right. It's about choosing which side you care to embrace as your workview. Chances are, if you choose the left, you will constantly be looking for and finding evidence to support your workview. Therefore, your energy and your attention will be focused on the negative, and your emotional response will certainly fit this view. Propensity for hijacking will abound. Besides, there is nothing about this workview that will solve any of your problems. It will only compound them. You'll go to work every day believing that people are stupid and insensitive and that management is out to get you. In fact, you'll no doubt perpetuate this workview. It's hard to imagine your being caring and helpful toward others if you believe that everyone around you is not helpful. We become what we believe. If, however, you focus on the right column, you will no doubt find examples to support this view, and your emotional energy will be focused on positive assumptions that should reduce your likelihood of being hijacked. The workview on the right will produce a different emotional energy that will affect your coworkers as well.

But wait again. Am I suggesting that we just deceive ourselves into thinking life is wonderful when in reality it is not? Of course not. If things are unbearable, you must take steps to change them. The question for your self-coach to help you determine is this: "Is it really bad, or do I just perceive it as bad because of my worldview?" It is your worldview or workview that frames how you take in information. Here's where your rational brain can help you sort through information to get to the truth. Your self-coach can help you look for contrary evidence.

I sometimes refer to this shift in workview or worldview as the shift from a critical heart to a grateful heart. Depending on how I look at the same set of circumstances, I can be disappointed or elated. For example, if you are a leader, a grateful heart will allow others to feel that you believe in them, feel that you support them, and feel that you care. We learned earlier that feelings affect behavior and productivity, but this has nothing to do with standards or expectations. I'm not at all suggesting that you lower your expectations. Consider the difference in the success between the leader who approaches her staff with a grateful heart and the leader who approaches her staff with a critical heart. Who's more likely to get her staff to produce more, care about quality, or treat customers well? It's workview that will frame how each leader will handle the discussion regarding quantity or quality improvements or enhanced customer care that will produce the result.

Your self-coach should be checking in with you to check your assumptions. How are you framing things? How are you looking at situations? Which heart do you carry around: the critical heart or the grateful heart? Even a quick shift in the moment will redirect your emotional response to avert a hijacking. However, this technique will serve you best if you focus on a total shift in your philosophy or worldview rather than to try to use it in the moment to avert a hijacking. If you shift your philosophy, you will experience the hijacking urge much less frequently.

EXAMPLE OF WORLDVIEW/WORKVIEW IN ACTION

If we take two common sets of assumptions and place them on a continuum, we can see how assumptions will affect our view of the world. For example, consider the following assumptions regarding self-doubt and confidence to be on a continuum (see Figure 11.4). Then consider another continuum around the assumption that we make regarding others (see Figure 11.5).

If you combine these continuums into x and y axes, the results would look like the chart in Figure 11.6. These assumptions would dramatically affect your worldview and your workview and would certainly affect your behavior.

Quadrant 1, The Pleaser: In this combination of assumptions, you would create a world in which you generally perceive others as better than you. In this situation, you would never feel equal. Power would generally shift to others, as you would not be willing to assume any power or control because you consider yourself unworthy. You would often defer to others, thereby compounding your power loss. You would generally not offer ideas for collaboration, although you would probably work hard to support the ideas of others, especially others who tend to show some type of support toward you. Fear would tend to be your most likely avenue for hijacking.

Quadrant 2, The Collaborator: In this set of assumptions, you would have the greatest opportunity to interact with others in a positive way. You would approach others in a manner that gives equal power to them and to you. You would be more likely to collaborate with others. You would be open to the ideas of others. In addition, you would offer ideas and approach life in a way that suggests you are a willing and helpful player. You would view questions from others as a way to help you gain clarity and to help you achieve your purpose. You would listen because you would have a true desire to hear what others have to say. You have mutual respect and honor for others, and this is a great source of your power. You are least likely to get hijacked when coming from this set of assumptions.

View of Self

X _____

I have little or no competence.	I am competent in many areas.
I am afraid that others see me as stupid.	I am able to understand things easily.
I have little or no confidence.	I am fairly confident in my abilities.

FIGURE 11.4

View of Others

Y _____

Most people are out to get me.	Most people are good.
Most people are only out for themselves.	Most people will offer help and assistance.
Most people like to see me fail.	Most people want to see me succeed.

FIGURE 11.5

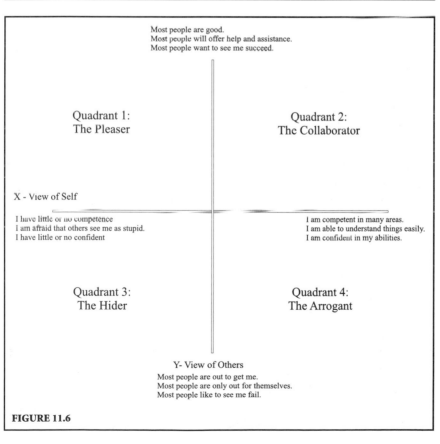

Most people are good.
Most people will offer help and assistance.
Most people want to see me succeed.

Quadrant 1:
The Pleaser

Quadrant 2:
The Collaborator

X - View of Self

I have little or no competence
I am afraid that others see me as stupid.
I have little or no confident

I am competent in many areas.
I am able to understand things easily.
I am confident in my abilities.

Quadrant 3:
The Hider

Quadrant 4:
The Arrogant

Y- View of Others

Most people are out to get me.
Most people are only out for themselves.
Most people like to see me fail.

FIGURE 11.6

Quadrant 3, The Arrogant: This combination of assumptions would set you up as a know-it-all. You would assume that because you are competent and others are largely negative and out to get you, you would have to protect yourself. You would tend to be arrogant. You would feel compelled to spend a lot of time proving your point. You would use power in a negative way. You would rely on the power that comes from position or authority rather than the power that comes from mutual respect, because you do not have mutual respect. You would view any type of questioning as a challenge. You would tend not to listen to others because you don't believe they have worth. You could easily be hijacked to anger because others may be viewed as challenging you.

Quadrant 4, The Hider: In this set of assumptions, you would find life difficult. Your self-doubt and your belief that others are negative and out to get you would cause you to hide. You would likely not speak up in meetings. You would create systems to protect yourself. You'd feel powerless and victimized. You'd believe that others have power and that their intention is to use it against you. You would tend to be suspicious and fearful. It would be difficult for you to live your intentions. You would likely be hijacked by fear.

This is just one example of the power of assumptions and how they can affect your worldview. There are many other combinations of assumptions that we haven't even addressed, such as assumptions about sadness and joy, despair and hope, and fear and courage. Each set of assumptions will affect how we view the world and our emotional reactions to the people and events that we encounter each day. Changing your workview or worldview will change so many things. It is by far the most powerful way to greater emotional intelligence. By shifting your view, even triggers that once seemed likely to hijack you will likely dissipate because it isn't the trigger, but the assumptions that your trigger activates, that causes the hijacking. For example, bad weather isn't what causes my hijacking, but my assumption that the world is a fearful place when roads are snow covered. The fact that it's snowing is just that. A fact. So by focusing on your assumptions, your self-coach will likely find many rewards to assist you in living a more emotionally intelligent life.

Act As If

Although psychologists confirm that our experiences influence how we behave today, they also tell us that we have a tremendous capacity to determine who we wish to be tomorrow. One simple technique rooted in psychological principles is to *act as if.* This technique is based on the assumption that our attitudes will follow our behavior. It proposes that "if we act as if we're happy, we smile," is as valid as "we smile because we are happy." This technique is based on personal construct psychology (PCP). Originally drafted by George Kelly in 1955, PCP has been extended to a variety of domains, including organizational development, education, business and marketing, and cognitive science.[14]

So if we act as if we are defeated, we feel defeated. Conversely if we act as if we can make a difference, we begin to make a difference. If we persist in the face of obstacles, we begin to feel that we can overcome the obstacles. If we act as if we have control and influence over our lives, we begin to feel that we have control and influence over our lives. Research supporting this theory suggests that our subjective emotional experience can be altered if we behave accordingly.[15] In addition, facial expression does seem to contribute to the intensity of our emotional experience and our overall moods.[16] This concept is fundamental to changing our worldviews and assumptions.

If you find yourself in a pattern of thinking that is destructive, the most significant way to change that pattern is to begin acting differently, even before you believe or feel like acting differently. Thought will then follow your behavior. Most of us recognize that peer pressure among some young people can cause them to act out of character. Suddenly, they begin thinking and espousing beliefs different from what they had previously held. You can use that same concept

---

[14] Neimeyer, R.A., and Bridges S.K. "Personal Construct Psychology." *The Corsini Encyclopedia of Psychology and Behavioral Science, 3rd ed.* New York: John Wiley & Sons, 2001.
[15] Mischel, W.; Ebbesen, E.; and Zeiss, A. "Selective Attention to the Self: Situational and Dispositional Determinants." *Journal of Personality and Social Psychology* 27 (1993): 204–218.
[16] LeDoux, Joseph. "Emotion and the Limbic Systems Concept." *Concepts in Neuroscience* 2 (1992): 87.

to help you break away from destructive thoughts. Use your self-coach and find positive peers who demonstrate the behaviors you desire. Begin emulating their new behaviors and soon you will be feeling and thinking these new patterns. Feel like a victim? Take one action instead *as if* you are empowered. Feel low self-esteem? Take one action instead *as if* you have confidence. Feeling afraid? Take one action instead *as if* you have courage. One action at a time will feed your sense of power and courage. Practiced long and hard enough, you will gain the ability to influence yourself. Brian Tracy states in *Create Your Own Future* that "What this means is that you can *act* your way into feeling the way you want to *feel*. You can program your subconscious by behaving as if you already have the qualities and characteristics you most desire."[17] Is it false to *act as if?* No, not if your intention is to change yourself. Yes, if it is your intention to change others. *Act as if* is a tool for you to change and influence yourself, not to manipulate others to be something else.

Shifting

Another technique for redirecting your emotional state is a technique called shifting. Shifting isn't a preferred technique and should be reserved for those occasions when, in the moment, you recognize that you are at serious risk of being hijacked but are unable to redirect in a constructive way. Shifting is the act of transferring your focus from triggers you can't redirect to some object unrelated to whatever threatens to hijack you. Shifting is about emotional suppression. Shifting will allow you to compose yourself in the middle of a negative encounter when you might be on the verge of exploding with anger or being reduced to tears. For example, imagine that you are a pediatric nurse working on a cancer floor. An angry co-worker or an unreasonable boss confronts you while you are in the middle of tending to a patient. Let's assume that you are on the verge of tears. Obviously this isn't a situation where you can very easily

---

[17]Tracy, Brian. *Create Your Own Future.* Hoboken, NJ: John Wiley & Sons, 2001.

excuse yourself and distance yourself from the situation. At this point, you are unable to redirect to a meaningful path, but you also know that you do not wish to be hijacked to tears. What options do you have? Although your options may be limited, you can use shifting.

This shift works to control the emerging emotion and suppress it for the immediate time being. Here's how it plays out in an example. As your coworker or boss confronts you, you notice that lump in your throat or perhaps your eyes welling with tears. If you think about it, you may find that you feel humiliated or hurt or somehow violated by this person's insensitivity. If you keep focusing on what the person is saying or if you continue to dwell on the immediate situation and the humiliation or other emotions that are surfacing, you will no doubt experience an overabundance of tears and therefore, your emotions will be ruling. However, remember that we said in this situation you are unable to redirect. Perhaps the hurt or humiliation in the moment is just too intense. In this type of situation, the best you may be able to do is shift your thinking. Shifting will require you to focus on something rational, even if it is completely irrelevant, just to stop your limbic system from getting too carried away by the emotion. So, rather than think about how miserable you are feeling and the apparent humiliation, you can begin to focus on the color of your patient's nightgown or on some details as you read your patient's chart or on the capital cities of various states. The objective here is just to stop your emotional reaction in the moment. By focusing all of your energy on rational thoughts, even though the rational thoughts are not relevant, you will at least buy some time so that you can deal with the situation constructively at some later point. Because it is so difficult for your mind to function at this rational level and also dwell on the emotional reaction you are experiencing, this technique will serve your immediate needs.

Of course, much about this technique is undesirable. It serves only to suppress an emotional reaction. We've said time and again that emotional intelligence isn't about suppressing emotions, but rather finding appropriate ways to express emotions. So, this technique should be reserved for those rare situations when you are just unable to redirect your path. Later, you will want to revisit the situation and determine how you can confront the situation and deal with the conflict. If not, suppressing emotional reactions can be harmful and can lead to undesirable behaviors.

So if it's harmful, some would argue, it isn't even a worthwhile technique in the workplace. I can think of a few instances when it would be useful for you to suppress your reaction in the moment. The example of the pediatric nurse may be one of them because in this example, if you keep in mind the overriding intention and purpose that drew you to this field in the first place, you recognize that your little patient has seen enough misery. Because moods are contagious, crying in front of the patient will more than likely not serve your purpose. Other examples would include instances when your duty to the public or the customer must come first and an emotional reaction in the moment would prove disastrous. I don't think we want our airline pilots or our surgeons or our police officers being hijacked in the line of duty. Therefore, emotional suppression can occasionally serve a purpose. Ultimately, if these situations are constant, and suppression becomes a way of life, we develop high risk for undesirable coping behaviors, such as drug and alcohol abuse.

IMPLEMENT IN THE MOMENT

Thus far this chapter has discussed the need to visualize the end result, or your intention, and the need to strategize and determine a technique that you can use. The final step is, of course, to implement the technique. And, just to make it challenging, we have to implement in the moment. Chances are that if you practice these techniques you will have some success as well as some failure. However, the trick is to keep trying. I distinctly remember trying to use the technique of shifting to my gratitude voice when I was being overly critical of my three-year-old daughter. The result was that I sounded completely ridiculous. I had already started down the hijacking path by stating a laundry list of things I was dissatisfied with, and then I tried to mitigate my own negative voice with some positive comments. Trouble is, my attempt was too late. She looked at me and said, "Make up your mind, Mommy, are you mad or not?" It was hilarious. Her humor served as a perfect, yet unplanned, way to change everyone's emotional reaction.

There's really nothing much to say about implementing these techniques except, just do it. Later, your attempts with both good results and failures will provide useful information during the next step, which is reflection.

CHAPTER 12

STEP 5: REFLECT

*We need quiet time to examine our lives openly
and honestly . . . spending quiet times alone
gives your mind an opportunity to renew itself
and create order.—Susan Taylor*

Ionce heard the statement, "There's a huge difference between
thirty years of experience and one year of experience repeated
thirty times." I love this statement because it captures the true
essence of wisdom. Wisdom is not about putting in time in this
thing called life. It is about the profound knowledge that can come
from life experience. I say "can" because I don't think wisdom is the
outcome of only life experience, for I know some children who are
quite wise with little life experience and some very old people who
are very unwise despite their long years of experience. So I don't think
it is truly about life experience. However, I think we can use our life
experience to create wisdom if we pay attention.

Reflection is the rain and the sunshine and the fertilizer that can
turn life experience into wisdom. Without reflection, our promising
seeds of wisdom will die. With reflection, they will sprout and bear
fruit that can be harvested and enjoyed daily. I know of no other area
of life where this holds truer than in the area of emotional intelligence. Sure, you can become a wiser gardener, a wiser cook, or a
wiser auto mechanic with experience; the years are bound to teach
you something. But to become a better parent, a better leader, a bet-

ter person will require thoughtful reflection on these intangible acts that make up our human interactions. The measures are also more obscure in the latter. As I become more adroit in the kitchen, I know that I can handle a knife better than I did thirty years ago. I can see the result. Yet how do I know that I am a better person?

Life will provide us with ample opportunities to practice becoming better people, but reflection will help us to decide what to do with those opportunities. Just as any sports team watches game highlights to rehash the plays that made them win or lose, your mind can watch your life highlights. Then, with the help of the coach, these sports teams decide what to practice to improve their game. After next week's game, they watch again. Although we may not have the luxury of having our game on videotape, we surely can benefit from the practice of review. That's what reflection is all about. Reflection is our opportunity to watch the tape of our daily experiences and interactions with others rolling in our minds. This tape contains all the moments of brilliance, as well as our moments of mistakes.

What is the purpose of replaying the tapes? Review and reflection of our daily interactions with others is our mental practice at becoming wiser. It is the opportunity to rewire our brains, to mentally practice different endings and to practice being our most inspired selves. It is our opportunity to work with our self-coach, who can provide the commentary and the direction for redirecting our actions in the next game. It's all about reflecting on what went well and rehearsing to make the rest of it better. Reflection will help to ensure that you aren't wasting those thirty years of experience, but rather building on those thirty years of life experience to continually improve. Reflection is a wonderful way to get you closer to understanding your emotional reaction in the moment, which is the true mastery of emotional intelligence.

Reflection is not about regret. Sure, you will experience some regret as you reflect, but regret in and of itself is a useless emotion. You can use regret as a signal to your self-coach that something requires improvement. Beyond that, let it go. If you use your reflection time solely for regret, and you practice beating yourself up for your errors, you'll accomplish nothing other than to become better at self-degradation. This will not serve as a means to greater emotional intelligence.

Reflection isn't about rationalizing or justifying. Emily Schultheiss, business coach and author of *Day By Day, A Journey Toward Thriving,* distinguishes the difference between reflecting to justify versus true reflection. She told me that too often we spend our valuable moments of reflection justifying what we've done, and why we did it. Rather, she suggests, "What could have been different? When you can get in touch with what's in back of your mind, then your reflection can serve a greater purpose." In an interview, Tom Kopler, internal organizational development professional, adds the thought that when in reflection, Stephen Covey's principle "seek first to understand rather than to be understood," holds true. So ask your self-coach to help you tune in to your reflection. Are you hearing your self-talk justifying your actions? When I hear much justifying going on inside my head, I probe in the opposite direction to ask: What else could this be? How else could I have behaved? Could there have been another way? Or as Schultheiss adds, "What am I missing?"

As I think about countless meetings in the business world, I hear much justification talk going on in these meetings. We've been trained and conditioned to find justification for the actions we take. However, I wonder how much of this has added to our skill of justifying and has detracted from our skill of reflecting. In one meeting I observed, every item that came up for discussion started with the phrase, "Well, I had little choice except to. . . ." And then the party would revert to the justification for whatever action was being discussed. If our mental reflections begin with that statement, then I'd suggest we have some work to do. Ask your self-coach to expand your thinking and to be creative during reflection and not to justify what actions you have already taken.

Reflection isn't about reflecting solely on our feelings. It is essential that we also reflect on the facts. I'm not talking about the fact that two plus two equals four, but the facts surrounding our interactions with others, not our feelings. Franky Johnson, of Johnson and Lee Consulting put it this way: "When we reflect, we must reflect on how others actually received the information or interaction, not what we intended for them to receive." He used this example: "Let's say I decide to give you a lollipop. My intentions are good. I think it is something that is good to do. And I feel good about doing it. So, I could go about this business of reflection feeling good about my decision to give you a lollipop. But the thing that I must consider is not how I felt about it, but how did you feel about receiving it? The 'fact' is how my intention was received. If you received it and were happy about it, then I have lived my intention. If you were upset about it, then I did not live my intention." So reflection should take into consideration not only what your intentions were and how you felt about your actions, but more importantly, how did others who were on the receiving end of your intentions view your actions. I'm not suggesting that good intentions are bad. I'm only suggesting that intentions alone are not enough. Intentions executed into actions that others perceive in the manner in which we intend truly align us. And the only way to determine this is to reflect on how others receive our behavior.

REFLECTION BASICS

So how should you go about this business of reflection? I'm a big proponent of free-flowing reflection. I think reflection should be practiced all day long. Reflection should bubble up, not be forced into a pattern. I think it's those momentary flashes, more like the quick flash of a firefly, that could provide important insight. Occasionally, you may experience the lightening bolt moments, but more often than not it will be subtle reflections that surface. It's those subtle reflections that we must be prepared to capture and incorporate into our learning. For those who prefer some structure, I've listed some questions that may help with your reflection. Select the questions that you think are pertinent to your day. Select a few. Don't allow reflection to become rote. Roteness isn't going to produce insights. Ask your self-coach to help lend his or her observation to the following:

> Q. What is my purpose? (I believe that every day you should ask yourself that question.)

Q. How well did I live my purpose in my interactions with others today?

Q. How did others receive my actions?

Q. What did I do well today?

Q. What did I do that could be improved?

Q. What did I do that I should stop doing?

Q. What voices did I hear from today?

Q. What voices could I have heard from today that I did not?

Q. What mood was I in today?

Q. What triggers did I notice today?

Q. Which of the Dirty Dozen permeated my thoughts today?

Q. Any averted hijackings today?

Q. Any successful hijackings?

Q. What assumptions did I carry today?

Q. What worldview/workview did I have today?

Q. What positive effect did I have on others today?

Q. What negative effect did I have on others today?

Q. What can I be proud of today?

Q. How many of my thoughts were dominated by a grateful heart? How many by a critical heart?

REFLECTION METHODS

So how does one go about the business of reflection? The answers to that question will be as diverse as the number of people who answer, but the techniques listed below may help. Your method of reflection will depend on many things, such as your personality preferences and your comfort level with some of these techniques. I would suggest that you experiment with a variety of things to determine what gives you the best results.

Journaling

Writing is the path to awareness. I'm not talking about anything fancy here. Neither spelling nor grammar count. Even logic doesn't count. I'm just talking about the act of putting words on paper. Raw flow. It makes life clear. It forces us to clarify our intentions. It forces us to confront what bothers us. It forces us to face up to our inconsistencies. It forces us to take a stand. It forces us to know ourselves. Write it down. Yes, it's that important. The best advice I can possibly give if you are interested in developing greater emotional intelligence is to begin to journal every morning. Julie Cameron, author of *The Artist's Way*, describes the act of writing what she calls Morning Pages as "spiritual windshield wipers." She writes "Once we get those muddy, maddening, confusing thoughts on the page, we face our day with clearer eyes. We are more honest with ourselves and others, more centered, and more spiritually at ease."[1] I concur.

The implication for emotional intelligence is great. Intention has been a common theme of this book. It is critical that we keep our intentions, our purposes, in mind. I can think of no better way to confront our intentions than to write every day about them. Also, we talked about the importance of mood and how mood can trigger emotional reactions. Yet so often, if you don't spend time reflecting on your mood, it's likely that you'll be taken by surprise sometime during the day by the powerful force of mood. I find that the best way for me to understand my mood is to write in the morning. The morning sets the stage for your day. I see it as the warm up, the mental rehearsal, and the time to clearly establish the boundaries that are you.

---

[1]Cameron, Julie. *The Artist's Way – A Spiritual Path to Higher Creativity, 10th ed.* Los Angeles: J. P. Tarcher, 2002.

Journaling is also a wealth of information for your self-coach. It allows your coach to peer into your soul. He will have first-hand knowledge that will help him do his job. Journaling is about many things. Sure, it's about thinking about our intentions, our moods, our hopes, and our dreams, but it's also about making sense of where we have been and where we are. It is reflection at its finest. Without reflection, there is no movement. Without reflection it is surely possible to repeat the same mistakes without even realizing that you are making the mistake. With reflection, we at least have an opportunity to review our mistakes and our successes and to decide, I'd like more or less please. Business coach Schultheiss says two critical things about this:

"When you notice that the same lessons or the same problems keep recurring in your life, you must ask yourself, 'What is it that you haven't changed?' Also, you must reread your journals to discover the progress, the repeated areas where we continually make the same mistakes, and for hints about the secrets still to be uncovered."

Only writing it down in a journal gives you the opportunity to have such access to the history of your inner thoughts. It's very powerful to have that kind of record in life. Besides, what else are you going to do on a rainy day?

Lessons Learned Log

If you aren't up to journaling, then the next best thing is what I call a Lessons Learned Log. Your Lessons Learned Log doesn't chronicle the journey so much as what destinations you visited. By at least pausing to record your lessons learned, you create an awareness of those flashes or lightning bolts. One person I know keeps her Lessons Learned Log in the form of quotations. She selects quotations that highlight something of significance, then jots down the incident in her day that caused her to select those quotations. Another person I know just keeps a notepad in his office and jots down a couple of words as a running record of his lessons learned. I'm not proposing anything fancy, just something effective at capturing the reflections. I am a strong advocate of some type of written record or log because it gives you an opportunity to look over your progress.

Mentoring

For those who prefer to reflect in the company of others, there are many avenues. Mentoring is one of them. If you have a trusted mentor, you could use this relationship to reflect. The beauty of doing this with another person is that he or she can help you make sense of some of your random thoughts and can point out inconsistencies or patterns. A mentor may also be someone to whom you feel accountable and therefore, for whom you feel an obligation to improve. Mentors inside the same organization can also understand the players and help you interpret what's going on. Besides, the statistics suggest that seventy percent of people with mentors report faster salary and total compensation growth.[2] Those in mentoring relationships also show gains in nine of eleven generic career and life-effectiveness skills.[3] Effective mentors will also share their own struggles and triumphs in conquering some of the same territory that you are working on.

Friends

How about reflecting with a great and trusted friend? "That's fine as long as your friend has the courage to tell you you're full of it," advises Schultheiss, "and as long as your friend doesn't indulge your sense of rationalizing or justifying." Just like a written journal, long-term friends can provide a sense of history for you. True friends will also love you in spite of your repeated errors, so you can feel free to indulge those same lessons. I'd encourage you to advise your friends to ask you the tough questions, such as "What role are you playing in this recurring problem?" Friends are also great for helping us clarify our voices. Voices come through with other people, so they can serve as a means to identify the voices in your inner choir. If you choose to reflect with friends, however, you'll have to determine if

[2] Qaddumi, Thora. "Study Shows Mentoring Is Key to Retaining Minority Leaders." *Houston Business Journal* January 4, 1999. http://www.bizjournals.com/houston/stories/1999/01/04/focus3.html

[3] Murray, Margo. "Energizing Employees with Mentoring." *Masters Series, Performance Improvement*, 40 (3): 34–38

their assumptions and worldview are so close to yours that they won't be able to challenge your thinking.

Dream Team

Many years ago, I had the privilege of being part of a small group of people who decided to form a "Dream Team." Our mission was and remains to nurture and challenge each other so we can live our dreams. Our Dream Team meets quarterly. Each member is asked to report on lessons learned, challenges, celebrations, and progress toward dreams. The process sounds so simple, yet to put this in practice takes quite a commitment. Of course, one of the functions of the Dream Team is to serve as a forum for reflection. Those reflections are powerful and, when forced to reflect quarterly, especially with a team who has a great memory, you can sometimes clearly see your progress or lack of it. Also, we state out loud our intentions to improve, so there is a built-in sense of accountability in our group. You might find a perfect forum for reflection in your own Dream Team.

Coaching

Working with a coach provides another avenue for reflection. A skilled coach can help you reflect, improve your accuracy, and save you the time of rationalizing or justifying. With razor-sharp accuracy, a coach can zip open your inner world and help you to see clearly. Your coach can call attention to the inner characters that dominate your thinking, challenge your assumptions, and point out the worldviews that help and hinder. Also, if you are struggling to determine your purpose or your intentions, a coach can be the perfect person to help you discover what you really want. Char Kinder, life coach and founder of DiscoveryWorks, talks about the concept of "showing up." She helps clients become clear about what their intentions are and asks them how they intend to "show up." Just like you decide what suit or sweater you're going to wear, Kinder helps clients discover what intentions or values they hope to live today. What a great way to reflect on the notion of purpose.

Volunteering

Other suggestions that may help the reflection process include spending time doing something outside yourself and outside your normal routine. "Volunteering, especially in situations such as hospices and homeless shelters, heightens your awareness about your life," says Schultheiss. Volunteering with those less fortunate than you allows your gratitude voice to surface. It also can serve as a powerful way to test your assumptions. For example, if you often come from the point of view that you're the unlucky one and don't get a fair share of life's breaks, volunteer and then go home and reflect on your good fortune.

Hobbies

Taking walks, woodworking, digging in the dirt, and other hobbies allow for reflection time that can produce good results because you are engaging in something that you enjoy. That process changes the chemistry of the brain and allows for thoughts to flow differently from when you just ruminate over things.

Tangible Objects

Another suggestion for reflection is to come up with tangible objects that remind you of or connect you to your lessons. You can surround your desk with these tangible objects to make those lessons real. Since his heart attack, a friend of mind keeps a rock on his desk with the word "HEAVY" written on it. The rock reminds him that carrying around other people's burdens can take a heavy toll.

Reading

For others I know, reading is a means of reflection. For these masters, reading isn't about reading to accumulate facts and information; it's about accumulating knowledge to reflect on and to decide how one's own life compares. That translates into the distinction between knowledge and wisdom.

Yearly Pilgrimage to a Favorite Spot

Another friend, Mary Butina, devised a clever way to reflect on her progress. Each year, she would go to a favorite spot with her camera and journal in hand. She would take a picture and reflect on the lessons she's accumulated in a year's time. These pictures and reflections, when placed in an album, make a powerful and interesting reflection tool that can serve as a tangible reminder of growth.

SUMMARY

Whatever your methods, reflection is a critical component of emotional intelligence. If you just keep in mind the premise that reflection should draw you closer to living your intentions, the insights will pour into your consciousness. By asking how you are progressing toward those intentions and what obstacles might be holding you back, you are on your way of turning your years of experience into true wisdom.

CHAPTER 13

STEP 6: CELEBRATE

Reflect upon your blessings,
of which every man has plenty,

not on your past misfortunes,
of which all men have some.

—Charles Dickens

Celebrate! The overachiever in me often wonders why we celebrate birthdays. After all, a birthday signifies nothing more than the passage of time. What has really been achieved? Don't misunderstand. I joyfully eat my cake and blow out the candles. I love the celebration. But in comparison, some of life's other achievements truly represent milestones that have taken great effort. Events or dates, such as graduations or anniversaries, mark some of those. However, I think we often miss the opportunity to truly celebrate those intangible achievements that aren't marked by a specific event or a date on the calendar. Yet if we think about it, some of the most significant breakthroughs in our thoughts or behaviors probably defined and changed us as much, if not more, than a graduation or anniversary. I'm suggesting here that we develop an appreciation for those moments and celebrate.

Why? Well, two reasons. First, celebration is fun. So, what other reason do we need? Second, celebration serves an important function of emotional intelligence. Celebrating hardwires our life experiences and changes the patterns in the limbic brain. When we associate pleasure with a particular circumstance, we tend to repeat it. Reinforcement works. In fact, we've adopted many of our present behaviors because others have reinforced them. Why do you put your napkin on your lap? Why do you lower your voice when in a house of worship? Why do you wait to be seated at a restaurant? (Okay, so maybe you don't do any of these things, but surely there are examples I could state that would apply to you too.) Most often we behave in a certain manner because somewhere along the way, that behavior (including unruly behavior) was reinforced. However, if you think about it, you've allowed others to determine how you should behave. And that includes behaviors that may not be serving us well. For example, most of the time when we do not voice our concerns in a meeting, it's because somewhere along the line, it was reinforced that stating our concern was not acceptable. This behavior could have been reinforced many years ago, perhaps even in another company or perhaps at the dinner table as a child; yet, it still affects the way we are today. That's fine as long as we are aware and deciding for ourselves the behavior that we choose. However, for those behaviors that no longer serve us, celebration can be a powerful way to reinforce the new behaviors we select in their place.

For celebration to promote new behaviors, we need a purposeful understanding of the new behaviors we wish to create. Your self-coach has been collecting great information throughout the earlier steps. The whole notion of directing your thoughts, inner characters, assumptions, and workview are aimed at understanding new behaviors that will serve you better. So your self-coach has been busy working to identify new behaviors that will create emotional responses that will help you live your intentions. Beyond that, during the reflection step, we've asked that you continually ask what you are doing that is working well. What have you improved? What are you proud of? What lessons have you learned? These are the seeds of celebration.

Our society is very focused on the physical trophies that we collect and that stand for our accomplishments: the bigger house that represents the promotion at work, the vacation to Europe signifying landing the big account, or the new car that symbolizes some other accomplishment. So much of what we celebrate comes from material achievement or at least tangible achievements, such as earning an MBA or Ph.D. Yet, from my perspective, the greatest gains in life are not about those tangible accomplishments but rather the intangible accomplishments. Their intangible nature makes them harder to recognize and therefore harder to celebrate. Ralph Cain, business consultant and organizational development specialist with Koinonia Consulting Group, introduced the idea of "Emotional Trophies." Emotional trophies are those moments or events we cherish, not because of some tangible reward, but because they represent some emotional memory that was a triumph, some moment when we truly lived our values and our life's intentions. That concept is valid because it allows for a tangible expression of intangible growth. Can you imagine a room full of emotional trophies that signify our accomplishments?

Yet what would those trophies in your life signify? I often ask people if they are somehow wiser today than they were ten or twenty years ago. By wiser, I mean not in an arrogant sense, but wiser in the sense of managing oneself and relationships with others. Most quickly respond that yes indeed, they are wiser. "So how do you know," I ask. That question is more difficult to answer, yet the answers I've collected all seem worthy of emotional trophies. The measures seem to revolve around four central themes. They are: Life Perspective, Self-Directed Living, Greater Skill Level, and Acceptance.

LIFE PERSPECTIVE

Many people I interviewed said they had gained perspective on what was important in their lives. In example after example, people said that a sign of their growth was the ability to discern what mattered and what didn't matter in life. This knowing they attributed to a greater understanding of their core values.

Perspective also allows for fewer emotional hijackings. Michael Boccia, Ph.D., an organizational consultant, talks about the intensity and frequency of emotional responses as his measure of success. "I like to think about emotions such as anger on a continuum of one to ten. If I used to feel a ten because someone cut me off on the highway, and now I feel five, I've made tremendous progress. It's the difference between road rage and annoyed. That's significant."

SELF-DIRECTED LIVING

With this increased perspective, people make decisions and life choices based on what they wanted, not on what peers, parents, spouses, or bosses wanted for them. This greater perspective allowed for self-directed living, which in turn, people believed led to better life choices. Instead of being driven by people, events, or things outside themselves, people found greater satisfaction in life because they were driven by their core values. Too often, people spoke of decisions that they made because someone else thought it would be best. Even societal or organizational pressures caused people to believe that they should act in a certain manner or go after a certain goal when, upon examination, it was not the right choice for them. When people took their life's direction in their own hands, they believed they had cause for emotional celebration or had acquired true emotional trophies. Please note that self-directed living does not mean selfishness. In many cases, the individuals that I spoke with felt that their decisions were much more selfless because they felt greater freedom in their lives. With the freedom that comes from living their own life, people felt more able to give to others freely rather than out of obligation or debt. Emotional trophies for many translated to better decision-making.

In *Don't Sweat the Small Stuff,* author Richard Carlson writes, "If you regularly take a minute to check in with yourself, to ask yourself, 'What's really important?' you may find that some of the choices you are making are in conflict with your own stated goals. This strategy can help you align your actions with your goals and encourage you to make more conscious, loving decisions."[1] That was echoed in our interviews regarding both big and small decisions.

Self-directed living also means freeing yourself from the most controlling of all partners—your own ego. When you finally let go of the notion that you must have the last word, or the best idea, or the largest staff because it feeds your ego, then you are truly free and

---

[1] Carlson, Richard. *Don't Sweat the Small Stuff . . . and It's All Small Stuff.* New York: Hyperion, 1997.

can live a self-directed life. Otherwise, you are living for the short-term emotional pleasure you get from the rush of winning. The problem with these ego-driven accomplishments is that there is always the need for the next accomplishment to fill the gap. Instead, when your choices are based on your values and your life's purpose, ego isn't part of the picture. It's about doing the right thing because it's the right thing, not because someone will notice and your ego will feel bolstered. When you've accomplished a sense of self-directed living, true emotional trophies are in order.

GREATER SKILL LEVEL

Many people reported a greater skill level in their relationships with others. Simple things, like getting acquainted, were done with greater ease, as people believed they acquired more emotional intelligence. One person I spoke with likened it to a dance. He said the choreography in relationships with others was more graceful and polished than it used to be. What used to feel awkward or strained now was a matter of routine. People also reported feeling more comfortable in conflict situations. For example, one person said that after a lifetime of handling complaints, he learned that it just doesn't pay to get upset. He had honed his skills in addressing conflict and complaints to the point where he most often was able to win people over. Another manager told me that in his earlier years as a manager, he became concerned if he had to address someone's poor performance. He said that although he wouldn't place that on the top of his list of favorite things to do, he had become much more skilled at addressing performance problems. Another manager reported that she felt much more skilled and comfortable at mentoring others. Earlier in her career, mentoring felt awkward and she was uncomfortable extending herself in a mentoring relationship. Now, she mentors others with ease. Without doubt, however, the most common declaration of progress was that people felt more skilled in creating and sustaining healthy relationships with those they loved. The measures were evident in the internal satisfaction they felt in their relationships with others and in the inner peace they felt.

ACCEPTANCE

Another common theme that people use to measure their growth is acceptance. People communicated a sense of peace they had discovered about life. With increased perspective and self-directed living, people were able to achieve a sense of acceptance of others, of life's detours, and of their own faults as they reflected on emotional trophies or measures.

Acceptance also allows you to enjoy the journey instead of always being concerned about the outcome. Ernie Emmerling, President of Broad Street Consulting, said he finds in golf, in life, and in business, it is easier to enjoy the journey. He relates a story about the annual two-day golf tournament with his brothers. He says that they were so intense about the outcome they forgot to enjoy the game. This year, he found himself able to enjoy the game. In the past, he, too, would forget to enjoy the journey, be it in golf or in other aspects of his life. Ultimately he says that the intensity and focus on the outcome affects performance. He says the idea of being more relaxed about life is a signal to him that he has made progress in his personal growth.

In fact, a common theme from my interviews was that acceptance of life's unplanned events was an important milestone in people's emotional growth. Many people I interviewed who had suffered personal and career setbacks said, "It's life; it isn't going to go exactly as planned. Accept that and move on." Many people that I interviewed had learned that eventually had to accept serious illness, death of a spouse, financial failures, and other life events or they would not be able to regain their lives. These same tragic events proved powerful triggers in helping them gain perspective and live self-directed lives. There was a circular feeling to their observations.

Along with revealing acceptance that life doesn't always go exactly as planned, my interviews proved that we have to accept that other people don't always behave as we would expect either, and that, too, requires acceptance. "I've learned that I can't, nor should I try to, control other people," one leader told me. He said that he knows his greatest learning as a leader came when he stopped trying to control his staff. "Once I stopped trying to control them, it's as if I had turned a switch, and they suddenly started to respond to me. It was then, that I learned what leadership was all about." Another leader said that, although this was a painful lesson, he had to accept that not everyone wanted his help in succeeding. He accepted that people had a right to make their own choices even if those choices could lead to termination. Both in the workplace and in people's personal lives, acceptance played an important role.

Acceptance is not about resignation. There is huge difference. Those who are resigned may withdraw from life, believing that they can no longer make a difference. They feel impotent in the face of life. Their energy is drained, as they believe they are unable to make a difference. Acceptance is another matter. It allows people to spend their energy wisely. It allows them to evaluate where to spend their energy so they can make a difference and live their live's purpose and when they should just accept the situation as it is. Acceptance allows people to know the difference so that they don't become depleted in trying to control things that are outside of their realm of power. Acceptance helps people to set boundaries on their efforts and energy. Acceptance allows people to move on to where they can contribute wisely. Acceptance can also lead to forgiveness, which is a powerful force of energy.

SUMMARY

These four central themes—Life Perspective, Self-Directed Living, Greater Skill Level, and Acceptance—are areas in which you can look for progress to celebrate your life's emotional achievements. I'd suggest you evaluate your interactions with the idea that each day it's the same program, but with a different ending. Imagine the same television program with the same characters and the same plot. Day after day it gets to be a rather boring venue. It's predictable. Growth is when you see yourself in similar situations, but you are no longer the same character. Deborah R. Bernstein, leadership consultant and executive coach, says that one of the key indicators of success is that you experience similar situations, but you bring a different person to the experience. This wiser person emerges because you consciously incorporate your past learning into the next situation. Using this definition of emotional progress is a wonderful way to measure your growth.

My interviews proved helpful in realizing that certainly there may be patterns, but everyone's lessons are unique and lessons learned depend on where you are in life—both metaphorically and chronologically. What I discovered is that emotional trophies depend on where we are and what we need to learn. I can't give you a list that will speak to you, only some examples of what other people have found to be worthy in their own lives. You must ask the question: What should I be celebrating?

Of course, you are a work in progress, and you haven't reached perfection. In fact, don't let the quest for perfection hold you back from recognizing your accomplishments. Don't let perfection be the enemy of the good. It's not about being perfect; it's about being better than you were. If you have learned to hush your Control Troll or to turn up the volume on your Gratitude Meter, then you're making progress. Or perhaps you're gaining skill in mitigating some of the Dirty Dozen such as "catastrophizing" or "negativity." Or perhaps you are able to recognize your triggers. So if you can honestly say that your awareness is greater today than it was before, then you are on your way to being hijacked less often. And that is cause for celebration.

How should you celebrate? However you like. The only guidelines I would suggest are that you are clear on what specifically you have accomplished and to celebrate as soon as possible. This will lead to greater reinforcement. Remember, there's a purpose to celebration, and that is to rewire your limbic brain (and to eat cake). In fact, during reflection, I'd suggest jotting down your lessons learned on festive looking paper, such as paper with pictures of balloons and cake and party hats. The idea here is that even when I make note of my lessons, it triggers a reinforcing thought in my brain. Another important thought, so that reinforcement takes hold, is to be sure that you are reinforcing improvements or advancements more frequently than you are chiding yourself for disappointing performance. If you are not, you are likely killing potential progress toward your emotional intelligence because your limbic system is registering negatives and failure. Your reflection time could be presenting you with information that further denigrates your efforts. Yes, you are going to make mistakes, but if you pay attention, you're also making progress. In fact, I encourage you to use the five-times rule. Think about things you have to celebrate five times more frequently than you think about setbacks in your performance.

We're all works in progress, and sometimes, it's just best to take a look at that work and admire it. And celebrate!

CHAPTER 14

STEP 7: REPEAT

It doesn't happen all at once. You become.
It takes a long time.—Margery Williams,
—The Velveteen Rabbit

Affirm the direction, then let go and follow the path. Life is a great teacher. It will provide the lessons if we are open to the learning. Emotional intelligence requires constant learning. The focus of that learning is to help us live our intentions. The more you imagine living your intentions, the more you will live them. Don't focus on being perfect. Quickly let go of that notion. Instead, focus on the path and enjoy the journey. If you have great desire to live your intentions, you will. If you have great desire to be perfect, you'll be disappointed. Disappointment will lead to negative reinforcement and thoughts that you are a failure, and soon you'll be living up to your failure expectation because you are reinforcing it. In the case of emotional intelligence, the journey is what matters most, because it is the journey that will produce the end result. If you focus on never being hijacked, you will fail. That's an impossible goal. You will be hijacked. You will continue to have emotional responses to things and have interactions that take you away from your intentions. I promise. It will continue to happen. The focus should be on taking the steps we've outlined here. If you do, you will have fewer hijackings and you will be more closely aligned and living your intentions. Michael Anthony, author of *The Mental Keys to*

Improve Your Golf, writes, "The vast majority of individuals has spent their entire lifetime chasing the outcome. However, you can train your mind to ignore the outcome and stay in the present by focusing on mastering the process. This is a major cultural change for anyone brought up in the Western civilization's belief system of materialism and winning. Ignoring the outcome is a huge undertaking, but it can be accomplished."[1]

All the steps we've focused on in this section make up the path. Have faith, desire, then relax. This step is about helping you recognize that the quest for emotional intelligence is a way of life, not a destination. You're never going to arrive. And that's a good thing. Remember what we said earlier: Each new life experience adds to our capacity for greater emotional intelligence. If we've arrived, that insinuates that we are having no more life experiences. Instead, our life experiences will teach us new triggers or combinations of triggers that we must master. New persons and relationships will enter our life, and each day we'll have a new opportunity to begin again. To repeat.

I continually think that now that I'm in my fifties I've gained some wisdom. Yet, I am anticipating that when I am in my eighties, I will probably think that I knew very little in my fifties. Why? Because I hope I continue to learn. Repeat is about renewing the sense of awe that life has to bring every day. If we view everything as "been there, done that," then what's left? The way I prefer to think of it is this: I've been there and done that, now I wonder what it would be like to be there and do it again with a fresh eye and a new mindset and a new set of life experiences that are continually changing the essence of who I am. Granted, there are certainly some experiences that I do not want to repeat, but I look at this as an attitude toward life rather than actually going back to repeat.

Most people recognize that new life experiences have added to their insights. I love watching new parents as they hold their infants and believe that surely this birth marks the first time anyone has ever done anything so miraculous. In the case of giving birth, it's

---

[1]Anthony, Michael. *The Mental Keys to Improve Your Golf.* Bolinas, CA: Anthony Press 2001.

that wonder and sense of awe in this new experience that changes the essence of who we are. Equally changing are life experiences such as tragic illness or death. But also changing are those subtle experiences. The best way to think of those subtle experiences is that they can accumulate and sneak up as wisdom. It's the difference between immersing yourself into a tub filled with water versus sitting in the bathtub as it fills one drop at a time. Each experience, as each drop of water, may seem small and insignificant, but when combined, can be equivalent to a lifetime of wisdom or a wonderful warm bath. All of these experiences can change you if you repeat and allow those experiences to accumulate into wisdom. But you have to be ready. The way to be ready is to always think about repeating the journey.

Life becomes more interesting when you have new experiences. But it can be equally interesting when you do some of the same life events year after year with a new eye. For example, holiday gatherings can be quite predictable. The same food, the same tablecloth, the same characters seated around the table. It's easy to fall into the same patterns of emotional reactions. Or you can repeat the event, but bring a different you to the experience. The same holds true in the workplace. You may have found that every Monday morning staff meeting is predictable. Everyone acts in the same patterns, says essentially the same things, and the outcomes are equally unsurprising. Everything is predictable including you, unless, of course, you focus on the process of emotional intelligence and choose to show up each Monday like a new person.

Repeat sets the stage for you to meet each encounter with a new mindset. It sets you up to become competent. But you can't become competent without knowing how. Knowing how requires practice and discipline until it becomes automatic. Thus far, we've devoted a great deal of time to suggesting how to become more emotionally intelligent, but becoming emotionally intelligent is about practicing those steps repeatedly. So jump back into the process and continue repeating.

PART 3 FIVE AREAS OF EMOTIONAL INTELLIGENCE AT WORK

CHAPTER 15

SELF-AWARENESS AND SELF-CONTROL AT WORK

Real knowledge is to know the extent of one's ignorance.—Confucius

SELF-AWARENESS

As a consultant for the past 23 years, I've found myself in many different organizations working with people to improve their effectiveness. I often have the privilege of working with many different individuals within the same company. Therefore, I am often privy to the thoughts of individuals who may be looking at and experiencing different sides of the same situation. Often, I am struck by the difference in the interpretation of the exact same situation. The contrast in their points of view often makes me wonder if they are talking about the same situations or the same organization. Sometimes my experience with these individuals leads me to conclude that in some cases self-awareness is painfully lacking. The following three examples are experiences that I witnessed first hand. Please consider them as examples of how lacking self-awareness can render us blind in various work situations.

Examples

EXAMPLE 1

Meeting Purpose: To discuss progress on a new assignment
Company: OSP Controls
Interview 1: The Employee

Q. How's it going with your manager?
A. Not good. My manager is ignoring my needs. I'm concerned that I won't be able to succeed if I can't get some answers.
Q. Have you asked for direction?
A. Are you kidding? Of course. When I go in and ask for some direction, she talks about things that are completely unrelated to my assignment. I'm assigned to work the West Coast. She keeps telling me how concerned she is about the performance of our company in Latin America. I ask her if she is telling me this because there are lessons there that I should be taking into consideration for my job here on the West Coast, and she says no, they are completely different markets.
Q. So, then what do you do?
A. I try to be more specific. For example, I went in yesterday and asked her to review the sales objectives that I set.
Q. And?
A. She ignored my request and said that she needed to go to a meeting. I asked when we could get together, and she said that she didn't think it would be necessary. She seemed irritated and angry that I even asked the question. I felt like I was bothering her.

Interview 2: The Manager

Q. How's it going with your new salesperson on the West Coast?
A. Great. I've been spending lots of time with him getting him up to speed.

Q. Does he understand what his objectives are?
A. Sure. I've given him lots of direction.
Q. Do you think he thinks he's had enough direction?
A. Yes. He is comfortable with his new assignment.
Q. Have you asked him?
A. No, not specifically, but we talk often, I'm sure if there were a problem he would bring it up. Besides, he knows I am easy to approach.

Example 2

Lunch Conversation Between Two Friends

Q. How's it going?
A. Awful
Q. Why?
A. I just got passed over again for a job posting. This system is rigged. You can't get ahead here. It's impossible. They tell you that they believe in advancing from within, but I don't believe it.
Q. Why do you think you got passed over?
A. Who knows? Probably because they have someone already picked for the job—one of their pets. They said it was because of my computer skills, but my computer skills are as good as the next guy.

Facts: The person was passed over for a job because he doesn't currently have the necessary computer skills to do the job. The job requires mastery over Excel spreadsheets and the ability to create complex spreadsheets. This person has never created a spreadsheet. He said he would if he had to. The person who was awarded the job has created many complex spreadsheets and, in fact, was able to discuss in detail how he would create a spreadsheet for an application that is currently needed. He also brought samples of some of the spreadsheets he has created.

Each of these examples presents a picture of some distorted self-awareness. In each case, two very different views emerged of the same situation. How could this be? Who's right? Who's wrong? It isn't a matter of who is right and who is wrong. None of these people were maliciously trying to distort reality. The fact is, they saw things completely differently. However, it is how we see things that will predict how we react to or behave in situations, and if we are not seeing things clearly, then our reactions or behaviors may not produce the result we want.

In Example 1, the boss wanted to be present for her new employee. She wanted him to be comfortable and succeed in his job. In Example 2, the person wanted to be promoted. He wanted to be successful. But for a variety of reasons, these people's behaviors did not produce the results they wanted. And in fact, they weren't even aware that their behaviors were not producing the results they intended. This blindness can dramatically affect our careers and our relationships at work. It's so unfortunate, because too often misunderstanding can be attributed to this lack of self-awareness. In fact, if any of the examples above continued, what kinds of long-term perceptions could develop? Possibly the West Coast salesperson would think his boss wanted to see him fail, which is exactly the opposite of her intention. Perhaps the employee seeking a promotion would begin to spread rumors that the company plays favorites and that their internal promotion policy was a hoax. None of these perceptions would be in line with the intentions of the other party, but, unfortunately, they may appear to be forged in stone.

In my interviews with hundreds of leaders in all types of industries, most of these leaders see themselves as believing in the "Good Boss" list generated in Chapter 1 and acting in a way that, most of the time, reflects it. Sure, they acknowledge that they may slip occasionally and exhibit a bad boss trait now and then, but they tell me that those instances are not the norm and they may have reason or provocation to slip. Similarly, most employees tell me that they indeed believe they exhibit the characteristics on a similar "Good Coworker" list and that perhaps occasionally they may slip and display a characteristic on the other side of the chart, perhaps when provoked by a negative coworker or unruly boss. Wouldn't all the workplace statistics on job satisfaction, morale, and the like be more positive if people exhibited these traits far more frequently than not? Could it be that we believe that we are acting and behaving in a certain way when in reality we are not? Or perhaps people are not seeing us for who we truly are and what we truly intend? Or both?

Surely at times both are true. That's why emotional intelligence is so powerful. It can help you live your intentions in the workplace by acting in a way that is consistent with what you intend, AND it can help you understand and see others more clearly. All of the steps addressed in Part 2 of this book are devoted to increasing your self-awareness. Self-awareness demands that we intimately and accurately know who we are. This includes our strengths, weaknesses, values, and beliefs. If, for example, the manager in Example 1 was aware that she had a tendency to be vague in her directions or that she sometimes didn't listen as well as she should, then perhaps she would have tuned in to her West Coast salesperson more and been able to avert the situation described above. Self-awareness also demands understanding and predicting one's emotional reactions to situations. Our friend in Example 2 may have been served much better if he had realized that he had a tendency to blame instead of look at his own behavior or skills in a situation. Maybe he would have been able to ask specifically how he could prepare for the next promotion.

A person with full self-awareness is generally not surprised by his/her emotional reactions. Also, self-awareness enables people to determine emotional triggers that will cause reactions. In the workplace, I hear people with high self-awareness use the expression, "I know that I have to be careful when . . . (in a particular situation), because I can say things that I will regret." As you know by now, the purpose of your self-coach is to raise your awareness of these triggers. One who is emotionally competent at self-awareness is also fully aware of one's values and core beliefs and knows the effect of compromising these core components. Understanding emotions is central to more effectively relating to people and creating a positive emotional climate with the people with whom you interact at work. People see you as having an understanding of how your emotions affect you.

Conversely, if you have low self-awareness, people may see you as emotionally out of touch or insensitive. You may not have a clear understanding of what you are feeling and, therefore, you may be unaware of how your emotions may be affecting others. You may not have a strong understanding of your strengths and weaknesses that could produce blind spots in your development. You are missing an opportunity to use your feelings for information that may be useful in advancing your goals and objectives. As you may be unaware of your emotions and/or your strengths and weaknesses, you may be unable to develop to your fullest potential without this useful information. One striking example that I recall was Jeremy, a manager who was prone to getting angry. Everyone who reported to Jeremy knew the signs. He would begin to fidget in his chair. He would get red in the face. He would clench his teeth. He would say that people aren't focusing on the important issues. His staff was able to list without fail all the signals that indicated that he was going to blow. But Jeremy had no idea that he was on the verge of an angry outburst. One morning, Jeremy was in a meeting with an outside audit team. The audit team was charged with two things: (1) reviewing data about reorganization and (2) assessing staff for the possibility of reduction. The audit team questioned some of the data that Jeremy was presenting. His staff watched as he began to fidget, his face got red, he clenched his teeth, and he said that the audit team wasn't focusing on the important issues. Then, he lost it. No one in the room who knew Jeremy was surprised, except Jeremy. He said he had no idea that he was getting angry and that he was about to lose his cool. Unfortunately, he not only lost his cool, he lost his job. How could it be that everyone saw the warning signs of his anger except him? In fact, this lack of self-awareness about our emotions is commonplace. We have taught people that emotions do not have a place in the workplace. Therefore, some people ignore their emotions to the point that they are unaware of their existence. However, emotions have a sneaky way of "leaking out" if we don't recognize their existence. These same people who ignore their emotions may be completely inept at knowing or understanding what to do with their emotional reactions. They simply don't have the skill of recognition and mastery over emotional reaction. Unfortunately, when we do not acknowledge that our emotions are present at work, our emotional reactions can be extreme, as in Jeremy's case. This lack of awareness can be damaging to careers.

In another example, David, a bright engineer, found that many of his peers had been promoted, and he had repeatedly been left behind. He was in an organizational culture that strongly rewarded those who spoke up and were able to articulate their ideas in front of others. He knew this, but even though he had many wonderful ideas, he was unable to speak up. He kept making excuses. He would say that the timing wasn't right, that someone else had started to talk, that he hesitated because he thought someone had already proposed a particular idea, or that he just wasn't feeling well that day. His manager coached him at length about this issue and kept encouraging him to voice his ideas. It took more than a year for this engineer to realize that the reason he didn't speak up was that he was concerned with what others might think. Once he became aware of his feelings, he was able to conquer this irrational thought. This company's culture truly did value speaking up. Not until he was able to recognize his feelings was he able to see how they were holding him back.

Self-awareness is one of the most difficult areas of emotional intelligence to tackle and, of course, most of this book has been devoted to this topic. However, if you think you are self-aware and are interested in checking your assumption, you can use a 360-degree assessment to give you some added insights. A 360-degree assessment allows you to rate yourself on a variety of items and then asks others to rate you on these same items. The beauty of a 360-degree assessment is that it allows you to check your accuracy by seeing yourself through the eyes of others. For example, if you think you are a good listener, a 360-degree assessment would ask you to rate yourself, and then would ask others to rate your listening skills. "Others" could include your coworkers and peers, your boss, your subordinates, or others who know you and interact with you in the workplace. This data, then, would serve as a way to help you understand what others see. The reason for obtaining 360-degree feedback is, of course, to uncover blind spots. Without this data, you may be missing important development opportunities. For example, if you think you're a terrific listener, then you wouldn't spend time trying to improve that skill. Now, on the other hand, if you thought you were a terrific listener and data from numerous other people said

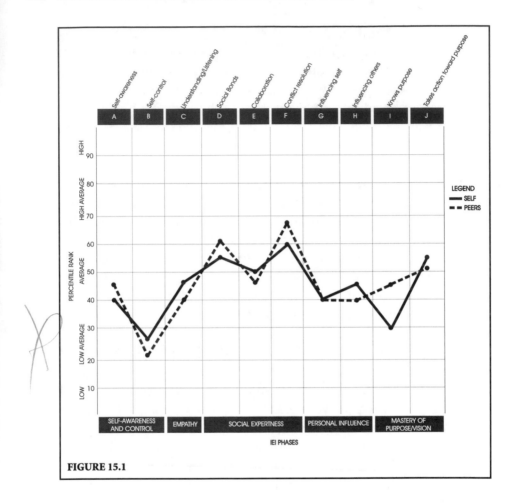

FIGURE 15.1

that you were not, then you may wish to spend some time developing in this area. Studies have linked 360-degree feedback and increase in managerial effectiveness because of an increase in self-awareness. One such study in the *Journal of European Industrial Training* reports considerable research to suggest that the enhancement of self-awareness leads to more effective managers.[1]

---

[1]McCarthy, Alma M., and Garavan, Thomas N., "Developing Self-Awareness in the Managerial Career Development Process: The Value of 360-Degree Feedback and the MBTI." *Journal of European Industrial Training* 23 (1999): 437.

Here are some examples of actual 360 data on emotional intelligence as measured by the Index for Emotional Intelligence. You can see from these charts that some people's awareness is accurate when compared to the views of others. In other cases, that is not the case. In Figure 15.1, for example, the person has an accurate view of his emotional intelligence. Conversely, in Figure 15.2 this person's chart indicates that he has a view of himself that is quite different from the view that others have.

Another pattern that we sometimes see in 360-degree assessments is that people rate themselves much lower than others see them. These people may have opportunities to leverage their strengths if

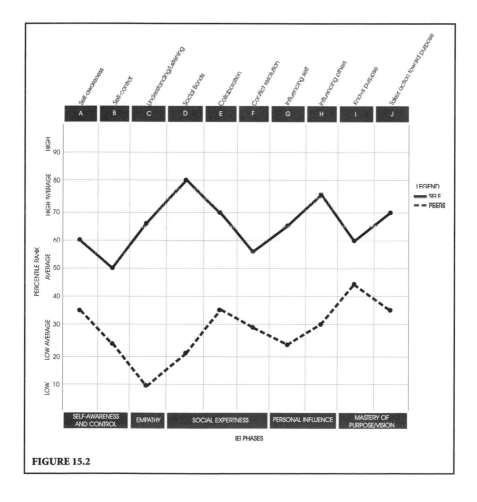

FIGURE 15.2

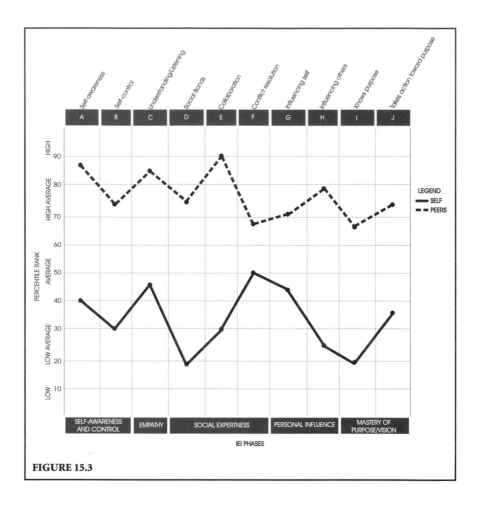

FIGURE 15.3

they realize that indeed they are competent in these areas (see Figure 15.3).

The more accurate our self-awareness, the better we can become in terms of emotional intelligence. Without this accuracy, we can continue to make the same mistakes. I compare it to being married for 30 years and coming home one day to find that your spouse has left you. When you ask why, she says it was because you left the cap off the toothpaste for the last 30 years and she couldn't tolerate that behavior anymore. If you had known, you may have chosen to put the cap back on, but at least you would not have been blind to the problems caused by your behavior. Awareness gives us choices.

We don't have to change, but awareness at least gives us the option to do so.

Some Suggestions for Improving EQ in the Area of Self-Awareness

- Read and practice living Part 2 of this book.

- Solicit feedback from your manager, employees, and peers about your strengths and weaknesses.

- Use 360-degree ratings and other performance feedback as an opportunity to learn more about how others view you.

- Spend time in personal reflection about your strengths and weaknesses.

- Keep a "lessons log" to journal the lessons that you have learned each day.

- Review your "lessons log" regularly to look for patterns. If you see that certain lessons are in your log on a regular basis, you may want to work harder to connect these lessons to your future actions.

- Before taking an action, review it in context with your "lessons log" and ask yourself if you could modify the action to be more effective.

- Look for supporting evidence that reinforces the lessons you've learned. Collect articles, quotes, books, or other sources of information that confirm your lessons.

- Keep visible reminders of your strengths and weaknesses so that you can check in and adjust your behavior before taking important actions.

- Ask to be mentored or coached in areas that you see as your weaknesses.

- In a problem situation, brainstorm actions that you could take to capitalize on your strengths.

- In a problem situation, brainstorm actions you could take to minimize your weaknesses.

- Observe your reaction to an unwanted change. What thoughts and feelings are you aware of regarding your reaction to change?

- What seems to help you accept an unwanted change?

- What seems to cause you to resist an unwanted change?

- List changes you have made that resulted in a better situation eventually, but that were difficult at first. How did you feel during and after the change?

- Take classes or other learning opportunities that will enhance your areas of awareness.

- Get involved in a broad range of teams, task forces, and other assignments that broaden your awareness.

- Do something unusual each week. Stretch yourself. You can learn new dimensions of yourself by deliberately trying new things.

- Practice naming your emotions.

- Ask yourself repeatedly, "What am I feeling?"

- Watch a movie and discuss your emotions about the movie with a trusted friend.

- Write down as many words as you can to describe your emotions. Sometimes we lump all of our emotions into one category when other words may better describe the true feeling. For example, the word "angry" is often used but may be more accurately described as "insulted," "hurt," "enraged," "furious," "put down," "belittled," "jealous," or "frustrated."

- When you have a negative encounter with someone, stop and reflect on what you are feeling and why you may be feeling this way.

- When you have a positive encounter with someone, stop and reflect on what you are feeling and why you may be feeling this way.

- When you find yourself in a particularly good mood, ask yourself how you feel and why you think you feel that way.

- When you find yourself in the dumps, ask yourself how you feel and why you think you feel that way.

- List circumstances in which you think you have benefited by changing the way in which you have expressed your negative emotions.

- List circumstances in which you think you have experienced doubt in the workplace.

- List circumstances in which you think you have experienced fear in the workplace.

- Pay attention to how you feel during a conflict situation. What effect are your feelings having on your actions? Your words? Your tone of voice and body language?

- Listen to your tone of voice when you are happy. How does it differ from times when you are stressed? Angry? Tired?

- Talk about your feelings with someone who is close to you.

- In the middle of a task or meeting, take a mental "time out" to assess your feelings. Try to determine how your feelings might be affecting your present task.

Exercises for Improving Self-Awareness

EQ EXERCISE #1: GIFTS AND WEAKNESSES

Make a list of your natural gifts.

Ask a group of others (manager, peers, subordinates) who know you well to do the same.

Any similarities?

Any surprises?

Make a list of things you perceive as areas for improvement.

Ask a group of others (manager, peers, subordinates) who know you well to do the same.

Any similarities?

Any surprises?

EQ EXERCISE #2: CHAMPION OR CHUMP

Take a piece of paper and divide it into two columns labeled champion and chump. As you think about your past work experiences, when did you feel like you acted like a champion and when did you feel that you acted like a chump? Think about a specific action you took, or specific words you spoke. When did you think you lived your values and intentions and when did you not? Some champion examples might be: I asked Sam how I could help him the other day when I noticed he was behind. I told Arnold how much I appreciated his department assisting in our project. I asked for Bob's opinion at the last meeting.

Some chump examples might be: I told Carl that I agreed with his position in the hall right before the meeting, but didn't speak up in the meeting when the issue came up; I blamed Darren for causing my department to be late on the reports because he didn't have his data in on time, even though we would have been late anyway; I told a customer that we could have a shipment out even though I knew it wouldn't happen.

SELF-CONTROL

I am,
indeed,
a king, because I know how
to rule myself.
—Pietro Aretino

When interviewing people, I often ask them to write a letter to their boss. Here are a few that capture the issues around self-control.

Letters to the Boss

LETTER #1

Dear Boss:

Here we go again. This is the fourth year that you have asked us to complete a 360 assessment on you. Do you know that we find this very amusing at the lunch table? Why? Because you keep asking us for our feedback, but you never change. This is obviously just a silly exercise for you. How about this year we just use the results from last year? In case you forgot, here's a recap of your results:

    a. You don't listen.

    b. You criticize people in public.

    c. When in meetings, you call on the same people for their opinions and ignore the rest of us.

    That's it, short and sweet. Save us all the bother this year.

Sincerely,
Your staff

LETTER #2

Dear Sarah:

As manager of our organization, you complain that people don't tell you what's going on. You constantly say that you don't want to be surprised. Yet, I just witnessed another incident where you chewed up and spit out the messenger once again. People are not going to tell you the truth when you hand them their head on a platter when they do speak the truth. I've noticed that more and more people are beginning to outright lie to you. You can't have it both ways. If you want people to be open with you, then stop going off on a tirade when you hear unpleasant news. Grow up and act your age.

Sincerely,
Elizabeth

LETTER #3

Dear Gary:

I'm confused. Before the staff meeting this morning, I spoke to you about the Halice account. I told you how the policy was getting in the way of our ability to provide the best service, and you agreed. Not only did you agree, you even gave an example of another account where the policy had the same effect. Yet, when the issue came up for discussion you said nothing. You just sat there in silence. When I suggested that there were other accounts that were being affected, again you were silent. Why? Was it because you didn't want to disagree with Humphrey? Or are you suffering from amnesia? Or what?

Disappointed,
Fred

Self-control requires that we master our emotions. This mastery enables us to channel both positive and negative emotions in a productive way and enables us to learn and gain from our emotions rather than be burdened by them. With self-control, we can both anticipate and use our emotional reactions to maximize our effectiveness. Angry outbursts are most often associated with a person who lacks self control, but emotional self-control is much broader than controlling our anger. Self-control also means finding productive ways to address self-doubt and other feelings, such as fear, that can be destructive to achieving our life's goals and objectives. Self-control requires us to know how to express emotions appropriately —both positive emotions and negative emotions.

Self-control takes our self-awareness to the next step. Self-awareness allows us to understand our limitations; self-control allows us to address them. In the first letter, the manager had heard about his limitations before. Understanding your limitations is a gift, but without taking any action, that gift just collects dust in the closet of your mind. With self-control, you can create the emotional climate that you and others will operate in rather than have knee-jerk reactions to situations. If truth is indeed the desired outcome, the second letter illustrates the damaging effect of knee-jerk reactions in the workplace. Anger expressed inappropriately can mute the truth. Instead, self-control can help you create an emotional climate that is consistent and honest. Self-doubt and fear, if not managed, can also create a climate that is inconsistent and dishonest. In the third letter, we can see a glimpse of how doubt or fear can hold us back. In this case, as doubt and fear ruled over Gary's behavior, he created a climate whereby his peers didn't trust him to speak the truth. He gave his peers permission to dismiss and ignore him as a unreliable player. These examples of emotional hijacking reflect the drama that we experience every day in the world of work. Hijacking, whether by way of anger, fear, doubt, or other emotions can cause inconsistency and disharmony. If you allow yourself to be hijacked regularly, you are missing important opportunities to build the emotional climate in your workplace that will help you get work done and advance your goals and your career. Part 2 is devoted to reducing the risk of hijacking.

Don't forget, as we discussed in Part 2, the volume control button on our emotions goes both ways—up and down. Positive self-control requires that we know when to express emotions that will enhance goals. Emotions however, must be expressed authentically. As an example, consider Ingram, the front-line supervisor in a manufacturing plant. Ingram was by nature very reserved and quiet. Ingram's company instituted a new measurement program, whereby each department was expected to post production measures and celebrate progress each week. The manner in which the celebration took place was left to the discretion of the supervisor. Some of Ingram's counterparts, who were naturally expressive, dressed up in costumes and arranged loud parties and celebrations each Friday near the end of shift to mark their team's achievements. Ingram was concerned. He knew himself well enough to know that if he tried to mimic his peers, his employees would surely think him inauthentic. Yet, Ingram was genuinely proud of his team's accomplishments. So, to let his team know, each week he wrote a personal thank-you note to employees who contributed to the production goal and specifically thanked them for their dedication. He asked the team to decide each week how they would like to celebrate. There were no goofy costumes from Ingram, just handwritten thank-you notes. Ingram's quiet enthusiasm, sincerely expressed, was effective. Turning up the volume on positive emotions such as pride or gratitude doesn't mean being something that you're not. Self-control simply means finding ways to express emotions appropriately. By appropriately, I mean appropriate to you and to the outcome that you intend.

Self-control is about selecting the words, appropriate time, and demeanor that will give you the results you seek. It is the means to a planned and thoughtful emotional climate. If you want to have a discussion with your teenager, you can't begin with your finger waving in the air and the words "I told you so." "When I was your age," will also lead you to a dead end. There will likely be no discussion. "When I was doing your job" will likely have the similar effect of killing any type of discussion in the workplace. These phrases do not invite discussion, they imply lecture. What outcome do you desire—a lecture or a discussion? It's not about what you want to blurt, it's about how you can craft your words to gain the desired outcome. That's not manipulation; that's effective living.

I often think about emotional climate in terms of a music metaphor. What type of music do you intend to play in the background? That music gives clues to the emotional climate that you create. Do you know people who are always playing the blues with whining steel guitars or droning violins? Do you know others who are playing "Flight of the Bumblebee?" How about others who always seem to be dancing to polka music? Still others who sound like background music to a good war flick or thriller? Self-control allows us to decide the emotional tone rather than have a station stuck that we can't seem to change.

Crafting the emotional climate takes skill and practice. Your self-coach can be instrumental in helping you by always asking what you intend and then by strategizing to determine the actions and words that will deliver the results, just as discussed in Part 2. One important concept here is that you are not powerless over your actions and words. If you choose, you can change.

Some Suggestions for Improving EQ in the Area of Self-Control

- Read and practice living Part 2 of this book.

- Ask yourself, "If I express my emotion here without thoughtful purpose, what is the risk?" Also ask yourself, "If I express my emotion here with thoughtful purpose, what is the benefit?"

- If you are reserved, practice expressing a positive emotion, such as enthusiasm or support, in a situation in which you would normally hold back. If you are usually outgoing, practice holding back a negative statement until you have taken time to get over the immediate reaction.

- The next time you are in a meeting, try on a new behavior related to emotional control. If you normally hold back expression, express yourself. If you normally just come out with it, hold yourself back.

- Ask a trusted friend to give you feedback regarding your emotional control. Ask him or her to observe and give you this feedback based on the way you conduct yourself in meetings, at lunch, or at other events.

- Practice positive expression of emotions. If you are happy or grateful, let others know.

- Try using the phase "I feel . . ." as opposed to "I think. . . ."

- Practice breathing techniques when you feel stress.

- Mentally rehearse staying calm in a crisis.

- Ask yourself, "Is this situation truly that bad?"

- Ask yourself, "How is my thinking distorted right now?"

- Recall a time when you felt you lost control of your emotional reaction. How did it affect you? How did it affect others?

- How would others describe you? As one who displays his or her emotions? Or as one who does not display his or her emotions?

- List ten situations in which you could have benefited by expressing positive emotions to others?

- Given your personality, think about ways in which you could authentically express positive emotions.

- Recall a time when someone expressed emotion to you in the workplace and it was a positive experience. Write down how you felt.

- Recall a time when someone expressed emotion to you in the workplace and it was a negative experience. Write down how you felt.

Exercises for Improving Self-Control

EQ EXERCISE #3: NEXT TIME

Think about the last time you experienced the following emotions at work: anger, joy, fear, self-doubt, pride, and overwhelmed. List what you actually did at work when confronted with these emotions. In Column 3, list how you might have improved your action.

EQ EXERCISE #4: MUSIC

Self-control creates the emotional climate in which we operate. Imagine emotional climate as a song or type of music that comes from us. What kind of music or songs do you create? What kind of music or songs do you wish to create? For example, do you know some people who sound like the blues because every time you are around them, they are whining? How about others who seem like they are constantly playing "Flight of the Bumblebee?" Think about the type of music you actually create. List the type of music you would like to create.

CHAPTER 16

EMPATHY AT WORK

He who knows only his own side of the case,
knows little of that.—John Stuart Mill

A common question on performance and development reviews asks managers to suggest areas for improvement. Some common answers are listed below.

Q. What could this person do to be more effective?

A. Ralph is a good doctor. He has excellent clinical skills. However, Ralph could be more effective if he would listen to his patients more. In the Jones case, Ralph would have gained information for diagnostic purpose had he listened and asked questions when Jones complained about pain in the tissue surrounding the area of the procedure.

A. Karen has excellent analytical skills. Her problem-solving ability on mechanical performance is outstanding. However, Karen could be more effective if she would talk to the operators and listen to concerns they may have when she is designing equipment modifications. The latest equipment modification on the spoiler proved to be ineffective because they had told her that her proposal would not be suitable.

A. Lu has excellent technical skills as a financial analyst. However, Lu must learn to understand the concerns of the floor traders. Also, when Lu tries to explain a new offering to the traders, he explains it in terms that are irrelevant to their point of view.

A. Madison's job is at risk if she doesn't begin to empathize with the customer. Madison needs to understand that the customer's concern is important. Madison needs to put herself in the customer's shoes before addressing a customer complaint. She must also gain information to understand the customer's problem. It is unacceptable for Madison to tell a customer who is experiencing a disruption of service, "If you'd pay your bill this wouldn't happen." As we've seen in the Dreit account, the customer had paid the bills, but we failed to record them.

Lack of empathy is costing lost revenue, lost opportunities, and even lost lives in the workplaces of America. Customers become angry, and they take their business elsewhere. They tell other prospective customers not to do business with you. In fact, consumers take the time to detail customer service complaints on widely read Internet sites with very popular Google rankings. These consumers are so fired up that they tell thousands if not millions of others about their bad experiences.[1] The words, "lack of empathy" are directly contained in the text of many of these "reverse testimonials."[2] Consider the following evidence presented in a study done by TARP (Technical Assistance Research Programs) presented in an article by John Goodman in *Competitive Advantage,* "On average, twice as many people are told about a bad experience than they are about a good experience."[3] According to another survey conducted by the A.C. Nielsen Co. and quoted in the *Journal of Marketing,* "Only 2% of unhappy customers complain, while 34% of all dissatisfied cus-

---

[1] Lincoln, Greg. Earthlink Debacle, http://www.mazin.net/adventures/adventures.php?week disp+15.

[2] Geer, David. Zenith Television, http://www.2xtreme.net/~dlgeer/Zenith.htm.

[3] Goodman, John. "Basic Facts on Customer Complaint Behavior and the Impact of Service on the Bottom Line" *Competitive Advantage,* June 1991.

Note: The research mentioned in this article was carried out by TARP (Technical Assistance Research Programs) and was originally delivered for a government study.

tomers switch brands."[4] And that's only the beginning. Salespeople who lack empathy lag behind their counterparts who demonstrate a higher level of competence in this area of emotional intelligence.[5]

In hospital emergency rooms, doctors who are more empathic and take time to listen to their patients are less likely to be sued for malpractice than doctors who do not demonstrate signs of empathy, regardless of the medical care given.[6] In fact, empathy is now being required as a competency in medical residencies throughout the country. In the most serious cases of malpractice involving death, 55 percent of patients' families stated that the patients had told the doctor of symptoms and the doctor had dismissed their complaints.

Lack of empathy is also the source of a variety of morale problems within organizations. Leaders who do not understand the perspective of those who work for them have higher incidences of turnover. Morale also suffers.[7] James Waldroop and Timothy Butler report in *Harvard Business Review on Finding and Keeping the Best Employees* that "An astonishing number of people have difficulty getting outside their own frame of reference and seeing through another person's. In other words, they lack empathy. In a sense, they never moved beyond the narcissism that is normal in childhood; they never got the instruction from parents and others that helps most people learn to understand the world from other people's perspectives. Having a well-developed sense of empathy is essential if one is to deal successfully with one's peers, subordinates, managers, customers, and competitors."[8] In another article in the *Harvard Business Review* by Tony Simons entitled "The High Cost of Lost Trust," Simons

---

[4]Kendall, C.L., and Russ, Frederick A. "Warranty and Complaint Policies, An Opportunity for Marketing Management," *Journal of Marketing* (April 1975): 37.
Note: The information in this article refers to a survey conducted by the A.C. Nielsen Co.
[5]Schwartz, Tony. "Coping: How Do You Feel?" *Secured Lender* 56 (November/December 2000): 108.
[6]Henry, Gregory L. "Continuing Medical Education for Emergency Physicians" *Medical Practice Risk Assessment Track,* Emergency Physicians Annual Conference 2000: audiocassette.
[7]Gerstner, C.R., and Day, D.V. Meta-Analytic Review of Leader-Member Exchange Theory: Correlates and Construct Issues, *Journal of Applied Psychology* 82 (1997): 827–844.
[8]Waldroop, James, and Butler, Timothy. *Harvard Business Review on Finding and Keeping the Best People—Managing Away Bad Habits. Harvard Business Review,* Boston: Harvard Business School Publishing, 2001.

correlated the level of employees' trust of the manager as the most significant factor that related to high customer satisfaction.[9] In my own research in *In Search of Honor, Lessons from Workers on How to Build Trust,* I found that empathy was one of the most significant factors that built high trust between leaders and employees.[10]

Coworkers who lack empathy cause unnecessary conflicts that cost millions in productivity. As an example, consider the case of Miller Supply, a small, profitable company providing cleaning supplies to commercial accounts. Miller had eight salespersons who spent most of their time on the road and three internal support representatives whose job was to process the orders brought in by the outside sales force. Things were going along smoothly until the day when Ruthann walked through the door to join the internal team. Ruthann bickered with the other internal staff. She complained that they were dumping on her all the jobs no one wanted. She complained that others took longer lunches than she did. She complained that the salespeople were not communicating with her. She also complained that the other internal staff were not giving her access to financial information that she needed to perform her job. And so it went. After several months, the two internal staff and three of the sales staff talked to the owner about Ruthann. The owner ignored their comments. He told them he didn't want to be involved in petty wars among staff members and suggested that they mature. Unfortunately things deteriorated. They deteriorated to the point that both internal staff resigned and the three salespersons also found other positions. But that's not the worst of it. Ruthann, now the dominant internal staff person, began to embezzle funds. Slowly at first, she would write checks to cover false expenses. At the height of the fraud, Ruthann was embezzling about $18,000 per month. The owner's lack of listening actually cost him his business. How the owner wished he had taken time to listen. Need we say more? Empathy is an essential component of success, regardless of your job

---

[9]Simons, Tony. "The High Cost of Lost Trust." *Harvard Business Review* 80 (September 2002): 18.

[10]Lynn, Adele B. *In Search of Honor, Lessons From Workers on How to Build Trust.* Pittsburgh: Bajon House Publishing, 1997.

or level within the organization. Empathy is understanding the perspective of others. Listening is a tool of empathy. Listening alone, however, is not empathy, because many people listen very well. But they listen with an ear toward disproving, discrediting, or somehow proving the other person's point of view incorrect or incomplete. Or they listen so that they know just the point they can make to sound important or knowledgeable in the conversation. Empathy occurs when listening turns to understanding—not necessarily agreeing—but full understanding of why people said what they said. When people listen with empathy, it is the single most powerful way of honoring another person. Listening leads to understanding, not only from an intellectual level, but also from an emotional level and is the essence of honoring others. These lines in the lyrics of the Disney classic *Pocahontas* beautifully describe empathy,

> "But if you walk the footsteps of a stranger
> You'll learn things you never knew you never knew."[11]

Knowing because I tell you is much different from knowing because you have empathy. Empathy calls for a completely different level of knowing. Empathy is the ability to understand how others perceive situations. This perception includes knowing how others feel about a particular set of events or circumstances. Empathy requires knowing the perspective of others and being able to see things from the value and belief system of the other person. It is the ability to fully immerse oneself in another's viewpoint, yet remain wholly apart.

The understanding associated with empathy is both cognitive and emotional. It takes into consideration the reasons and logic behind another's point of view, as well as his or her feelings. Empathy is essential to our interactions with employees, customers and most other members of the human race. The payoff is great. When you are adept at understanding the perspective of others, you create an

---

[11] © 1995 Wonderland Music Company, Inc. Colors of the World, Music by Alan Menken, Lyrics by Stephen Schwartz.

environment in which others feel respected and valued. People feel a sense of importance and honor in your presence. Empathy alone will not cause people to follow you, however, it is an essential foundation for leadership because empathy increases the likelihood that people feel respected. When people feel respected, they are more apt to listen and to reciprocate, are less resistant to change, and more open-minded.

Without empathy, people perceive that you are insensitive to them. Others may think you do not respect them or value their point of view. Pushback may occur. In a classic example, I watched a group of formerly industrious caseworkers become unproductive after a few months under the reign of a new supervisor. This supervisor's lack of empathy was evident daily. Some of his favorite expressions were, "This bunch of lunatics (referring to the caseworkers) are worse than our clients. If I had a dollar for every time you made a mistake, I'd be rich." He also sent subtle messages such as not looking them in the eye when he spoke to them, interrupting them in mid-sentence, and walking out when they were speaking. This group's performance went from 350 completed cases a month to 97. Although this supervisor's behavior went way beyond lacking empathy, it speaks loudly about the effect that insensitive leaders have on performance.

So what stands in the way of empathy? Many things, but certainly one of them is emotional hijacking. We are less likely to listen when we are feeling angry, rushed, overwhelmed, threatened, or another emotion that short-circuits the listening required for true empathy. One study looked at seminarians at Princeton Divinity School. Seminarians were divided into two groups. Both groups had just finished a lesson on the Good Samaritan. Individuals from each group were told that they had to make a presentation in a building across campus. Individuals from one group were told that they were running late for the meeting, and individuals from the other group were told that they had plenty of time. On the path to the meeting location, researchers planted a person who appeared to need help. As each of the divinity students passed, this person asked for assistance. Only 10 percent of the students who were told they were running late stopped to help the person in need. A full 90 percent literally stepped over the person. Feeling busy and hurried dramatically affected their behavior. Of those who were told they had plenty of time, 63 percent stopped to help.[12] Sound familiar? So, understanding our feelings, paying attention to the triggers, and using the other methods described in Part 2 are essential.

Another common obstacle to empathy lies in our assumptions and worldview/workview. Our assumptions are blinding. It is virtually impossible to see the other person's perspective if we do not have an open mind. For example, one of the assumptions we talked about is "my coworkers don't pull their fair share. I do all the work." If that is what you believe, then you will look for evidence to support your assumption. Empathy requires us to be devoid of assumptions, to listen with an open heart. So when a coworker approaches and asks for help, and if you are already convinced that coworkers don't carry their share and you do all the work, you're likely to respond without empathy. Or you will agree to do it, but silently resent the coworker. I'm not suggesting that empathy requires you to be used or stepped on. I'm saying that empathy requires you to experience each situation anew and not allow past assumptions and views to draw conclusions about the present without exploring the whole situation.

Experience, of course, helps shape our assumptions, but experience and assumptions can prove wrong if we project them onto the next situation. For example, in the returns department, you'll meet all kinds of customers. Some customers, unfortunately intend to take advantage of you and your company. They may berate or belittle you. Let's say you've had a string of negative customers this morning. Some were even outright fraudulent in their claims. In fact, one person said that she wanted to return something that she had purchased at the store and didn't have a receipt. You investigated the merchandise and learned that your company did not and never did sell the brand she was attempting to return. Another person entered your returns department with a forged receipt and was asking for

---

[12]John Darley, and Batson, Daniel. "From Jerusalem to Jericho: A Study of Situational and Dispositional Variables in Helping Behavior." *Journal of Personality and Social Psychology* 27 (1973): 100–119.

cash back on an item. Again, after investigating the situation, you learned that the person had lied. Then along comes Mary. Mary complained she had just purchased a computer ink cartridge and that the ink cartridge wasn't working. She said that she had thrown away the receipt because she had no intention of returning the item. Of course the package was open because she had tried to use it in her printer. It would be easy to assume that Mary, too, was lying, but that assumption would stop any type of empathy for Mary. In fact, I watched a customer service person tell Mary that she didn't believe her. I heard her say, "We have customers that bring back their empty cartridges and claim that they weren't working all the time so they can get their money back. Sorry, next please." Each situation is different, and when we let negative past experiences and assumptions affect our interactions, empathy erodes.

Empathy can be improved. Our life experiences can be crucial in supplying us data that will help us become more empathetic. Scientists at UCLA Neuropsychiatric Institute and Brain Research Institute have studied how mimicry of others can jump start empathy.[13] We've all experienced a sympathetic wince when someone we love is in pain. Our sympathetic wince can be prompted by our child falling from her bicycle or by seeing the needle used to inoculate her against disease. We also grin as loved ones tell us about their triumphs and joys. This wincing and grinning is empathy. Scientists are able to pinpoint the exact area in the brain that controls these reactions. Additionally, the Consortium for Research on Emotional Intelligence reports studies that validate that empathy can be increased. One study in particular trained medical students in empathy.[14] Students were observed before and after significant training that included medical interviews, case studies, and role plays of patients and patients' families and the impact of the interpersonal interface

---

[13] Page, Dan. "UCLA Imaging Study Reveals How Active Empathy Charges Emotions; Physical Mimicry of Others Jump-Starts Key Brain Activity." *UCLA News*, April 7, 2003.

[14] ——— "Interpersonal Effectiveness Training for Medical Students." The Consortium for Research on Emotional Intelligence in Organizations, www.eiconsortium.org/model_programs/interpersonal_effectiveness_training_medical.htm.

in the doctor/patient relationship. Those exposed to the training, as compared to a control group, demonstrated significant and lasting improvement in supportive, empathetic behaviors. So, our goal is to use our life experiences and the people we encounter as a laboratory where we can stimulate our brain center responsible for empathy. That can only happen if we consciously choose to consider their perspective. Your self-coach should be on the lookout each day for experiences that will add to your database.

Some Suggestions for Improving EQ in the Area of Empathy

- When someone is talking to you, ask yourself what emotion is underlying his or her words.

- Try to put yourself in the other person's shoes. Can you understand his/ her point of view even if you don't agree with it?

- Try to anticipate the emotional reaction of people in a team meeting or in another work situation.

- Watch people's nonverbal reactions to you. What do you think they are feeling?

- When someone says something you disagree with, active listen his or her statement. Do so in a nonjudgmental way. Notice the reaction that this precipitates.

- When someone says something you agree with, stay silent about your views and draw the other person out and ask them to tell you more.

- Watch a television without the volume. Record it for later review. Try to read the emotions that the characters are portraying. Watch the show again with the sound to determine how accurate you were in your assessment.

- When listening to someone, ask that person to clarify the feelings behind his / her statement, not just the facts.

- List ten people you think are extremely empathetic. Observe their interactions with others and list the qualities, both verbal and nonverbal, that you observe.

- List ten people who you do think are insensitive to others. Observe their interactions with others and list the characteristics, both verbal and nonverbal, that you observe.

- Ask someone who you think is very empathetic to coach or mentor you.

- Role-play and video tape situations in which you would like to discuss an issue or concern. Watch the tape with a coach and look for ways to improve your skills.

- Think about the people you work with. What do you think you could to do to improve your service to them?

- Ask others what you could do to assist them.

- Think about your department's encounters with customers and anticipate how you could improve the service level your customers are experiencing.

- Ask your internal customers what you could do to assist them.

- Come up with some suggestions to improve service to your internal customers and ask them if they think your suggestions would be useful.

- Study others in the organization who are trusted mentors or advisers. How do they interact with people? What "secret formula" do they seem to have that draws people toward them?

- Assess how you are similar to those most trusted mentors in your organization. How are you different?

- Shift your focus and think of others when a problem situation comes up. Rather than think about the effect of the problem on you, think about the problem from the point of view of others—customers, suppliers, peers, other employees, the boss.

- Survey peers, employees, superiors, and others and ask them how you could be of greater service to them.

- Seek out people you normally don't talk to. Ask their opinions. Determine the effect your questions had on them.

- Walk a different path to a meeting, lunch or break. Stop and take the time to talk to people along the way. Active listen to determine their feelings and concerns.

- Express your gratitude, even for simple things like emptying the trash. Watch to determine the effect of your words.

- Express gratitude genuinely and sincerely and as often as is appropriate. Watch for the affect of your words.

- Think about ways that people have gone out of their way for you.

- Think about how a request might make someone feel before asking.

- Recognize other people's reaction to an unwanted change. What reactions do your observe?

- Try to determine a person's reaction to a change before it is announced.

- Think about diverse people you have met. How have their views surprised you?

- Think about things you have learned about people who are different from you. How can you use this information in your next encounter?

- Think about times when you have jumped to a wrong conclusion. What can you learn from these experiences?

- Watch for the nonverbal signals in your next conversation. What do you think these nonverbals are expressing?

- Watch the nonverbal signals at the next decision-making meeting. Can you see clues to what people are thinking?

- When in conversation, remind yourself to ask what the other person is thinking and feeling.

EXERCISES FOR IMPROVING EMPATHY

EQ Exercise #5: Importance Meter

Empathy gives people a sense of importance because they feel understood. List people you interact with on a regular basis in the workplace. Think about each as having a meter that indicates how much importance you place on them through empathetic interactions. What could you do to increase their sense of importance by your interactions with them?

EQ Exercise #6: The Subtle Signs of Empathy

Think about all the subtle ways people can display a lack of empathy. Examples include not making eye contact with someone during a meeting and asking for one person's opinion at a meeting and not another's opinion. Make a list of experiences you have had when you felt a lack of empathy by others. Make another list of times when you may not have displayed empathy to others.

CHAPTER 17

SOCIAL EXPERTNESS AT WORK

No matter what accomplishments you make,
somebody helps you.—Althea Gibson

S ocial expertness extends your emotional intelligence to develop relationships with others. The definition of social expertness is the ability to build genuine relationships and bonds and to express caring, concern, and conflict in healthy ways. Once you have a firm understanding of yourself (self-awareness), know when and how to control your emotional reaction for the desired outcome (self-control), and can be empathetic about another person's viewpoint (empathy), then you are perfectly positioned to create social bonds, collaborate with others, and resolve conflicts with others (social expertness).

SOCIAL BONDS

Telephone Call #1

Brrring. . . .

    MIKE: Automation Department, Mike speaking.

    NICK: Hey Mike, How's it going?

    MIKE: It's going fine, Nick, and you?

    NICK: Well, not so good. I just lost my job because of our recent merger. In fact, that's why I'm calling. I was wondering if you might be able to meet with me to help me put together a list of people I can call to begin to job hunt? I know you know lots of people in the field. What do you say?

MIKE: Of course, Nick. I'd be happy to. I'm free for lunch on Friday.

NICK: Thanks so much, Nick. I don't know how to repay you.

MIKE: Don't even think about it. That's not what it's about. Besides, you already have many times over.

Telephone Call #2

Brring. . . .

MIKE: Automation Department, Mike speaking.

PETE: Hey Mike, How's it going?

MIKE: It's going fine, Pete, and you?

PETE: Well, not so good. I just lost my job because of our recent merger. In fact, that's why I'm calling. I was wondering if you might be able to meet with me to help me put together a list of people I can call to begin to job hunt? I know you know lots of people in the field. What do you say?

MIKE: Gee. Pete. I really don't know of anyone who's hiring right now. If you send me a resume though I'll keep you in mind.

PETE: O.K. I'll send you my resume.

MIKE: O.K. Good luck.

PETE: Thanks.

Why might Mike react so differently to essentially the same phone call? It could be that Mike is just an inconsistent kind of guy, but my hunch is that it has something to do with the different social bonds that have been established between Mike and the callers. I think of social bonds as the giant Roll-a-dex® of people that you know. But I don't think about it as the number of entries that you have in that Roll-a-dex®, but rather the response that you get when you pick up the phone and call the people. Are they delighted to hear your voice? If so, you've created strong social bonds with that person.

Your skill in establishing and maintaining relationships causes others to be available to you. When you've built relationships based on honor and respect, others are willing to help you, share information, communicate problems, and give you guidance. In the telephone call examples, in one case, Mike was willing to help, while in another case, Mike was polite, but didn't offer much assistance. Who's going to gain access to Mike's knowledge, associates, and advice? Of course, Nick will. We are not willing to share our relationships with others with people in whom we are not confident. What is the nature of the confidence, and on what do we base our decision to share it? Well, we base it on our experience with that person. The kind of confidence depends on the situation, and what the person is asking for. For example, in the case above, one quick kill might be if Mike's experience was that the person was incompetent. Another might be if Mike's experience was that the other person might be pushy, rude, or otherwise dishonorable in his interactions. Would you want to open your trusted associates to someone you thought might abuse them? What if you had sufficient experience with the person to know that he complains and whines? Would you want to expose your honorable associates to a person who was going behave this way?

Even in terms of offering knowledge and information, we are selective—perhaps less so than in sharing our relationships, but still protective. In a study of high performers at Bell Labs, conducted by Robert Kelly and documented in *How to Be a Star at Work,* Kelly found that the most exchange of information occurs between high performers.[1] High performers respect other high performers and are more willing to share information with them than with others. They see it as an efficiency issue. They have only so much time, so they prefer to share information with other high performers who are more likely to act on the information to solve problems or create new products.

I'm not suggesting that you seek and build social bonds only with high performers. I'm stating that, in reality, those who are high performers and who bring something to relationships are the people who create high regard in our social stratum. Those that are perceived as the "takers" do not. Reciprocity is not the goal of creating

---

[1]Kelley, Robert. *How to Be a Star at Work.* New York: Times Books Publishing, 1998.

social bonds. It is the outcome. If we look for relationships and main-tain relationships because we believe we have something to gain, we have the wrong assumption and worldview. Think "give," not "take."

On a practical note, a survey of 209 top selling professionals cited in *Sales and Marketing Management* by Erika Rasmusson presented traits that were identified as essential to be successful in sales.[2] Of these respondents, 72 percent said that the ability to build relation-ships is key. In the area of sales, the idea of building social bonds seems obvious, but more and more research points to social bonds as an essential component in success regardless of occupation. Engi-neers engage others for information and answers that lead to quicker and better solutions, sales professionals increase their performances because of their social bonds, and even millionaires use social bonds.

Although wealth is not necessarily the measure to success in life, Stanley Thomas, Ph.D., author of *The Millionaire Next Door,* dis-cusses the importance of strong social bonds in achieving wealth.[3] He devotes an entire chapter in his book to what he calls "The 900 Club." In it, he disputes the idea that wealth can be obtained only by those with heavy-duty brainpower. He describes millionaires who achieved 900 or below on their college boards and says that their wealth is the result of their social skills and their ability to build last-ing social relationships with others. These social relationships serve them well in business and have in turn created great success, includ-ing wealth, as their reward. As a personal example, I live my life pur-pose because others have been willing to help me. Even as I write this book, I pick up the phone and call people and ask their thoughts and opinions. Their willingness enables me to refine and upgrade my thinking. Without them, I would be much less. I also would be more than willing to reciprocate. Not because we keep track of the debt, but because it would be my honor. I learned another way to look at it from a wonderful lady I met on the streets of Paris when I was still in my teens and hungry. She bought me a loaf of bread. I said I

---

[2] Rasmusson, Erika. "The 10 Traits of Top Salespeople." *Sales and Marketing Management* 152 (August): 34–37.

[3] Stanley, Thomas, and Danko, William D. *The Millionaire Next Door.* Atlanta, Longstreet Press, 1998.

wanted to repay her. She said to buy someone else a loaf of bread someday, and that would be repayment. So continue to buy loaves of bread and give them away. Don't buy them to eat, buy them so that others may eat. That attitude will serve you well in developing social bonds.

Some Suggestions for Improving EQ in the Area of Social Bonds

- Keep records and contact information on people you meet. Record simple notes regarding people's skills, interests, and abilities.

- Make an effort to stay in touch with people you meet. For example, if you talked about a certain subject, send a news clipping regarding that subject or an e-mail about the subject or event.

- Connect regularly with your contacts. Don't expect to call on someone for assistance if you haven't spoken to him or her in 10 years.

- Seek quality, not necessarily quantity, in your social bonds.

- Try to converse with people on a level other than the normal conversation that usually occurs. Talk about subjects other than work, talk about feelings related to work, share concerns that you have regarding business, or talk about family and friends.

- Offer unexpected assistance to someone today.

- Think about your company and come up with a list of ideas that could help the company function. Volunteer your services to make these ideas a reality.

- When you talk with people, make it a point to remember something about what they said.

- During your next conversation, recall some information the person conveyed during your last conversation and bring it up if it seems appropriate. People will be impressed that you cared enough to remember.

- Always smile and say hello in passing. You can't and are not building bonds if you don't even take the time to say hello.

- Remember people's names. Call them and greet them by name.

- Recall significant family members and events occurring in employees' personal lives. Ask about these situations.

- Join and become involved in professional groups and organizations.

- Take time to learn about other people's interests.

- Be genuine in your alliances. If you align yourself for personal gain, your credibility will suffer.

Exercise for Improving Collaboration

EQ EXERCISE #7: YOUR ADDRESS BOOK

Quickly list the first fifty people who come to mind with whom you interact at work. How many of those people would you be willing to ask for help? What type of help would you be willing to ask of them? Also evaluate that list to determine when the last time you offered assistance to them. Answer these questions:

Do I feel like I have a strong support system in my work life?

In what areas do I feel I am alone or not supported?

What could I do to help others on my list?

What do I need to do to gain greater support at work?

Note: Many people feel a strong sense of independence and asking for help from anyone may seem to them to be a sign of weakness. The purpose of this exercise is not to encourage you to be needy and ask for help. It is to help you evaluate whether or not you have developed strong social bonds that would result in assistance if needed.

COLLABORATION

Dear Team,

I have served on many teams in the past, but my experience on this team was a highlight of my career. I have never seen such cooperation. There were no egos at our meetings, only the common goal. I think you'll agree that everyone went out of their way to listen to others. We have all commented that our final product is a brilliant combination of everyone's ideas. Also, absolutely everyone pulled their weight. When the assignments were made, everyone volunteered even if they were overloaded with other responsibilities. But I think the thing that amazed me the most was how everyone was complimenting each other at the team presentation to management. No one was taking credit. Everyone was "blaming" the other person for our success. It was my honor to serve on this team. Thank you teammates for an extraordinary experience.

Paula

Collaboration is not limited to working on teams, but the team experience is one area that magnifies the ability of people to collaborate. If you've ever served on a team where your teammates were slouches and credit hogs, and in-fighting and ego displays were the background music for your meetings, you can appreciate the difference that collaboration can bring to the work experience. Collaboration is born from the parents of equality and helpfulness. The assumptions that collaboration makes are that people's ideas are worthwhile and that others can help you reach goals.

Collaboration is an invitation to others. It requests the honor of their presence in your thinking. It invites people to sit at the table with you. If we think of inviting others, then their presence and their ideas are not viewed as intrusions, but rather as gifts. Collaboration then, has the potential to enrich our goals and our intentions. It is the natural offspring of social bonds. Once we have created strong social bonds, then we invite these people into our thoughts, ideas, and goals. Your sense of collaboration makes others feel valued. When you believe in collaboration, you recognize that you are more powerful in concert with other people. Collaboration will add to your ability to advance your goals and ideas. However, collaboration is a two-way street. You can't expect people to collaborate with you if you are not willing to help others toward their goals and intentions, too. In fact, this sharing sets up a win-win attitude that reduces conflict and sets the foundation for true influence. Without collaboration, you may not be fully using the resources and ideas of people who can advance you toward your intentions. Also, you may be viewed as a lone wolf who isn't willing to work with others to accomplish things.

Some Suggestions for Improving EQ in the Area of Collaboration

- Get people in touch with one another. If you've met two people who have a similar interest in a subject, invite them to lunch.

- Follow through on your promises. If you say you will send something or do something, then by all means do it. Come through for others. If someone asks you for help or assistance or referral on something, do your best to respond. If you can't personally come through, get them in touch with someone in your network who may be able to help.

- Share the wealth. If you have a good idea, it may pay you to call others and include them in your effort.

- Find ways to collaborate. Collaboration strengthens your social bonds and allows you to give and take at the same time.

- Practice genuinely inviting people's ideas and opinions. Ask questions. Do this before you state your opinions or ideas.

- Seek out the value in what others have to say.

- Always respect a different view and be willing to change your view when a case is made for the good of the organization.

- Facilitate rather than dictate. Ask questions.

- Identify a mentor who is a good collaborator. Strategize with your mentor to determine who can help you to move your ideas forward in a collaborative way.

- Don't expect people to rescue you. Do your own work. Others are there to strengthen your efforts, provide information or insight, not to be a dumping ground.

- Offer assistance to people without waiting to be asked. If you have information or contacts that can help someone, offer them.

- Form a "Dream Team"—a team of people who support each other in their dreams, goals, and aspirations. This strong collaborative group will vastly multiply your resources.

- Consider a present goal that you have. Now, consider several different paths to obtain this goal. Don't evaluate them; just recognize that several paths may exist to reach the same goal.

- Pay attention to the path of decision-making in your organization. Who is involved early? Who is involved later? Who is usually most influential? Least influential? Understanding the decision-making process in your organization is very important and can save you work in the long run. For example, if you don't get your boss's input early, will it put the project at risk later? Sometimes collaboration means being politically astute about the decision paths.

- Think about a time when you were surprised about a decision. What happened? Why were you surprised? Who ultimately influenced the decision?

- Help others link their ideas to other popular positions in the organization.

- Build a case for others' ideas or positions if you believe their ideas supports the organizational goals.

- If you know that someone's idea or position may be unpopular, discuss it up front with that person. Listen carefully and try to understand his or her perspective. See if you can help them if you believe it is the right thing to do.

Exercise for Improving Collaboration

EQ EXERCISE #8: CURRENT PROJECTS

Think about five current projects or tasks at work that are currently assigned to you. Who is affected by the project or task? What could you do to include those affected that would serve to solicit their ideas and/or opinions? Or think about tasks that you currently perform whose results are used by someone else. What could you do to improve the quality or timeliness of your task that could help the next person in the chain? Discuss your ideas with others.

CONFLICT RESOLUTION

Conflict resolution often appears as a common area for development on performance and development reviews.

Q. What could this person do to be more effective?

A. Ruth needs to see both sides in a conflict situation. She tends to get narrow-minded and doesn't see that there may be another way to solve a problem other than her own.

A. Steven needs to listen in a conflict situation. In previous conflicts, he has not allowed the other person to state his opinion. If the other person states his opinion, Steven quickly dismisses it. In the latest conflict with the shipping department, Steven said, "That's not the way I want it," without even listening to why the shipping department was proposing a different solution.

A. Tom does not listen to other points of view in a conflict situation. He is stubborn about his opinion and won't allow others to express their views. Tom has insulted others in conflict situations by saying, "That will never work, and if you had thought about it, you'd see why." Tom must learn to understand the concerns of others when in conflict and to listen with an open mind.

A. Vera sees customer complaints as conflict situations in which she is challenged and must prove herself right. Vera must change her perspective so that she views her job as helping to resolve complaints in a win-win manner. Vera must stop reacting personally to what the customer is saying and try to solve the conflict. It is inappropriate for Vera to raise her voice to a customer even if the customer provoked the situation. Vera must maintain calm and manage her emotions when dealing with difficult customers.

Nothing tests our emotional intelligence as much as our ability to resolve conflicts. Conflicts set the stage for triggers and stressors to hijack our emotional response. Yet, all relationships are prone to some disagreement, so learning to resolve conflict in a way that maintains healthy relationships is central to our well-being and productivity at work. When you can resolve conflicts without damaging relationships, you are viewed as reasonable, open-minded, and flexible. Resolving conflicts is also an essential foundation to influence and leadership.

Two M.O.s tend to emerge in dealing with conflict. One suggests that conflict is a challenge to what you know or what you stand for and that you must win to preserve your ego. All energy is focused on winning. If you listen, you listen to prove the other point wrong. If you speak, you speak to prove your point and discredit the other person. If you ask the opinions of others, it is for the sole purpose of supporting your position. The only vision for conflict resolution is the vision of your point of view prevailing. I'm sure you've encountered people like this. I once observed executives at a meeting, whose purpose was to decide which of two product lines to fund for the next fiscal year. One executive strongly preferred one line over the other, and she cut off others when they began to make a positive statement about the other line. She would question any numbers that seemed to support an opposing opinion. She even went so far as to suggest that the numbers may have been rigged. In addition, she belittled those favoring the other product line, saying they were obviously unable to see the big picture. This woman's argument may have been correct. She may have indeed been supporting the product line that was best for the company, but her obnoxious behavior made it difficult for others to see beyond her attitude. If emotional intelligence is about living our intentions, and this person's intentions were to support the best product for the company, her win-lose MO made it impossible to discuss the matter.

Another M.O. for conflict resolution is the conflict avoidance. A person who avoids conflict doesn't engage in conflict resolution at all, because he is concerned that expressing opposing opinions or ideas will not be heard or will somehow displease others. Therefore, he either keeps his opinions to himself, or worse, pretends to agree when indeed he does not. This disagreement unfortunately surfaces later, either in a quiet lack of support for whatever decision was made or by stirring discontent with others pointing out the absurdity of the decision. Another common possibility is that the conflict avoider supports the situation but somehow feels resentful of himself for going along. This resentment can manifest itself in general discontent on the job, feeling a lack of empowerment, self-criticism, or other destructive behaviors.

In either M.O., damage occurs in work relationships. The inability to resolve conflicts can be a career stopper in many organizations. This inability damages relationships that are crucial for getting things done. In the first M.O., others may shut down, draw sides by garnering support for their position, or create subversive ways to get around the conflict. In the second M.O., the person may be dismissed as a serious player because he lacks the courage to engage in healthy conflict. He may also gain a reputation for not speaking the truth and, therefore, will not be trusted. In either case, he may be passed up for promotions based on his inability to resolve conflicts in a healthy way.

All areas of emotional intelligence build on one another. In conflict resolution, the building nature of emotional intelligence is certainly obvious. If you are not aware of behavior in a conflict situation, then you cannot recognize how you are coming across. If you are aware and at risk for being hijacked either by anger or by fear, then you cannot control your emotional response in a way that will enable the conflict to be resolved. If you do not have empathy, you can't listen and understand the other person's perspective. If you don't have strong social bonds with others, your ability to resolve conflict is lessened. Figure 17.1 shows how the areas of emotional intelligence combine to enhance conflict resolution:

Emotional Intelligence and Conflict Resolution		
Emotional Intelligence Factors	**How it Applies**	**Action**
Self-Awareness	It is essential to be aware **in the moment** of how you feel in a conflict situation because your feelings may hijack your rational brain and impact the outcome of your conflict resolution.	Ask: **In the moment** What am I feeling in this situation? What is my typical M.O. in this type of conflict? What is my intention in this situation? How is my limbic brain at risk of hijacking my intention in this situation?
Self-Control	You must exercise self-control if your emotional reaction will undo your intention. Self-control can be accomplished through breathing, self-talk, suggesting another meeting time, or other centering techniques.	Ask: **In the moment** What is my potential impact on others given my M.O.? What is my intention? What do I need to do to limit the risk of hijacking?
Listening	Active listening is an essential skill in de-escalating a conflict and coming to resolution.	Ask: **In the moment** Am I employing my active listening skills? Am I listening without regard to proving my point?
Understanding the Perspective of the Other Person	In a conflict situation, it is important to try to understand the other party's perspective, not for the purpose of disproving it, but rather to build on it.	Ask: **In the moment** How can I use my empathy to understand this situation? Has my life experience taught me anything that can help me relate to this situation?
Social Bonds	Respect and dignity in the conflict is important to resolution.	Ask: **In the moment** Am I respecting this person? Are my words and actions building bonds or destroying them?
Collaboration	Inviting others to solve the conflict helps them retain some sense of power and control over the situation.	Ask: **In the moment** How can I invite this person into the solution? How can this person's perspective be included to solve the conflict?
Conflict Resolution	All of the above must be present.	

FIGURE 17.1

Some Suggestions for Improving EQ in the Area of Conflict Resolution

- Always, always actively listen during a conflict. Take a listening class if you need a refresher, then put it in practice.

- Do not assume that because someone has an opinion contrary to yours, that you are automatically in conflict.

- Don't think about issues as win-lose. Inside, find the common ground and find out how that opinion may make the organization stronger.

- If you tend to avoid conflict, practice speaking your opinion.

- Take time out if you think your emotions are getting out of control. Negative emotional reactions harm your ability to think clearly and can damage the relationship with the other person, thus making conflict resolution much more difficult.

- Work with a mentor to determine how you can more readily state your position. If you tend to avoid conflict, you can greatly increase your effectiveness and provide valuable input if you realize that your position has value.

- Think about a time you were involved in a conflict situation that turned "ugly." What happened? Make a list of things you could you have done differently.

- Think about a time when you addressed a conflict and were able to resolve the conflict, yet preserve the relationships of all parties. What did you do that was successful in this instance? Write it down.

- Think about times when you avoided conflict. Why did you avoid the conflict? When was it the right choice? When was it the wrong choice? Reflect on your M.O. related to conflict avoidance.

- Think about people you think address conflict situations negatively. What do they do that diminishes their effectiveness?

Make a list of things you do not want to do in conflict situations, given their example.

■ Think about people who you think address conflict situations very well. What do they do that adds to their effectiveness? Make a list of things you would like to incorporate in your conflict resolution skills.

■ When considering addressing an issue, determine if the issue is connected to your core beliefs. If so, develop a strategy that will most positively address the conflict.

■ The next time you are in conflict with another person, make it a point to determine common ground. Ask what the two of you agree on. Find agreement and try to build resolution based on the common ground.

■ Take time out if you think your emotions are getting out of control. Negative emotional reactions can harm your ability to think clearly and can damage the relationship with the other person, thus making conflict resolution impossible.

■ Stick to the issues. Do not attack the person.

■ Write down the pros and cons of both parties. Put distance between the arguments by putting them on paper. Also write down your areas of agreement.

■ When in conflict with someone, encourage them to speak and state their views. Do not dominate the discussion. If anything, do more listening than speaking

Exercise for Improving Conflict Resolution

EQ EXERCISE #8: CONFLICT RESOLUTION M.O.S

Think about conflict situations that you've encountered in the past six months. Whether at home or at work, list at least six conflicts that have occurred. Think about how you behaved during these conflicts. Which M.O. below described your behavior in the conflict?

Was there a difference in how you behaved if the conflict involved family and friends versus a situation at work?

M.O.#1: CONFLICT STIRRER

- Feels challenged.
- Energy is focused on winning.
- Listens in order to prove a point.
- Speaks to prove a point.
- Discredits the other person.

M.O.#2:CONFLICT AVOIDER

- Doesn't express views.
- Avoids conflict situations by keeping quiet.
- Pretends to agree to avoid controversy.
- May feel anger toward self for not speaking opinion.
- Will try to appease both sides of a controversy.

CHAPTER 18

PERSONAL INFLUENCE AT WORK

The extent to which you are able to transform your "self-concern" into "other-concern" will determine your effectiveness in getting others to follow along.
—*Anonymous*

Personal influence, the area of emotional intelligence that addresses both our ability to influence ourselves and our ability to influence others, is the essence of leadership. Inspiring others through example, words, and deeds requires a firm foundation in all of the areas of emotional intelligence already discussed. The ability to lead others requires that strong social bonds have been developed. Personal influence is the ability to read situations and exert influence and leadership in the desired direction. A person with a high degree of personal influence will look for creative ways to get others to buy into her concepts and ideas. He or she will understand what it takes to move an idea or suggestion forward and will mobilize others to his or her point of view. Personal influence is also the ability to pursue issues that are important or debilitating to relationships, goals, missions, or visions. If a person realizes that something or someone prohibits a goal that he or she believes in, he or she will determine how to overcome those obstacles rather than crumble in defeat. Overcoming obstacles and maintaining optimism is essential to emotional intelligence. Researchers have found that people who have a positive outlook tend to have better morale and a greater adaptive capacity. Because they are more resilient in the face of stress, adversity, or loss, they actually suffer less, even in the worst circumstances. They respond to challenges more flexibly and creatively. They are likely to be ready for trouble when it comes, and they have learned how to confront and overcome rather than avoid it. They succeed because they persevere.[1] Persons with strong personal influence are optimistic. Their optimism even affects their health. They live longer than pessimists.[2] A person with strong personal influence exhibits motivation for one's visions, missions, core values, and beliefs. Therefore, influence is directed in two directions, internal to self and external to others.

INFLUENCING SELF

Profile 1

Name:	Marsha Cromley
Age:	37
Education:	B.S. Liberal Arts, Podunk State University
Family Background:	Hard-working, poor, blue-collar in large urban area
Position:	CEO, Specialty Toy Manufacturing Company
Favorite expression:	Plan, persist, and prevail!
Assumptions/Workview:	I can do it if I try. The world will reward your efforts. Other people will help you if you meet them more than half way.

---

[1]Miller, Michael Craig. "The Benefits of Positive Psychology." *Harvard Mental Health Letter* 18 (January 2002): 6.
[2]—— "Mayo Clinic Study: Optimists Report Higher Quality of Life." *FDA Consumer* 36 (November/December 2002): 7.

	Every obstacle presents an opportunity to learn. Life without challenges would be boring. Try another path. Don't quit.
Obstacles to Overcome:	Too numerous to mention. But to give you an idea: Financing without equity. Breaking into a tight, competitive market. Getting others to take me seriously. Raising two children and running a successful business.
Biggest Challenge:	The biggest challenge was believing in myself and having the vision that I could do this. Once I overcame that challenge, nothing could stand in my way.

Profile 2

Name:	Marsha Boosley
Age:	37
Education:	B.S. Liberal Arts, Podunk State University
Family Background:	Hard-working, poor, blue-collar in large urban area
Position:	Currently unemployed after a series of difficult, low-paying jobs in the service field.
Favorite expression:	Some people have all the luck.
Assumptions/Workview:	You have to be connected to get the right jobs. The world is stacked against me. People are out for themselves. It's nearly impossible today to make it.

What's the use?
There's nothing I can do to improve my
situation.

Obstacles to Overcome: People who won't give me the time of day.

Biggest Challenge: Surviving and getting enough money to
                            pay the bills.

What can we learn from our two fictitious Marshas? First and fore-most, influencing self is related to our assumptions and worldviews/workviews. If we are unable to get at the core assumptions and worldview/workview that affect our daily behaviors, our success in all aspects of life will suffer. Yes, it's that important. Of course, hosts of different factors influence our assumptions and worldviews/workviews, but, regardless of how we obtained our views and assumptions, if we don't do something to address destructive views, our happiness will suffer. In *The Pursuit of Happiness,* David G. Meyers, Ph.D., lays out the traits of happy people.[3] Three of the four traits are contained within our worldview and assumptions. They are a sense of personal control, self-esteem, and optimism. If we begin to work on any assumptions and views we hold that are contrary to these, progress will occur. The personal control that Meyers speaks about is similar to believing that you have power over aspects of your life—and then exercising that power. We must be confident and persistent in our actions and move ourselves toward goals. When we stop persisting, we stop living.

In the workplace, there's a double jeopardy. If we give up taking actions because we feel defeated, we suffer not only from an internal sense of lack of power and control, but others see us as unmotivated, lacking conviction, and otherwise unable to persist in difficult times. So, our influence within the organization goes down. In fact, I've witnessed rising young stars who hit a career block because of how they handled an obstacle or setback. When things were going well,

---

[3]Myers, David G. *The Pursuit of Happiness.* New York: Avon Books, 1992.

they were in their stride, but when things got difficult, they lost their balance and stumbled. Everyone stumbles, but how fast you can get up, dust yourself off and join the race again is what separates the winners from the rest.

How do you address those assumptions and worldviews/workviews that are holding you back? First, you have to recognize them. This is where your self-coach can help you to understand what voices, assumptions, and views dominate your self-talk. Of course, some of these traits are rooted in genetic predisposition and in the social environments in which we have grown. Beyond that, the technique of *act as if* discussed earlier may be the best way to influence your behavior.

Some Suggestions for Improving EQ in the Area of Influencing Self

- Find a mentor who understands the organization and can help you use your strengths. This person should also be someone you could talk to when you feel discouraged or doubtful.

- Surround yourself with optimistic people. Don't feel defeated by others, allow yourself to feel inspired by them.

- Brainstorm ideas on how to circumvent obstacles. Everyone faces obstacles, but the more you can effectively learn ways around them, the more effective you will be.

- Watch your reaction to failure. Are you suffering from paralysis due to past failures? Work to change your attitudes about failure so that you can learn from your mistakes and move on.

- Develop contingency plans so that if one method fails, you are left with another avenue.

- Ask others for help in selling your ideas and offering strategies for how to get things done. It is often easier to move toward your goals with the help and support of others.

- Work to your strengths. Gain a good understanding of what you do well. Use that information to advance your ideas, to keep yourself motivated, and to persist. Your strengths will deliver your desired outcomes if you persist long enough.

- Ask yourself, "Am I giving up too soon?"

- Watch your reaction to failure. Are you learning from your mistakes?

- Be a role model for learning. Let people know what development needs you are working on. Ask for their help or advice in your development.

- Recognize your progress in reaching objectives.

- Reflect on how far you have come rather than on how far you have to go.

- Develop learning objectives and write them down. Develop an action plan for achieving your learning objectives.

- Before implementing an idea, think about how different people might react to your plan. Where would you get resistance? Where would you get support? Come up with some different ways to implement your plan that would take into consideration the issues raised by your resistors. This will reduce the obstacles that you face when implementing your actions.

- Seek sponsors for your position or idea before the decision is made. The thought that others believe in you will help you maintain focus.

- If you do not have definite goals, take the time to develop them. You may need to seek assistance or coaching to home in on the things that are important for you and deserving of goal setting. What kind of goals are we talking about? All kinds— career goals, department goals, life goals, financial goals. Do you homework here. It is worth the effort.

- When you set your goals, decide on more than one plan of action to achieve them. Have contingency plans ready in the event that your original plan is sidetracked.

- Seek assistance and support for reaching your goals.

- State and speak about your goals often. Also, write them down.

- When you experience a setback on your way to a goal, step back and analyze what caused it and whether or not you could have avoided it.

- Have a bounce-back strategy in place. How will you regroup if you get off track?

- Have a support system in place if you fail. Call on your support system to get you back on track.

- Take a time out if you are experiencing multiple setbacks on your goal attainment. Reevaluate the goal.

- If you are struggling with a goal, by all means, ask for help. Don't go at it alone.

- Engage a mentor or trusted friend to call you on your goal attainment and to hold you accountable.

- Analyze what personal qualities are holding you back from attaining your goal. Come up with a plan to overcome or minimize these qualities.

- Include others in attaining your goals. What one person can't accomplish in a lifetime, an army can do in a day.

Exercises for Improving Influencing Self

EQ EXERCISE #9: IDENTIFYING MENTORS

Others can play a vital role in helping us stay motivated toward goals and persist when obstacles arise. Even success toward goals, such as developing an exercise regimen, is greater when you involve others in your plan. According to *Aerobics and Fitness Magazine,* exercising with a coach, trainer or friend increases the likelihood of staying focused on your goal by 37 percent. Of course, if your friend is a slouch who encourages you to eat ice cream instead, your performance will suffer. Persistence, self-motivation, confidence, determination, openness to criticism, contingent thinking, focus, and resilience reflect qualities associated with influencing self. So, when you think about staying motivated and persisting toward your goals, who do you know who displays these characteristics? Ask some people if they would be willing to mentor you in your quest for greater influence of self.

EQ EXERCISE #10: *ACT AS IF*

Within the next month, keep a log of each time you practice "*act as if*" in relation to influencing yourself. After the first entry, mark on a scale of 1 to 10 how difficult it was for you to "act as if." After thirty days, evaluate the last entry on a scale of 1 to 10 to determine how difficult it was for you to "act as if." Typically, it gets easier as we practice.

INFLUENCING OTHERS

Dear Carlos,

You were the true leader in our group. It's amazing how one person can make a difference. It's great to see a peer get promoted, but we're going to miss you. You were the one who kept us on focus. You were always optimistic. Also, when we started to gripe, you always cracked a joke to lighten the mood and kept reminding us that we didn't have it so bad. You always came through. I never once was delayed on a project because you didn't have your piece done. I remember when our group was working on the CSE program with you. I wasn't sure if we'd ever get done with all the problems and changes. You said, "Okay, we're a smart group of people. We can do this." Then, you asked all of us to make a list of the things about this project that were a problem. You listened and then took the list to management and started one by one to get the obstacles taken care of. We were just spinning our wheels and spending some of our time being frustrated. You took it to action. You sure deserve that promotion. You're already a great leader. Congratulations!

We'll miss you,
Your Work Group

Dear Boss,

I heard you went to training the other day to be a leader. What do they teach you in leadership school? Whatever it is, it's not working. For starters, you can't expect us to follow you when you don't even say good morning. That's just a common decency, but somehow you put yourself above that. Then, you expect us to listen to every word you say. Well that's great, but you don't listen to our ideas or opinions. The meeting the other day was a perfect example. You asked our opinion about the job opening in the department, but you shut us down when we started to express ourselves. You just kept talking about how you thought Scott was the best person for the job. Also, we told you last week that Line 5 was going to go down because we thought the pump was going bad. You said to keep pushing it. Well, what happened? The line went down. Now, you're on us about getting the production rolling because we're behind. We could have fixed it in two hours instead of losing a whole shift. Another thing that really gripes us. . . . You brought customers in here, and we heard you say that you're trying to straighten up "this mess." You were referring to us. You think we want to support you when we hear things like that? Go back to leadership school, boss; you need lots of work.

Sincerely,
The Day Shift

Dear Boss,

Consider this a thank you note. You are an inspiration to us. At first we were skeptical. You came in and said that you cared about our opinions. Well, we've heard that line before. Yet, you proved that you meant it. You listen to us. You actually believe we have brains. When you came in and showed us the numbers that said that we were performing the worst of all the sites in the company, we weren't sure what to think. Our other boss never showed us those numbers. He just kept saying that the company was going to shut us down if we didn't improve. But you said it differently. You said that you believed we were working hard and that you believed in us. You said that if we put the same amount of effort in, but worked on the "right" things, you believed we could be the best in the company rather than the worst. You didn't insult us. You kept us focused on doing the right things. You kept cheering us on. You believed in us. I can't believe it's been a year since you came and we've improved to Number 2 in the company. Yesterday's celebration was great. You thanked all of us and you really meant it. Well, it's our turn now. Thank you boss. You're a great leader.

Sincerely,
The Staff

Influencing others is easy. Influencing others to willingly take actions in the direction you think best is another story—and one worth pondering. With every action you do or do not take, you are influencing others. The question is: In what direction am I influencing them? When you don't say good morning, others will feel your influence. When you forget to say thank you, others will feel your influence. When you get hijacked at a meeting and begin to blame someone, others will feel your influence. When you share the credit with a peer, others will feel your influence. When you ask someone's opinion and stick around for the answer, others will feel your influence. Everything you do or don't do creates influence. Mastery of this competence however, puts you in the position to create influence in a way that serves you, your life, and work goals, and allows you to live your intentions.

So often I see well-meaning people do things that have exactly the opposite effect of what they intended. Parents want to open the dialogue with their children, so they lecture them. Leaders want employees to support a new initiative, so they release a memo or policy demanding it. Coworkers want peers to pitch in, so they complain to management that someone isn't doing his share. None of these actions influences the target to do as intended. Yet all of these intentions can be considered good. So, what's the mystery? The mystery is rooted in emotional intelligence.

If you want to influence people in a certain direction, you must master some basics. Those basics are everything we've covered thus far, plus one. We must be aware of our impact on others. How are we coming through? We must realize and control our own limbic hijackings because hijackings do not get people to follow us over the long run. You may get a short-term result, but you're not building loyalty, which is the foundation of influence. You are building fear. You must be able to empathize with their perspective, which means genuinely listening for the sake of understanding. And you must have strong social bonds with others, invite them into your thinking through collaboration, and respectfully resolve conflicts if they arise.

Sound familiar?

Beyond that, you need to demonstrate that you are willing to support your own goals and objectives. You must influence yourself before you can influence others. If you're not putting energy into a goal, don't expect others to. One sure influence killer is to play golf while you expect others to work toward your goals. The last thing on the table is that your influence must be honorable. If you are influencing others for self-serving reasons, it will show. Others will not follow. We've all experienced a time when someone in a position of influence treated us dishonorably. This person's behavior dampened our spirits and killed our desire to perform. I call these types of people spirit killers and soul suckers. Their techniques are sure-fire ways to kill influence. Here's what I've observed.

Spirit Killers and Soul Suckers

CELEBRITY EGO

It is hard, if not impossible, to influence someone if we can't get the focus off of ourselves. If we see the world as an extension of ourselves, then we're going to have a difficult time honoring others. Or if everyone else's place has to be secondary to our own, others will not follow. If you humble yourself to others, your influence will skyrocket.

HOG THE CREDIT

If you can't share the credit for a job well done with others, then you don't understand the concept of influence. Influence demands that you give others the spotlight. The credit will come back to you as the force behind the effort.

BLAME

It's your fault. Why did you do something so stupid? How could you be so shortsighted? Why didn't you realize the impact of what you were doing? Why would you do something like that? Didn't you realize what was going to happen?

Not inquiry, blame. The difference is in the delivery. If I deliver it with judgment and ridicule, with just the right gesture and facial expression, I have successfully blamed. Sophisticated blamers are very subtle. You have to listen carefully, but if you do, you will find all the elements of blame. The aim of blame is shame. If your aim is to inspire or influence others, they must accept and ultimately believe in what you have to say. You just can't get there from blame.

BEING "TECHNIQUED"

Phony. People see through it, and they just don't like it. If anyone attempts to manipulate others by building pseudosocial bonds, by pretending to empathize, or by bogus collaboration, it doesn't work. You must deliver this from the heart. If you don't believe that these things are the right things to do, then you can't do them effectively. Even when you believe it is the right thing to do, it takes practice to make it feel smooth and unrehearsed. You have to develop your own natural interpretation of what is presented here. There are no 1, 2, 3 steps.

GRATITUDE FOR GAIN

"Thank you" is a wonderful expression. When sincerely expressed, it builds the infrastructure of influence. Beware: If you use gratitude for gain or manipulation, people will see through it. We repeat: The sole purpose of gratitude is to honor the other person by acknowledging his effort, attitude, skill, or experience. Yes, influence could be a payoff to well-meaning gratitude, but if you do this with the payoff in mind rather than the real purpose, you will corrupt the results. People will see it as a manipulation tool.

YOU CONTRIBUTE, I'LL PLAY GOLF

Energy toward the goal that you are espousing is essential. You can't accomplish anything without energy. If your interpretation of influence is to get others to work toward your goals so that you can take it easy, that simply is wrong. Words are powerful, but action says you're in the game. Demonstrate. Show others the way and allow them to see you working toward the goal. The longer the lag time between stating a direction and supporting action, the greater the likelihood that it will fizzle and die.

INCONGRUENT ACTIONS

If you set out on vacation and tell everyone you're headed South, it doesn't inspire much confidence if your On Star keeps pointing North. We don't like to follow people who don't know where they are going. Herd animals follow the beast that confidently shows them direction. Congruent actions inspire others to know that you know which direction you're headed.

LACK OF ENTHUSIASM

When you talk to others to influence them toward your goals and you sound like verbal ether, how can you expect others to follow? If you want to put fire in someone's gut, you'll need to provide the spark for the flame. Haven't got a spark? Then find a spark, make a spark, set a fire. How? If you find it difficult to be enthused, it's probably time for a soul-searching conversation with yourself to establish what you really care about. This goes far beyond leadership, but is an essential step toward happiness. Discovering that which arouses our passions deep within is an essential part of life. It's worth the effort to spend some time here if you find yourself without enthusiasm. But for sure, if you can't find or make a spark, then others aren't going to follow you.

BULLYING

As if we can't generate enough fear on our own, insensitive, insecure tyrants add to our fear through intimidation and bullying tactics. If you care to influence others, put away the whips and chains. They will only work until we can find a way to escape. Influence requires a velvet hand.

PREACHING

Influence isn't about preaching. Just as most teenagers tune out preachy messages, so do most adults. When you try to influence by telling people what they *should* do and why they *should* do it, that's not influence, it's telling. A person with true influence helps people recognize and come to their own conclusions.

Without influence you are missing important opportunities to encourage others to action. With influence, you are skilled at enlisting, encouraging, and allowing people to follow. You have built a community in which others believe you are helpful and supportive. As a result, they are willing to follow you. You are flexible, yet direct. If you can't influence people who have untapped potential, you will lose input from many who could provide important resources toward achieving your goals and objectives. Regardless of your position within the organization, influence is important for everyone to understand. To understand influence is to understand emotional intelligence.

Some Suggestions for Improving EQ in the Area of Personal Influence

- Find a mentor who understands the organization and can help you positively use information to influence decisions that you believe are for the benefit of the organization.

- Do some soul searching to make sure your ideas and positions are not self-serving but rather provide a genuine benefit to the organization.

- Give honest feedback. Honest feedback given in a supportive way will help people understand you.

- Be a role model for learning. Let people know what development needs you are working on. Ask for their help or advice in your development.

- Recognize your progress in reaching objectives.

- Reflect on how far you have come rather than on how far you have to go.

- Listen carefully. Always and foremost, the primary skill underlying influence is expert listening. Do whatever you can to increase your skill in this area.

- Always include people when you can. This is an essential influencing skill.

- Before you speak, think about the words you will use. Will some words produce a result that will be better than what other words will produce?

- Watch for hot button words. List hot-button words of the people you work with. Edit these words from your vocabulary.

- If you have an important message to give, take time to write it down. Write it using many different variations of words. Evaluate which words will have the best effect on the listener.

- Key into the word choices of your audience. What words do they use? Can these words effectively be used in your message?

- Listen for the values and feelings that underlie other people's messages.

- Respect other people's differences and ask them to respect yours.

- Exercise empathy to determine where people's ideas are rooted. This will help you craft a message that is sympathetic, yet persuasive to another point of view. People will change their points of view when they feel more likely that their feelings or values are being honored.

- Before implementing an idea, think about how different people might react to your plan. Where would you get resistance? Where would you get support? Come up with some different ways to implement your idea that would take into consideration the issues raised by your resistors.

- Talk to people—many people and different people and include them in the planning process.

- Seek out people outside your usual circle of confidants. Ask for input from these people on your next project or idea.

- Encourage and seek input even from those you think will disagree with you.

- Seek sponsors for your position or idea before the decision is made.

- Think about your participation on a truly satisfying and accomplished team. What elements were present to cause this reaction?

- Think about your participation on a dysfunctional team. What elements were present to cause this reaction?

- Think about both informal and formal teams in which you are participating. How could you make that team experience more positive?

- If you will be participating on or leading a team in the near future, give considerable thought up front to your role. How will you encourage and support the team?

- As you participate in informal or formal teams, volunteer. Take on responsibilities and come through for your team members.

- Include other team members in your work. When the time comes, give them credit for the results.

- Encourage all team members to participate and voice opinions.

- Act as a role model for the perfect team player.

- Voice your concerns or positions early. Don't surprise your team with Monday morning quarterbacking.

- Encourage lessons learned from team experiences. Ask people to evaluate what the team did well and what the team could do to improve.

- When your team is at a low energy or commitment level, brainstorm ways to reenergize the team.

- Recognize team contributions and gratefully acknowledge accomplishments.

- State and speak about your goals often.

Exercise for Improving Influencing Others

EQ EXERCISE #11: INCREASING YOUR INFLUENCE

Identify five people you influence. You can select employees whom you currently lead, peers or your boss. Write down your current methods of influence with them. List additional or different methods that may be useful to increase your influence.

CHAPTER 19

MASTERY OF PURPOSE AND VISION AT WORK

To attempt to climb—to achieve—without
a firm objective in life is to attain nothing.
—Mary G. Roebling

KNOWS PURPOSE

If you look at your life as a story, what is the message? At the end of the book, what will we know about you? What will your story have contributed to the world? How is your story unique? Each life begs for a read. Sure, the book has subplots and supporting characters, but what story did you tell about yourself? Can we grasp the essence of who you are and what you stand for? Or is the characterization fuzzy? When we close the book, is the main character the person you want him to be? Or does he require a rewrite? Are you satisfied with the story you told?

Mastery of purpose requires that you know who you are and what you want to do with your life. It is about being guided by a strong personal philosophy that sets your life's direction. It serves as your inner script, fixing on the plot and giving you constant stage directions for living that purpose. Your purpose comes through in each line you speak, each action you take, each decision you make, and each secondary character and subplot that enters the pages of your life. When you're eighty years old and reading your life book, each chapter speaks to your purpose. What it says will either be unintentional or directed. Mastery of purpose requires that it be directed.

When we align our lives with this sense of purpose, we are authentic and happy. When misaligned, we suffer stress and discomfort. Your life purpose requires a set of deliberately chosen values that support your purpose. But purpose is deeper than merely living your values. You can live a code of values, yet not be sure of your purpose. For example, many people live by a set of religious values that espouse caring and concern for others, honesty, integrity, and so forth. These values are definitely worthwhile and provide a great compass for guiding behavior. And surely living your life according to these values is a significant accomplishment. But purpose requires you to live by a set of values for a particular reason or mission. It requires you to direct those values toward something. Purpose is the mission to which you have been called.

Many people who lived lives of deep purpose have made profound contributions to humankind, such as Mother Teresa's mission to serve the poor and suffering, Martin Luther King Jr.'s mission to achieve equality through nonviolent protest, and Christiaan Barnard's mission to save lives by developing successful surgical procedures for heart transplants. Each set upon a path, put their resources, energy and values toward it, and fulfilled a purpose. Yes, we live ordinary lives by comparison. We are ordinary people. Most of us are not sainted nuns, beloved civil rights leaders, or great surgeons. We are Joe, the factory worker; Pete, the computer programmer; Anna, the front line supervisor; Velma, the middle manager; or Jim, the student. How can a discussion of purpose speak to us, and what does it have to do with emotional intelligence?

Each of us has a purpose to which we are uniquely called. Plato first spoke of it in his Myth of Er in *The Republic*.[1] The Romans called it your *genius*.[2] Laurie Beth Jones, in *The Path*, calls it your mission.[3] Your purpose is your reason for being here. Purpose is not

---

[1]Plato first spoke of it in his Myth of Er in *The Republic*.
[2]Hilman, James. *The Soul's Code–In Search of Character and Calling*. New York: Random House, 1996.
[3]Jones, Laurie Beth. *The Path*. New York: Hyperion, 1996.

about your job or the roles you have in life. Purpose is larger than that, and it transcends roles and jobs. Jobs end, roles change. Purpose does not.[4] For example, my purpose is to touch and affirm people so they can reach their highest levels of inspiration. I can attempt to live my purpose in a variety of roles or jobs. I can do that in the corporate world, I can do that as a mom, I can do that as a friend, I can do that as a Girl Scout leader, I can do that as an accountant. Where I am or what role I have is irrelevant. Occasionally role may conflict so greatly with purpose that you will be forced to find another role, but those instances are rare. For example, if my job were executioner at the local penitentiary, I would more than likely struggle and feel conflicted between my role and my purpose. But most people can live their purposes regardless of the role or job they hold.

Consider Hank. Hank is an accountant in the purchasing department of a big company. When I met Hank, he had just taken the Index for Emotional Intelligence, which measures several factors of emotional intelligence, including "knows purpose." Hank scored himself particularly low on this item. He talked at length about how he felt that his job was empty. He said he felt bored and had little energy to expend toward work. He said he found little meaning in purchasing widgets and preparing contracts. After several discussions, Hank said that what he found to be meaningful in life was helping and teaching others. He wanted others to see that things could be straightforward. He loved to strip away the complicated and make things simple. Work came easy to Hank. He had a knack for understanding things, and he had a gift for explaining things to others. Hank agonized over his discovery. Because Hank realized that what he enjoyed was helping and teaching others, did this mean that he needed to leave his job? After all, his job was purchasing widgets. After a few more discussions, Hank's agony turned to delight. He realized that his job could provide many opportunities to help and teach others, but he kept focusing on the wrong things. Yes, preparing contracts and paperwork was part of his job, but by focusing on the paper, he

---

[4]Bateson, M.C. *Composing a Life.* New York: HarperCollins, 1989.

felt doomed and unsatisfied. Like a kaleidoscope, he shifted the view to human interaction and offered himself as a teacher. As a result, he gave his work a completely different meaning. His purpose, once discovered, consumed his thoughts and his actions. At work, at home, in the community, Hank kept creating opportunities to live his purpose. His values didn't change, but they had a sharper edge. Everything was clearer once he reframed his world. Two years after his discovery, Hank was promoted. Here's what his performance review said:

> Hank's technical skills are outstanding. He understands the purchasing process and accurately prepares contracts. However, Hank's willingness to share information and help others less familiar with the process is of particular note. Without asking, Hank has volunteered to help new employees in the department. He has put together a easy-to-read manual for new hires that thoroughly explains the complicated department process for purchasing supplies for the IST lines. In addition, others have commented on Hank's attitude regarding sharing his knowledge. Two department heads wrote memos regarding Hank's willingness to explain the purchasing procedure to their employees. Hank does this willingly, without arrogance and with no expectation of reward.

Purpose is the foundation of emotional intelligence. It gives new light to everything else, including emotional responses to situations. When we understand our purpose, our emotional response is much easier to craft. Think about Hank. Sure, he still may get angry or frustrated, but because he can quickly review his purpose, the seeds of anger or frustration are less likely to take off in a full-blown hijacking. He realizes that if he's hijacked, these emotional reactions will impede his ability to help and teach others. Most of us would not respond well to a teacher who has angry outbursts or constantly shows frustration. Clarity of intention produces a picture of appropriate emotional response. This works for our lives as a whole and it works in our daily situations. If my intention is to be a team player at work, and I must talk to a coworker about something he or she did not give me for a needed task, my intention will serve as the basis of that encounter. As a team player, I'll discuss it in a civil manner. If my intention is to be a team player and I can't come through with something another team member needs, I'll let her know in advance, work with her to come up with alternative actions, and take responsibility for the situation rather than place blame. The congruence between what I say I believe in and what I actually deliver is essential. If you examine the gaps between what you say you believe and what you deliver, you will often find those gaps are a result of emotional response.

Let's say that Joan thinks she is a team player, but she finds that she can't come through on something for the team. As soon as she realizes this, she feels pressure, perhaps embarrassment or even fear. Her voices kick in as well as her assumptions. Her emotions take over her rational thought. If only I had had the information sooner, I could have gotten my portion done on time. (The Blame Voice.) I hate it when people don't come through. (Assumption.) What am I to do now? It's not my fault I have so many other things to do. (The Victim Voice.) I'm not going to say anything because I know the team will be upset with me. (The Hide Voice.)

Joan is hijacked into inaction. She doesn't have her portion of the work done, and she doesn't let the team know in advance. This inaction causes the team to miss the deadline. The team labels Joan a nonteam player. Joan's actions (inactions) are inconsistent with her intention. Throughout this book, we talk about living our intentions. It is the vital link to closing the gaps between inconsistencies in what we believe and how we act. Intentions in everyday situations as described above are one level to examine. The deeper level is how all those everyday situations combine to paint a picture of our purpose. Every action is a brush stroke contributing to the form that takes shape on the canvas. Every color selected determines the final work of art.

Mary Frances Lyons, in *Becoming Who You Are*, looks at physicians who are living in an industry with sweeping changes and emotionally charged work environments. She provides an example of a physician who was able to separate his emotional reactions from the work for a more purposeful look at his life. He says, "I was a practicing OB/Gyn taking a leading role in the development of a system-sponsored physician network. To put it mildly, I got sucked in to the negative dynamics that always attend any discussions in depth where physicians are concerned. It was making me ineffective until—one day, for no particular reason that I can identify—I realized that all of this contention had nothing to do with me, personally. It was all about the issues and not at all about me. With that insight, I began to take steps back from the fray, listening and offering ideas and working with people, but all from a different, saner perspective. It was a revelation and a relief to get out of the emotional abyss."[5]

A schoolteacher said something similar. "When I realized that all the fuss about testing and holding teachers accountable for scores had nothing to do with me personally," she said, "I completely changed my attitude. Rather than feel defensive and attacked, I began to focus on the real issue—the children. Suddenly, my mind was free to come up with ideas that could raise scores, teach children, and satisfy administrators. The trick was getting back in touch with the real purpose of education and the reason I was called to education in the first place."[6]

Mastery of purpose crystallizes our intentions. We can continuously review our intentions by touching this base. Remember playing tag as a child? You knew you would always be safe at home base. Home base is our purpose. We know that when we come from this place, everything is aligned. We feel comfort. We live authentically. The most discontented people I see in the workplace are people who feel trapped or stuck, who feel as though they are selling themselves for a wage. They feel that their values are compromised on a daily basis. Sometimes these people may need to look for other employment to feel aligned, but I also believe that many times people could reframe their thinking about their present situations. They can focus on the values and purpose they can live within the confines of their present job or role, as did Hank in our earlier example.

---

[5]Lyon, Mary Frances. "Becoming Who You Are." *Physician Executive* 24 (November/December 1998): 62.
[6]Jamison, Laura. Interview regarding purpose and teaching, October, 2003.

Your self-coach can serve as the guardian angel of your purpose. He can help you align your purpose and take away the conflict between who you are and what others see. He can help you sort through values and other important clues that provide meaning to life. Purpose orders our values. Sure, we derive our purpose by examining which values are most important to us. We also develop our purpose by gaining intimate knowledge about our likes and dislikes, as well as our natural gifts. But once we understand our purpose, it serves as the ordering force. Decision-making is easier because we have the compass read that shows us true north. This compass also helps us understand the emotions that will promote our purpose, as well as those that will detract from it. Therefore, it helps us to know which emotions will serve us so we can turn up the volume on those. For others, we will know to turn the volume down. Purpose adds a deeper meaning to all that we've discussed thus far. Purpose is the base of the triangle in our model in Figure 19.1.

Purpose also requires that you use your natural gifts and talents. Sometimes negative emotional responses are a result of the frustration that we feel when we are trying to do things outside our natural gifts. For example, if you are naturally mechanically inclined, it's easy and fun to fiddle with the broken vacuum cleaner. However, if you have no gift for things mechanical, chances are you would find the task frustrating. Sure, you can learn it, and many of us perform tasks every day that are outside our natural gifts, but if you constantly work to your weaknesses instead of your strengths, you are likely to be less happy and more prone to hijacking.

In *The Pursuit of Happiness,* David Myers talks about "flow." Flow, as applied to work, is a term created by Mihaly Csikszentmihalyi. It means we are in an optimal state of work, where our challenge and our available time and skill are perfectly aligned. If we are called upon to do things that are outside our skill, we will feel stress. If we are not using skills we have, we are bored.[7] By uncovering purpose, we must assess our natural gifts, talents and skills and work to match these with available challenges. By definition, our potential for emo-

---

[7]Csikszentmihalyi, Mihaly. *Flow: The Psychology of Optimal Experience,* New York: Harper-Collins, 1990.

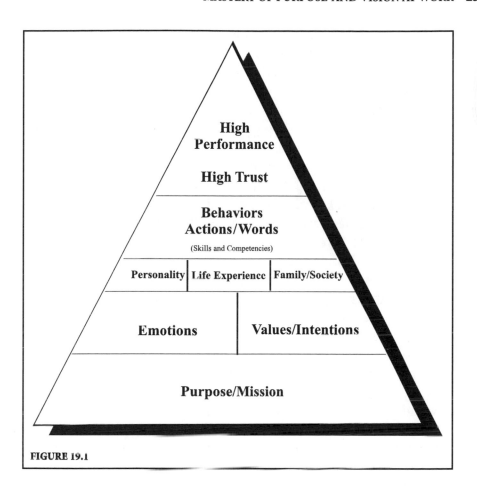

FIGURE 19.1

tional hijackings will wane because we will be more satisfied. But why work at all? Wouldn't we all be happier without work? Not according to Myers. He says in his book that meaningful work is one of the ingredients to a fulfilled and happy life. When Robert Weiss, a research professor at the University of Massachusetts, asked people in a survey whether or not they would work if they had inherited enough money to live comfortably, eight out of ten people said yes.[8] When *Fortune* magazine asked scores of managers, from CEOs to warehouse supervisors, why they worked, the three most common

---

[8]Dumaine, Brian. "Why Do We Work?" *Fortune* 130 (December 26, 1994): 196.

reasons cited besides paying the mortgage were to make the world a better place, to help themselves and others on their team grow spiritually and intellectually, and lastly, to perfect their technical skills.[9] The *Financial Times* also reported that regardless of employees' interests in lifestyle and income, one thing employees have in common is they want interesting, involving jobs.[10] Purpose rather than income is apparently driving actions in the workplace.

Discovering purpose is not for the faint of heart. It's hard work. It takes lots of pondering and an ability to put together all the pieces of our lives. Skills, knowledge, gifts, values, resources, likes, and dislikes all offer clues about our purpose. True discovery, however, is another matter. It requires deep reflection and reevaluation of all that we are. It also requires sacrifice. But the payoff is profound.

One of my favorite examples is Wally Cromwell. Wally was a corporate attorney with a six-figure income and a young family to support. However, a muse that lived deep inside tormented Wally. He found corporate law boring. Very boring. Wally thrived on making people laugh. He had been doing it since grade school. Yet, he went into corporate law because it paid well and, besides, his dad was a corporate attorney. He could live his life as a corporate attorney and make people laugh in his spare time, or he could radically reorder his life. Wally chose to radically reorder his life. He wrote his mission statement, which was, "To make people's hearts as light as a feather." He kept his day job for a while, but slowly he began to gain experience and credentials that were aimed at his passion: laughter. He literally went to clown school. Yes, really. He started practicing various routines on family and friends. He volunteered at events as a comic. He made public appearances at local hospitals. He wrote jokes and submitted them to professional comedians. Finally, after two years, Wally quit his job at the law firm. His parents were devastated. His new life consisted of writing comedy for two professional comedians, speaking engagements that left his audience in stitches, professional appearances as a clown, and consulting to teach corpo-

---

[9] Dumaine, Brian. "Why Do We Work?" *Fortune* 130 (December 26, 1994): 196.
[10] Weaver, Jane. "Job Stress, Burnout on the Rise." *Financial Times*, September 7, 2003.

rate America to laugh. Three years after Wally left the firm, he was making more than he had been practicing law. But the true reward wasn't in the money. He is aligned and delighted with who he has become.

When it all comes together in one neat package, I think of Jack Roseman. Jack heads the Roseman Institute, serves on a number of boards, and spurs entrepreneurs at Carnegie Mellon University. Jack is a living example of a person connected to his purpose and strongly living his core values. What led me to his door was his reputation as a man who goes out of his way to help others, his outstanding reputation as a leader, and his success as a serial entrepreneur. Shortly into our interview, he paused and said, "Look, there are a few things you need to know about me." He listed a few facts for me such as: he had a very serious heart attack many years ago that left only half his heart functioning; he grew up dirt poor; he had family members killed in the concentration camps; he had been raised by a mother who was consumed by the fear that her son, daughter-in-law, grandchildren, and siblings in Ukraine would perish during World War II; and he left home at eighteen to make his way in the world with a few parting words of wisdom from his father. (I thought to myself, I've interviewed people with similar backgrounds, but they don't always end up as successful as Jack—what's different about Jack?) His father's parting message was, "Always act as a gentleman." These words, spoken decades ago, called Jack to develop a sense of values that his father would be proud of. "Fifty percent plus more" is Jack's motto for the way in which he lives his life. He believes that it is his obligation and his privilege to meet people more than half way in his encounters. He brings his sense of values to everything he touches. He lives his purpose daily in the business world and makes a difference in his own life and in the lives of many others. What's different about Jack? Jack refers to himself as one of the "Privileged Poor," as described by A. Singer.[11] The privileged poor have inherited a sense of values and worth far more valuable than money. His worldview

---

[11] Singer, Amy, and Pascual, Jean Paul, eds. "The Privileged Poor of Ottoman Jerusalem," Conference papers "Pauvreté et richesse dans le monde musulman méditerraneén," Aix-en-Provence, France, 2002.

enables his success. He doesn't sit around feeling miserable about his childhood; instead, he demands more of himself (fifty percent plus more); and the success (and money) follows.

What does this look like to others? These Workplace Letters shed light on the power of purpose in the workplace.

LETTER #1

Dear Sid,

I've worked as your peer for many years. I believe you have taught me more about life and work than anyone else I've known. You taught me to live my word. There has never been a time when you didn't speak and act the truth. There is no inconsistency between what comes out of your mouth and how you act. You are the most authentic person I have ever met. Through the years, we've all seen examples when others have taken the easy way out. They say to your face one thing because it is easy, but do something opposite. You don't do that. Remember the time when the general manager polled the staff individually when he asked if we were in agreement with his decision? All of us outside the meeting were saying that we disagreed; yet, you were the only one who had the courage to say no in the meeting. I thought your career was doomed that day, but instead, the GM had more respect for you than the rest of us. Your courage taught me an important lesson. You are human and you didn't always come through on things, but you told us when you would be falling short. You didn't blame anyone; you just let us know. Again, you don't pretend. You somehow have managed to figure out that you don't have to play games. We get caught up in the games. We try to outdo one another. You try to outdo yourself. What a difference. Thank you for all these years and the wonderful lessons you've taught me.

With Gratitude,
Geoff

(One employee's true sentiments are expressed in the following letter. He realizes, of course, that it would be inappropriate to send this letter, but it illustrates the importance of aligning purpose with actions.)

LETTER #2

Dear Boss,

You're a fraud. I heard you in a meeting the other day talk about how you believe in treating people with respect. You said that your most important value was how you treated others. You said that nothing was more important to you than the aura you create when you are in the presence of others. You said it so eloquently; you said that you want that aura to be one of dignity, caring, and respect.

Hello? Who are you kidding? Obviously yourself. Let's get down to some examples:

- Last week you told Beverly that she was "dimwitted" because she couldn't find the answer to a problem. (That was your word, not mine.)

- You told Corey that he couldn't have Friday off even though he is getting married on Saturday.

- You said in a staff meeting that our biggest customer was a "pain in the butt."

- You passed me in the hall the day after I came back from burying my mother and the first thing you asked was whether I had time to run the proof today.

I'd suggest you either keep your mouth shut about what you say you believe in or start aligning your words and actions with what you say. I'd have more respect for you if you at least admitted that you didn't care about people.

Sincerely,
Kim

Some Suggestions for Improving EQ in the Area of Mastery of Purpose and Vision

- Think about times when you are truly your best and happiest. What defines these times?

- Think about times when you feel compromised. What defines these times?

- Take an inventory of the things in life that you feel passionate about. How many of these things are things you do daily?

- Think about times when you are most energized. What defines these times?

- Take steps to rearrange your life based on your life purpose.

- Continually evaluate your life purpose and the actions and activities you are involved in. Are they aligned? Evaluate which actions are closely aligned and which actions are not.

- If you are unsure of your life mission, take a personal inventory of your life and assess your true interests and motivations. This requires hard work and introspection. You may need help from a life coach. The goal of the assessment is to determine your purpose, your calling, and your mission.

- Assess and challenge your values. What do you truly believe in? What beliefs do you hold because others around you expect you to believe them? Find a dear and trusted friend to help sort through your values.

- Think about your present position and your life mission in a new light. Perhaps you are the purchasing manager of a large company and your life mission is to inspire people to treat others in a caring manner. You may find creative ways to live your mission within your present job if you approach it with an open mind.

- Evaluate your actions to determine which ones are closely aligned with your purpose and which ones are removed.

- If your purpose and your occupation are at odds, come up with a plan to align the two.

- When possible, take an assignment based on your interests.

- Do not accept excuses from yourself if you feel you are betraying your purpose.

- Keep a log of lessons learned.

- Check your lessons learned for information about how you can improve your effectiveness in the next situation.

- Make use of your strong points. For example, if you are excellent at organizing, volunteer to organize things.

- Enlist aid when dealing with things that are not your strength. Get coaching, feedback, and assistance to improve.

Exercises for Improving Mastery of Purpose and Vision

EQ EXERCISE #13: YOUR GIFTS

Think about your natural gifts. What skills, knowledge, values, or special attributes do you have that makes you unique? Reflect on your gifts and list them below.

EQ EXERCISE #14: YOUR VALUES CREST

Draw a crest containing the elements that you value most. For example, your crest may have fire to represent passion, a lion to represent great strength, and ears to represent the ability to listen.

EQ EXERCISE #15: A LETTER TO YOUR MOST INSPIRED SELF

Write a letter to your most inspired self. Tell your most inspired self what you see that you admire. Tell your most inspired self what he/she has to bring forth into the world.

TAKES ACTION TOWARD PURPOSE

Can you imagine a symphony conductor without passion for music, a football coach without passion for the game, an artist without passion for his canvas? How do you know that people have passion for what they are doing? Generally, people spend an enormous amount of energy when they care deeply and have committed themselves to something.

The energy and passion that we speak of need not be exuberant enthusiasm. Shouting, cheering, and jumping up and down aren't necessary to show fervor. When we are truly committed to something, quiet passion works just as well. This commitment to our purpose, to something we truly feel called to, is our reason for getting out of bed each morning. In fact, purpose becomes our master. Our workplaces, our homes, our communities, our houses of worship, serve as a backdrop, a setting if you will, where we go to commit and spend energy toward our purpose. Every rote task we perform, every routine detail, every word and action, all serve a purpose. Let's think again about Hank, the purchasing person. He felt bored and viewed his job as mundane when he thought of himself as just another purchasing employee. He saw himself as a guppy in the sea of work, surrounded by massive amounts of paper and perhaps a couple of sharks. Given that vision, his energy level and commitment reflected the hopelessness he felt. However, as he changed his perspective about his gifts and how he could use his workplace as a setting for living his purpose of teaching and helping others, he gained a renewed energy toward work. All of a sudden, work became a place to go to live his mission. All those rote details had new importance. Hank wasn't ever a poor performer, but with this new view, he poured himself into every task, no matter how small, because it supported his vision and purpose. Most of us spend at least a third of our time at work. Just by default, then, work matters. But it matters most when we connect it to something important to us. It becomes more than the pursuit of a paycheck. It doesn't matter if that work is widget making, hamburger slinging, or ditch digging; assuming that it's legal and moral, work can provide a useful outlet for living our purpose.

You must be able to mobilize your energy toward your purpose. When you do that in the workplace, you set an example for your peers and/or your employees. Remember, moods are contagious, and if you are engaged and inspired, others may catch that bug, too. Lots of the apathy and negativity we see in the workplace are because too few people have connected their work with meaning in their lives. That perception and that trend are what you can stop. If you are a leader, not only *can* you stop it, but you must stop it. The first "baby step" toward breaking that trend is for you to walk through the door each day with your soul and your spirit in hand and a driving passion for what you are doing.

Consider Jim. Jim was a front-line supervisor in a government bureaucracy. This bureaucracy was so well established that it may have been the inventor of bureaucracy. People labored over endless paperwork, much of which seemed useless. They lived in a world of "i"-dotting and "t"-crossing. It was difficult, if not impossible, to make any impact on the people or the system. To top it off, they lived under the constant scrutiny of the media. But for more than thirty years, Jim came to work each day and focused his group on the task at hand. His motto was "making a difference today by doing the best we can." For thirty years, he kept repeating that motto to himself and to his employees.

He knew what he could change: very little. He also knew, however, that the most positive thing he could do each day was to keep his crew focused on positive contributions and a positive outlook. He was there to support his staff. At his retirement dinner, people inside and outside the organization spoke about how he kept everyone positive. Keeping people positive is a wonderful mission. The world would certainly be a better place if more people adopted Jim's attitude.

In terms of emotional intelligence, keeping focused on our mission and working toward our mission leaves little time for pettiness, which may lead to exaggerated emotional responses. When we focus and expend our energy on things we consider to important, we simply don't get outraged about the little things. Mission gives us perspective. Others see this in us and are amazed at both the energy expended toward goals and the conviction that the goals are right. If we truly know our intentions and care to live them, emotional intelligence becomes all the more important. How else can we influence others toward our purpose except by being aware of and manage our emotional reactions, demonstrating empathy, creating social bonds, collaborating, and resolving conflicts?

One memorable person provided an excellent example of someone living her purpose and living an emotionally intelligent life. Eva, a self employed cleaning contractor, found joy and purpose in sparkling bathrooms. Eva scrubbed for a purpose. Eva rarely missed a call. She would double check each room or office before leaving to make sure things were perfect. When I interviewed her, Eva explained to me that cleaning was one of the most important things in life you can do. "If your house or your office looks like a hell hole and stinks, you stink. You see," she explained, "when something is clean it sets the stage for everything else. When people walk into a clean bathroom, they walk out feeling more pride, feeling more important, feeling more like they should do a good job, feeling more like they should do perfect work. That is what I do for people and for business." Eva went to work every day with a tremendous sense of purpose, and the energy she put toward her purpose was remarkable. And so were the bathrooms.

What is exciting for you? If you can't answer that question without much thought, then you probably have some work to do to define your purpose. But if you can answer that question, do you find yourself bouncing out of bed in the morning eager to get to your studio? Are you spending energy and taking actions each day toward your purpose? If so, you are on the path to fulfillment.

Perhaps you read this and it all sounds good on paper, but you lament that your reality is different. Perhaps it is. I am well aware of some work situations that would make it difficult if not impossible to live a purpose. If that's the case, you may consider leaving. Sometimes though, what we must leave are our assumptions and workviews, not our jobs. If Eva thought of her job as cleaning toilets, she may not have been able to muster much passion for the job, but her workview allowed her to think differently about her tasks. What assumptions do you have that are holding you back from putting energy toward your passions? Your self-coach can guide you through those assumptions and perhaps test or reframe what you believe. Perhaps there are other things holding you back. Once I realized what I wanted to do with my life, it took me five years to change my direction. I lacked the courage to act, weighed down with financial considerations and lifestyle changes that I knew would be a reality if I changed my course of action. My internal voices of self-doubt, famine, and fear erupted in a cacophony. Slowly, I learned to quiet them. I learned to develop new voices of hope and optimism, which served to jar my inertia. If I was afraid to take action and embrace my purpose, it was ridiculous to expect myself to inspire others.

Until I took steps toward my purpose, I wasn't fully alive. Knowing your purpose is one thing, but taking action toward that purpose completes the picture. As mentioned, sometimes we are robed of our purpose by our assumptions, our worldviews/workviews, or our voices. Some common "robbers of purpose" include:

Victim Mentality: This worldview and its supporting voices say that we can't take action toward purpose because we are a victim in the scheme of life. Living a purpose would require power, and we have none. As long as we are in this frame of mind, we are rendered impotent in terms of taking action toward our purpose.

The Warrior Shield: Some people go though life looking for a fight. I'm not talking about people who have taken up a cause they believe in and fight for it. I'm talking about people who find a fight in everything that touches their lives. If you say the sky is blue, they are the first to argue that it's not. If you say it's a nice day, again they are the first in line to prove you wrong. Fighting to gain nonessential ground depletes this person's energy to the point where they have nothing left to pursue a purpose.

Waiting for Tomorrow: Sometimes people believe that they will live their purpose tomorrow. Tomorrow, when the kids are grown; tomorrow, when the job duties are done; tomorrow, when time allows. The problem with this assumption is that sometimes tomorrow never comes. Living your purpose is something that requires your attention today. Taking actions today toward your purpose is the path to fulfillment.

Martyrdom: Some people believe that they cannot live their purpose because they must suffer "for you." They must put all of their interests aside "for you." They must stay quietly in the background and provide "for you." Trouble is, these people are harboring resentment and let you know it. This resentment is a powerful force that robs them of their energy. Often, when people live their purpose, they may put others first, but it is done out of love and it is energizing, not depleting.

When you view your life through your purpose, you will have a greater understanding of where to put your energy and resources. Energy is a finite, so the actions you take will be directed and focused rather than a random drain of your resources. You will also discover that when you feel tired, it will be a different kind of tired. You'll be tired but satisfied that you are accomplishing something, contrasted with the tired you can feel from sitting in front of the television day after day. Your emotional energy is directed toward something vital to you. This causes a sense of vitality in you. You will know, too, how to direct your resources. Your monetary donations will have meaning and focus. In *Fund Raising Management*, Michael Maude writes about self-actualized people and donating money to causes. He describes them as knowing precisely what is important to them, so they focus on issues or problems outside of themselves. He also says they devote their energy to a chosen mission with a passion that is inspirational. Self-actualized people are mission driven, and they thrive on being part of something significant. They are the most generous in terms of giving funds to causes they believe in because they are giving for internal reasons, not external reasons. In this case, it's about taking action with the wallet to support your purpose.

Some Suggestions for Improving EQ in the Area of Action Toward Purpose

- Listen to yourself talk. When do you hear yourself hedging or sounding unsure of your position?

- Listen to yourself talk. When do you hear yourself speaking with conviction?

- What actions do you take with extreme confidence?

- What actions drain you? Make a list of actions that deplete you.

- Think about times when you have taken actions most aligned with who you are.

- Listen to others as they speak. What makes someone sound confident? What makes someone sound unsure or wishy-washy?

- List people you think are arrogant; others that you think are confident. Define the difference.

- Listen as someone speaks with confidence. What feelings do you hear behind their words?

- When you state a point of view, determine first the feelings you have regarding your point. Could you improve your confidence by improving your feelings?

- When you're not sure of your position in something, don't pretend. State that you are not sure and are still contemplating your decision. If you pretend, you not only sound like you lack confidence, but you also risk losing credibility.

- Think about a time when you did not act on something you believed in. How did you feel?

- Think about a time when you took an action on something you believed in. How did you feel?

- Sometimes we are taking actions, but we're not focusing on our progress toward our purpose. Instead, we focus on what we haven't accomplished. Be sure to take time each day to reflect on your progress toward your purpose.

- Show more passion about things that are important to you. Sometimes we're just not showing our energy, so others think we're not committed. You can show your energy in many ways—by doing more, by encouraging others to see value, by constantly focusing on what's been accomplished and why it's important.

- Keep your focus even when things aren't going well. Sometimes we stop taking action because obstacles seem to overcome our power. If it's something you believe in, keep going. Every baby step will help you get there.

- If you feel defeated or are questioning your purpose, develop a cadre of people you can contact for support.

Exercise for Improving Taking Actions Toward Purpose

EQ EXERCISE #16: THREE IMMEDIATE ACTIONS

List three immediate actions that you plan to take to live your purpose. If you are unsure of your purpose, those actions should be aimed at gaining clarity about what is important to you.

BIBLIOGRAPHY

Bell, Chip. *Managers as Mentors*. San Francisco: Berrett-Koehler Publishers, 1998.

Blanchard, Ken and Michael O'Connor. *Managing By Values*. San Francisco, Berrett-Koehler Publishers, 1997.

Canfield, Jack and Jacqueline Miller. *Heart at Work Stories and Strategies for Building Self-Esteem and Reawakening the Soul at Work*. New York: McGraw-Hill, 1996.

Chermiss, Cary and Adler, Mitchel. *Promoting Emotional Intelligence in Organizations*. American Society for Training and Development, 2000.

Conger, Jay A. *The Charismatic Leader*. San Francisco: Jossey-Bass Publishers, 1992.

Cooper, Robert K. and Ayman Sawaf. *Executive EQ Emotional Intelligence in Leadership and Organizations*. New York: The Berkley Publishing Group, 1997.

Covey, Stephen. *Principle-Centered Leadership*. New York: Summit Books, 1990.

Goleman, Daniel. *Emotional Intelligence Why it can matter more than IQ*. New York: Bantam Books, 1995.

———— *Working With Emotional Intelligence*. New York: Bantam Doubleday Dell Pub.

Goleman, Daniel, Boyatzis, Richard and McKee, Annie. *Primal Leadership*. Harvard Business School Press, 2002.

Harmon, Frederick G. *Playing for Keeps*. New York: John Wiley & Sons Inc., 1996.

Hawley, Jack. *Reawakening the Spirit in Work*. New York: Simon & Schuster, 1993.

Herman, Stanley M. *The Tao at Work*. San Francisco: Jossey-Bass Publishers, 1994.

Jones, Laurie Beth. *Jesus CEO*. New York: Hyperion, 1995.

Kaye, Les. *Zen at Work*. New York: Crown Trade Paperbacks, 1996.

Kelley, Robert E. *How to be a Star at Work.* New York: Times Business, Random House, 1998.

Kouzes, James and Barry Posner. *The Leadership Challenge.* San Francisco: Jossey-Bass Publishers, 1987.

Lynn, Adele B. *In Search of Honor—Lessons From Workers on How to Build Trust.* BajonHouse Publishing, 1998.

———— *The Emotional Intelligence Activity Book.* AMACON. 2001.

Salovey, Peter, PhD, and John Mayer, PhD. *Emotional Development and Emotional Intelligence.* Basic Books, 1997.

Sashkin, Marshall. *Becoming a Visionary Leader.* King of Prussia, PA: Organization Design and Development, 1986.

Sterrett, Emily. *The Managers Pocket Guide to Emotional Intelligence.* HRD Press, 2000.

Weisinger, Hendrie, PhD. *Emotional Intelligence at Work.* San Francisco: Jossey-Bass, 1997.

Dear Readers,

Quality of life is essential. Defining it, however, depends on the individual pursuing it. Some would consider it to be good health. Others may desire ample leisure. Still others would define it as possessions and material wealth.

Just by reading this book, however, you have indicated that you value another type of wealth—emotional wealth. Emotional wealth may be the most important asset of all, because, in times of material poverty or poor health, our emotional wealth will sustain us. The dividends that we reap from investing in our relationships and the comfort we find in those relationships can often make all else bearable. Rich relationships, coupled with the strong inner peace that comes from managing ourselves, is the hallmark of emotional intelligence and, hence, our emotional wealth. Unlike material possessions or health, our emotional wealth is not only immune to the rise and fall of the markets or the ravages of disease and age, but it continues to grow and pay dividends. Others cannot take it away. It is the one thing we can truly possess.

As you continue to write the story of your life, I urge you to go deep within yourself and to ask that inner bird dog of yours to flush out the possibilities. Just like those turkeys, George and Harriet, you have all the resources to fly. The amount of emotional wealth you can accumulate is unlimited. Perhaps, at times, you just need to be reminded of your potential. Or perhaps you need your inner bird dog to move you to action—to set the stage for flight.

Carefully consider your words and actions. Honor your relationships with others. Honor the whisper in your own soul regarding your purpose, and expect it to grow into a roar. Honor yourself.

Take off and soar.

Adele B. Lynn

INDEX